N

TA

GR

How a near-dea

Injury showed n

COVID-19

How to dev

NEVER TAKE FOR GRANTED

How a near-death accident and a Traumatic Brain Injury showed me how much I'd taken for granted.
COVID-19 proved we ALL take things or people for granted.
How to develop an Attitude of Gratitude.

Debbie Grosser

Published by Best Seller Publishing®, Pasadena, CA
Best Seller Publishing® is a registered trademark.
Printed in the United States of America.
ISBN: 978-1-956649-04-8

For more information, please write:
Best Seller Publishing®
53 Marine Street
St. Augustine, FL 32084
or call 1 (626) 765 9750
Visit us online at: www.BestSellerPublishing.org

DEDICATION

This book is dedicated to the two people I wished most would still be here to witness my finished product, so I could make them proud. They were two of the most selfless human beings, who lived for their children and for each other. Their love for one another was so great that it's not surprising they died only a short time apart (a mere 164 days), after having been married for sixty years while on this earth. The void created by their absence is enormous. They are together again, and they will be forever more. Thank you, Mom and Dad, for all you have given us, for all you inspired me to be. I never thought I could do this without you, but you never quit, and that's what you taught us. That allowed me the ability to see this through, and I will be grateful to you and love you forever more.

TABLE OF CONTENTS

PREFACE

Who knew COVID-19 and all its attendant aftereffects would dovetail so perfectly with the theme of my book: Never Take for Granted. Perhaps it will provide both real-world and real-time proof, giving examples of how much we *all* take for granted. Attending family or friends' weddings, funerals, birthday parties, graduations, communions, bar and bat mitzvahs, and retirement parties. Just moving about freely, without fear of breaking rules or laws. Visiting a friend or loved one at the hospital or at a nursing and rehab center, especially when they're dying, or are about to die. I'm currently living at Gurwin Jewish Nursing & Rehabilitation Center, in Commack, Long Island, New York. To relieve my stress and anxiety, I took to posting about it on Facebook (one of my outlets).

Okay, guys and gals, the dreaded coronavirus has hit Gurwin. As a nursing facility in New York State, Gurwin was mandated to accept "recovering" COVID-19 patients. The new residents were placed in the 2 North and 2 South units. Once inside the facility, and despite fastidious precautionary steps taken, the virus spread quickly: first on 2 North and 2 South, but then to 4 West, 4 North, and 4 South. Within a few weeks, several residents had succumbed to the complications that accompany the virus. In mid-March 2020, Gurwin was placed on lockdown! No visitors, and nobody could go out on a pass. That meant no church on Sunday for me. Even worse, the lobby gym was quarantined. Thus, no recumbent bike, my only physical stress outlet, for me. Rather than complaining, I am commiserating. And I know unhappiness is inevitable but misery is an option! I'm just trying on the idea that this current state of emergency might turn into a three- to six-month (actually, over a year-long) SNOW DAY! And we know that snow days can seem like freedom for the first few hours, but they can rapidly become like *The Shawshank Redemption*—you know, the movie at the prison in Maine with Andy Dufresne (Tim Robbins) and Ellis "Red" Redding (Morgan Freeman): "You either get busy living, or get busy dying."

Choosing life, I try to stay as busy as possible. Having no choice but to obey the rules, I have now rented the movie *Bombshell*, with Charlize Theron, and I'll also watch the movie I refer to so often, *The Shawshank Redemption* (always a favorite of mine). Well folks, I'm just gonna do what I gotta do to stay busy: take as many walks as possible, do exercises in my room, and watch the movies I've rented, thanks to Amazon Prime! That is all. I'll be back. By the way, this outbreak sets the theme in this book, *Never Take for Granted*, just perfectly. Every simple thing we take for granted—going out to visit a friend, freely moving about the town, going to work, maintaining our livelihood to support house and home and put food on the table—all of this is in question for some yet-to-be-determined period of time. God bless everybody!

Just like my accident, I don't know that anybody could've seen this coming. I do think that, like my accident, the most important thing will be how I/we react and how we deal with things going forward. We can't control what the rest of the world will do; all we can control is our own reaction. Do I follow the lead and engage in all the panic and fear? I know, I won't. Just like with my accident, I've dealt with everything that's come my way: the nineteen surgeries, constant delays in moving forward with any plans I might have for my life, disappointments, the lack of immediate financial resources. These past nine-plus years, very little has been in my control. Thankfully, the clarity of thought that's become part of my life has shown that worry, panic, and fear do nothing to change situations; they only fuel the fire of negativity. And I don't want, or need, that. Instead, I seek solutions, and follow advice and execute upon the best ideas that are presented to me. I've had many setbacks, countless disappointments, and overall disruptions to my plans and goals. However, I've dealt with them. Not alone—yes, it takes a village. Thankfully, I've had many good friends in my village, and I'm so grateful they've been there for me. It is at this time that I'd like to dedicate some space to list the names of those who have so generously given of their time and resources to allow this book to come to fruition.

Special Acknowledgments

Tim Foxe & Ernie

Peter Petas & Ted Jones

Jim Foster

Jeanne Cusack Placido

Jim Asselstine

Jim Ivey

Bill Exiner

Barbara Germain

Sean & Fiona Duffy

John Sprofera

Mariel Clemensen

Lee Taylor-Vaughan

Brent Shum

May Pai

Cathy DePaola

Heather Roff

Nancy McFadden

Rich Barthelemy

Marjorie & Dominic Devito

Leigh Creamer

Michael Quinn

Stephen Balog
Scott Stark
Janis Mayors
Donna Pennacchio
Lauren Sharabi
Carol Sileo
Ruth Harrison
Gail Caccavale
Matthew Leblanc
Fran Bakker
Margaret and Alex Gregorek
John Leddy
Christopher Sadler
Keith Lambrecht

INTRODUCTION

Framing the Story: It All Depends on Perspective

By definition, nobody's perfect. We all make mistakes. Some of us make mistakes SO big that we'd never think of trying to come back from them. That is not me. Much had to change about me, and my life, to even consider the idea. But I have changed; I've changed virtually everything about myself, and my life. Out with the bad things and keep all the good things. Consider all of the things in question. Hopefully, I've developed the wisdom to know the difference, and that takes time. Which is all I've had, for nine-plus years, since the accident that changed everything. If I chose not to come back, that would be all about my ego. Being too embarrassed to acknowledge all my mistakes would be arrogance personified. Again, that is not me. Instead, I've had to humble myself, acknowledge my wrongs and transgressions, my foibles. I now have the opportunity to present the real me, the woman who's been bruised but not broken, nearly dead but now alive, once lost in the haze of alcohol, but now alert and clear-minded. Add to that, now, a keen desire to give back for all that's been given me. My life continues, when many believed it would not, and now, my key motivation is to demonstrate that I've learned from my mistakes, and I can possibly make my life, and the lives of those around me, better for having survived. It's been a nine-year journey, so far. The possibilities are endless from here. I must know my strengths and weaknesses and play with the hand I've been dealt.

No one likes to admit that they take things or people for granted. In all fairness, most people don't realize that they are taking things for granted, until those things are taken away. As a result of the coronavirus pandemic, everyone is beginning to realize just how many things, or people, they took for granted. So it was, in my own personal story.

In life, almost nothing is ever "granted," although our God-given gifts are the only true "givens." Most all things have to be awarded or loaned, and then be cared for and developed. As a survivor of a near-fatal accident, I've begun to see the world through a grateful set of eyes. I've been changed forever.

As Dr. Wayne Dyer, a wise man, once said, "When you change the way you look at things, the things you look at change."

As Ashlyn Llerandi, a wise young woman, once said, "I have found gratitude to be the very source of blessings too numerous to count."

Many people subscribe to a "conscious living" or "mindfulness" school of thought. In reality, the view that one must be truly conscious, or present, for each moment of one's life is optimistic. Instead, most people do not live their lives present for every moment, grateful for everything, until they have a life-altering experience that causes a dramatic shift in their view of the world. So it was with me.

I've developed a new perspective, all related to gratitude, and it's made a world of difference for me. I'd say I've had a spiritual metamorphosis.

In the current pandemic environment, we're beginning to acknowledge that we, indeed, take things for granted, and we need to be much more grateful for many of the simple things in our lives. On social media (I use Facebook) I found this recent post. Just a picture, that sums it up well.

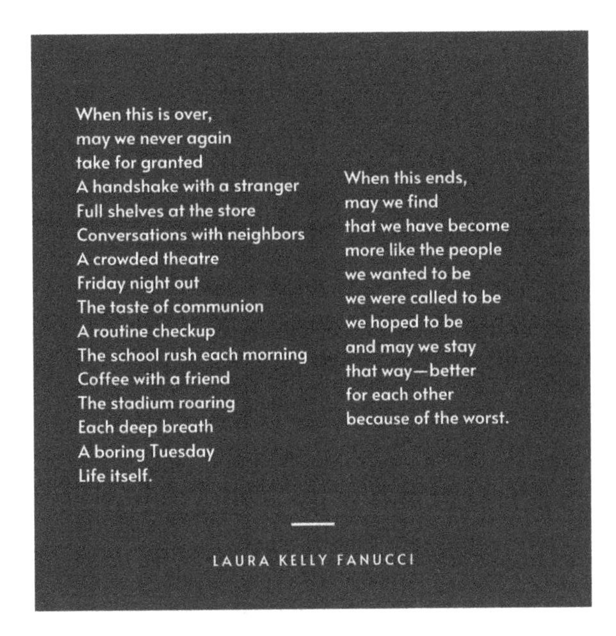

I like the last line of this picture: "May we stay that way—better for each other because of the worst." (Used with permission of Laura Kelly Fanucci.)

After the September 11, 2001, terrorist attack on the World Trade Center, it seemed like the United States changed into a kinder, gentler nation. For weeks, even months afterward, drivers during the rush hour to downtown Manhattan actually let other drivers cut in line in front of them (something unheard of in the past). People seemed to genuinely be happy when approached by others to speak, asking, "Where were you during the attack?" "Did you know anyone who was there or were lost in the attack?" People seemed to be kind to each other, for some time. Ultimately, they returned to their old ways, but it was nice while it lasted.

Inevitably, there will be other crises to confront us, and wouldn't humankind be better off to have learned from the 9/11 attacks, and now the coronavirus pandemic? We were created as social creatures, and it's been proven, time and again, that we need each other. Much as there are those who have an aversion to depending on others, it's really more of a strength, and can actually get one further to their goals by enlisting the help of others.

In my personal experience, my accident was horrific, and my resulting injuries were awful. But because of them (not despite them), I've been able to see my life, and my basic physical functions, as gifts. To breathe freely, to walk, to talk, to eat independently are all now gifts to me.

Further, to work on my physical abilities, and have glimmers of things coming back, are all new gifts for which to be grateful.

Now, I'm not suggesting that a near-fatal accident is necessary to achieve a complete "attitude of gratitude." But it sure was for me. Generally, I believe that something has to be life-altering for most people to develop an attitude of gratitude. I think it is hard for most people to maintain a complete attitude of gratitude until things are taken away from them, like basic freedoms. That's been the case with national "stay-at-home" orders. These have dictated people's ability to go out of their homes, or even go to work (as many businesses, unless essential, are closed). I don't wish my accident and injuries on anyone, but my newfound gratitude for my "gifts" make life like it's Christmas every day. And that perspective, and the gratitude that comes from it, I wish for everyone in the world.

Instead of a world filled with hate, contempt, and injustice, there'd be a new appreciation for our basic "gifts." That could lead to a changed world. If only people could see things differently, they'd be grateful. See Kelly's story in the next chapter as an example of, no matter your woes, how things could always be worse.

In the recent turmoil brought about by the murder of George Floyd, on May 25, 2020, by police in Minneapolis, coupled with the global pandemic, one wonders how much people can bear at one time. It turns out that humankind is resilient and capable of making sweeping changes, long overdue, to the criminal justice system. The violence that ensued following George Floyd's death, in some ways, seems entirely justified. After all, his death was so cruel and thoughtless, yet he was just one in a long line of Black individuals killed by the police. In memorials at his funeral, his family spoke of George as a gentle giant, and that "he had such a big heart," yet

George was not an angel. He had decades worth of criminal history, some of it violent. But no matter. George did not deserve to die in the unspeakable way that he did—crying out that he could not breathe while a Minneapolis police officer's knee was on his throat for about nine minutes, staying there long after George's body became limp and unresponsive. Nobody deserves to die like that. Nobody.

A Tale of Two Criminal Justice Systems

Let me just preface that I have the utmost respect for our law enforcement officers in this country. The police, as well as all first responders, run toward the danger: the crime or the fire, or other hazardous situations. We need them; we depend on their existence and their desire to serve and protect, but there are those who individually make bad decisions. We ought not paint the whole force with the same prejudice; this is the very thing we want corrected.

Sadly, we've been witness to yet another tragic and horrific example of excessive use of force by police, this time in Kenosha, Wisconsin, in the August 23 shooting of Jacob Blake, a Black father of three young boys, who watched in horror as their father was shot in the back seven times, for reasons that are unclear. The boys, aged eight, five, and three, will have untold trauma that will remain long after this senseless shooting.

Two nights later, also in Kenosha, a seventeen-year-old self-identified white supremacist shot two demonstrators. It was reported that Kyle Rittenhouse walked freely through the area of demonstration, carrying an AR15 long-gun rifle, walking past police, who did nothing to stop him from continuing on to his shootings! They actually offered him a bottle of water! Ultimately, he now faces first-degree homicide charges, but the difference in law enforcement reaction is stunning.

Sadly, there's also the tragic case of Breonna Taylor, a twenty-six-year-old beautiful Black EMT who was killed, in her apartment, by Louisville police in a botched police raid, on March 13, 2020. On September 22, a grand jury indicted one of the three police officers who fired multiple rounds at Breonna Taylor and caused her death (as detailed in her autopsy), but the indictment cited "wanton endangerment for human life," not the killing of Breonna. Breonna led her life with good intentions by caring for others in distress, yet her death by police was not met with justice. Nothing will bring Breonna back to her family, her boyfriend, and her life again. Perhaps it is only the civil unrest caused by the reaction to the grand jury indictment by thousands across the country that will demonstrate that a bigger movement to restore justice in this flawed system will happen this time. As a result of this incident, at least "no-knock" warrants have been outlawed.

Twenty-six-year-old Breonna Taylor
(www.theguardian.com/us-news/2020/jun/14/)

I digress. Back to my story. It's time to take my mess and make it a message. Or, it's time to make a miracle out of my mistakes. And I need to share my message with others. If it could benefit just one person, then my efforts in writing this book will have been worth it.

A wise person once said, "Any journey that opens our eyes and softens our hearts is worth taking."

My greatest wish is that my book will be a journey that is worth taking.

Words Have Power

Words can inspire and influence. If acted upon, they can live on, long after those who uttered them. Witness the powerful words of Dr. Martin Luther King, Jr., and his iconic "I have a Dream" speech, which launched thousands of other peaceful protests.

"No Words" Has Power

It is through the lack of action, in response to direct instructions. Witness Rosa Parks. Her refusal launched so many other peaceful protests, which spawned new civil rights legislation.

On December 1, 1955, in Montgomery, Alabama, Parks refused to obey bus driver James F. Blake's order to give up her seat in the "colored section" to a white passenger, after the whites-only section was filled.

Rosa is quoted as saying, "*You must never be fearful about what you are doing, when it is right.*" And, "Memories of our lives, of our works and our deeds will continue in others." "Happiness will never come to those who don't appreciate what they already have."

Rosa Parks being arrested
(https://www.loc.gov/item/today-in-history/december-01/)

I'M NOT DESERVING OF A HALO

It might sound like I have such a great attitude about my plight in life. There are times, however, when I feel like screaming about everything. I want to run and light my hair on fire to get someone to listen to me.

Whenever I grow impatient and wish that things could move at a faster pace, and I could be free again, I pause, and remember that I put myself in this entire situation. Had I not been drinking and fallen down the stairs, breaking my skull and suffering a traumatic brain injury, I would not have lost most of my last decade. I was fifty-two when I had my accident, and today, I'm sixty-one. I've had to grapple with a tremendous amount of self-loathing, being angry at myself for what I did to myself, my family, and my life. All that line of thinking does nothing. It's counter-productive and does nothing to propel my life forward, which is where I want and need to go: up! I make the choice every day to make progress on "rising from my ashes." My prior life, left in smoldering ruins, is gone. My new life must be rebuilt from scratch. Am I up to the task? I say yes. Can I do it alone? No, and I don't have to. I have Jesus back in my life. I also have a loving family and great friends who can help me in this likely-to-be-long journey.

Today (pre-COVID-19), Jesus answered my prayers, without me having to ask for anything. My sister-in-Christ, Kerry Rohe, texted me from LaScala Pizza and asked if I was up for a quick visit, a slice of pizza, and half of a cannoli. I couldn't have asked for more! When I met Kerry in the Brown Bag Room, with pizza and cannoli in tow, I couldn't have hugged her any harder—it felt *so* good to have my sister-in-Christ, my friend, actually in my presence, after several months of absence. We caught up on family stuff, how her boys were, the twins of one and the children of the other, and we fell into the comfortable dialogue of a truly dear friend! Hallelujah! Thank you, Jesus! You answered my prayers!

While this book will go into great detail about my life, how it got me to where I am, and made me who I am, I believe my message will pack a powerful punch and resonate with many.

Even when I view my story objectively, as writers are instructed to do, I ask myself: *Will my story grip the reader in the first few pages?* And my objective answer, upon reading it for the thousandth time, is yes.

All of my experiences, along with my description of them, should keep you wanting for more. Now, I don't know how many authors have spoken so candidly, but I believe in keeping it real. Many may want to sugarcoat their stories, make them look pretty, and show themselves in the best light. But my life wasn't always pretty, and so my adherence to the "truth" was my objective throughout. Even if it shows me in my worst light.

A recent re-post of mine on Facebook says: "It is through our worst times, that we can learn to be our best." And it is by sharing the lessons learned during the worst times that our words have depth and weight, and we can maybe inspire others and reach for our true purpose. Every step I take, every breath I breathe . . . for those simple things, I am ever grateful. Having come back so far, while painful, I believe God will help me go the distance.

Gratitude Is Now My Watchword

I am just so grateful for all the blessings in my life. It took being brought to my knees to see these blessings. Many would see them as horrors and pain, and there have been those things, but I choose to take the narrow, positive road, the road less traveled. I am grateful that God has been with me. I feel blessed in the early morn. I choose to lead a happy life.

I Had an Epiphany While Writing this Book

As I neared the end of writing this book, I had a moment of clarity. Reflecting on all the events that I've been through in my life, I began to realize that I did not fear failure, but rather, I fear success. With the amount of things that had gone wrong for me during my life, I realized that I am not afraid of failing; I've done that way too many times. Between my near-death accident and getting fired from a job I loved, my husband's untimely death, needing to go to rehab three times, and so many other embarrassing occasions (including three DUIs), I'm not boasting when I say that I've come to see how strong I am, getting up each time, learning from my mistakes, and rising from my ashes; I've come to realize that I am a very strong and determined woman. Yet, having the fortitude to pursue my goal, see it through all the way, and bring a long-hoped-for dream to fruition, what could be required of me if that happens? There's a popular Bible verse, Luke 12:48, that says: "To whom much is given, much will be required." If this book project turns out to be all that I envision for it, a big part of it will be to give back for all that's been given me. God gave me talents, both mental and physical: intelligence, reasoning, and wisdom (mental). He also gave me the ability to run, bike, and swim (physical). Another of my goals for this book is to position myself as an advocate for those who have suffered brain injuries. Hence, the basis for The Deborah F Grosser Foundation for traumatic brain injury (TBI) research.

WHY THE TITLE "NEVER TAKE FOR GRANTED"?

When considering my title, I had to explore the meaning a bit more. If something is "granted" to you, it is given without expectation of its return or repayment of its value. Thus, taking for granted is to give little attention to, or to underestimate the value of, and to fail to appreciate, whatever has been "granted." Usually, the epiphany of taking something for granted comes after it's already gone. Joni Mitchell had that epiphany when she lamented that we don't know what we've got till it's gone, in her song "Big Yellow Taxi/ Paved Paradise."

My book's title is a cautionary statement because we all take things or people for granted...and I have been learning a lesson about taking things for granted the hard way.

From the day I was born, after taking my first breath, my instincts kicked in and every other breath followed automatically. It was the same for my first step, my first word, my first bite of food, and my first suck on a bottle. I never questioned those instincts. For the last eight years, however, I have been in and out of hospitals and living in nursing homes with acute and sub-acute nursing care. I've had nineteen surgeries over the last eight years, one lasting thirty-two hours, all necessary to put my physical body and brain back together into a form that can function.

THE COVER PHOTO FOR MY BOOK: THE U.S. CAPITOL

No building is more emblematic of our democracy than the U.S. Capitol building. On January 6, 2021, our democracy came under attack. Thus, the picture of the Capitol suggests that our democracy is just one more thing we Americans take for granted. The attack was perpetrated by Americans; not a foreign country as many might suppose. No, these were home-grown Americans, purporting to "love their country," who were capable of desecrating our cherished symbol of our democracy, and who were threatening violence against many governmental officials. The picture of me in front of our nation's Capitol was taken in 2009 (two years before my near-death accident). We'd been to DC to visit with Senator Olympia Snowe (R-ME) to discuss a project on which we were working at the time. Never did I ever think that this picture would fit so perfectly with the theme of this memoir, a book I would write twelve years later.

My Lawyer's Wise Counsel

My lawyer's name is Arnold Reiter. I'd remembered that he was Gary's and my attorney for both closings of our homes in Mahwah. Thus, our relationship spans back to 1988—thirty-two years. Years later, it was Arnie I thought of shortly after my husband Gary's death, in 2006, when I was badly in need of calm and wise words relating to the handling of Gary's estate and proceeds from his life insurance, combined with retirement accounts. These assets would be managed by a financial advisor named Gary Goldberg, whose offices were housed in the same building as Arnie's office.

A Little Bit of History Surrounding My Lawyer and His Office Location

Montebello

(https://en.wikipedia.org/wiki/Montebello,_New_York, September 2018)

In the 1860s, Suffern, New York, experienced a growth in the development of elegant country estates thanks to its scenic and wooded landscape surrounded by the Ramapo Mountains. One such estate was that of wealthy New York financier Thomas Fortune Ryan. The Ryans called their estate "Montebello" (beautiful mountains).

In 1951, the copper mining giant Phelps Dodge Corporation bought the prominent mansion and used it as a corporate records headquarters for the next thirty-one years. After a relocation move, Phelps Dodge sold the mansion to Gary Goldberg, president of the investment/financial planning firm which now bears his name. After a year of extensive renovation, Montebello became an office park.

After my husband Gary's death in June 2006, followed by my August-to-September stay at Crossroads Rehab in Antigua, I often sought refuge in the relaxing and beautiful environment of meeting with Arnie at his office in Montebello in Suffern.

Retaining Arnie as my counsel turned out to be one of the wisest decisions I ever made. Gary and I were finally going to "get our affairs in order," something we'd always planned, but never did, until 2006, and Gary was no longer here.

Working with Arnie, we finally proceeded to put my will together, and some other documentation such as health care proxies (advance directives, including do not resuscitate [DNR] orders), durable power of attorney, and some others. I would not realize how important this was until my near-death experience! I wouldn't be typing this book were it not for those documents! After my accident, Arnie effectively became "me," handling all of my finances and other needs for the last eight years. This was all done in concert with my family's involvement. My brother and sister-in-law, John and Kelly, proceeded to move me out of my townhouse (in Ramsey, New Jersey), in which I nearly fell to my death. I had just moved into my new townhouse, which I loved, in December 2009. I was there only twenty-one months, until my fall on Wednesday, August 31, 2011. Moving me out after my accident was a herculean feat, with all the furniture and clothes (including shoes, bags, scarves, and all other accessories; pots and pans; dishes; personal products; pictures; and everything I had crammed into that townhouse). Fortunately, it was nearly three thousand square feet, allowing for most of my furniture and other material acquisitions I had made while at 17 Seminary Drive. No wonder John and Kelly were exhausted after that champion feat! Arnie had even considered nominating John and Kelly as CNN Heroes for having gone above and beyond any normal actions/call of duty, for having been unprompted in their efforts to move me out, when no one else could have ever completed that gargantuan task!

Flash forward eight years, Arnie and his wife of nearly fifty years, Sherie, came to visit me at Gurwin. Arnie gave me some additional wise counsel (free of charge, I hope) regarding some specific points I need to drive home in the writing of this book. He said, "First of all, it's a miracle that you are sitting here having a conversation with me and Sherie, because you were effectively dead, but you also have to articulate what it is that continues to drive you, motivate you, to go on and do all you're doing, when many others would have given up and wished to die with all you have to confront. Whatever it is that you need to put in your book to get people to know what you've been through, and where you've come from, to continue to get better. I mean, look at you, you look great! You're a different person, you're talking, you're articulate, you're getting close to walking (almost independently) and you just keep going! So many people would have quit so long ago, but you don't quit! How you do that is what you need to write in your book, to convey that message, and to inspire people!" I told him that I was doing that, and there are many sections of my book where I discuss that very topic. I'm taking my "mess" and making it my "message" (to quote Joyce Meyer). And here are some of the thoughts of what allows me to do what I'm doing.

Arnie continues as my lawyer today. He and his staff have worked tirelessly on my behalf. That includes his paralegal, Joan Tie; an associate attorney, Candice Dahan; and an office assistant, Cheryl Puso. They get me the answers I need in a timely manner, and they are always kind and courteous. They were the ones who filed the reams of paperwork necessary to obtain IRS approval for The Deborah F Grosser Foundation for TBI research. Without that, the foundation wouldn't have any of the enticement to attract funding sources. The pandemic has been an impediment to attracting large amounts of funding, given massive job loss and a shift in priorities to health and life and death concerns, versus charitable donations, no matter how worthy the cause. I would be continuing my efforts in earnest in the fall/winter of 2020. The motivation for tax deductions would increase toward year end 2020.

My longer-term desire is to return to a somewhat normal life. I plan to live independently again, perhaps with an aide living with me. I know that that will take time, and arrangements will have to be made, but that is part of my overall plan. Previously, in 2012, I lived with my aide, Yolanda, in an apartment in Garden City. But it was premature. I made some bad decisions, and my finances dictated that I return to a nursing facility environment. This time, I'll be ready. Importantly, alcohol is no longer part of my life. That important factor can help ensure that this time I will be ready!

I know that sounds ambitious. Some might say it sounds impossible, but a few key things have changed for me. Arnie asked if I had any religious or spiritual beliefs that contribute to my drive, and that answer is yes. I cover it in a later section of my book, on my path back to God, but I can say wholeheartedly that there have been huge changes in me since I have been studying the Bible and restoring my relationship with God. I've also been assisted by some wonderful relationships with my sisters-in-Christ. They have been a significant help to me in my long journey; all of it has been worth it, in part, because of them.

I also discuss my longer-term plan to return to school and study for a new profession, possibly to become an RN or a paralegal—all seemingly impossible, but now, I know it's not. I don't envision my role as an RN to include being an OR nurse, assisting surgeons with instruments during surgery, but a role in a nursing care facility might be a more feasible role for me. At this point (early 2021), I'm keeping all of my options open.

Having lived at Gurwin, I have learned that accomplishing goals at an advanced age is a definite possibility. I reside with women who are thirty-five to forty years older than I am (sixty-one), and in one case, this woman started businesses well into her sixties and seventies, and she retired at eighty-four! She turned 101 in January 2021, and she shows no signs of slowing down (although she does live at Gurwin Jewish Nursing & Rehabilitation Center). I am heartened by that example. You'll read more about Mae Guldin later in "The Centenarians." What is most impressive is that she still has all her cognitive skills: a great memory, an awareness of all current events, names, everything. She agrees, however, that having your mind is great, but losing your physical abilities is tough. That's why my efforts to improve upon all that was given back to me shall not go unused ever again!

This Just In

As of January 2021, I can report that my longer-term plan to return to school and pursue a nursing degree has begun! When I graduated from high school forty-three years ago, I took several Advanced Placement courses and exams, in biology, chemistry, and physics. Those are primary prerequisites toward a nursing degree. I was told that the only courses missing were human anatomy and physiology, 1 and 2. In Summer 2021, I will commence my first anatomy and physiology class, online. It will be instructor led and is accredited to allow it to matriculate into all my other courses to go toward a nursing degree. After this prerequisite course is completed, I plan to participate in on-campus classes to complete my nursing program. This was a huge step to allow me to state, with authority, that my plan to go back to school to ultimately achieve my RN has commenced!

And there has been help for me to do this. I need to thank Jerry Brimeyer, a former colleague at Lehman Brothers, for assisting me with some financial aid toward my goal. Thank you, Jerry! Jerry was a highly ranked pharmaceutical analyst at Lehman Brothers. He covered all of the large-cap (market capitalization) pharmaceutical companies, aka "Big Pharma" (i.e., Merck, Schering-Plough, Bristol Myers Squibb). After leaving Lehman Brothers, Jerry made several moves to other firms, and also to other countries, like the UK. Before he left Lehman, I was fortunate to have attended Jerry and his wife Dianne's wedding, in Newport, Rhode Island, on May 25, 1996. It was the first wedding I'd gone to that had an itinerary! There was the rehearsal dinner at Goat Island, there was the church on Saturday, followed by the reception at Hammersmith Farms (where John F. Kennedy and Jacqueline Bouvier were married on September 12, 1953), and topping it off, there was a farewell brunch at The Inn at Castle Hill for all of the guests to say goodbye to the newlyweds, Jerry and Dianne Brimeyer! It was a great weekend affair, enjoyed by all, and will be remembered forever!

Dianne and Jerry Brimeyer, in Paris

Fortunately, I love anatomy and physiology, and I can't wait to get started. I'm sure it will be a challenge, but I relish this one!

Positivity Works

I make a conscious choice, every day, to be positive. It hasn't always been the case for me, but it is now! And that has come with a lot of hard work, changing virtually everything about myself, and refusing to believe that things *won't* work out!

I remember a woman who delivered premature triplets in 1998, and, at the time, everyone was cautious and seemingly negative about the babies' low birth weights and potentially low odds of survival. She said that she and her husband never considered that their triplets would *not* survive. Today, those triplets are seniors, attending Ohio State and Syracuse Universities, with bright futures ahead of them. Clearly, the power of positive thinking does work!

I will share with you what happened to me, and what I do know is this: it is my positive attitude that keeps me going—always being grateful for what I have, not focusing on what I lost. The glass is half-full, not half-empty. I have come to believe that God kept me alive and did not let me die (even though the odds were against me) because I have an important message to share: I have overcome alcohol addiction, finally (for today), which I suffered with for nearly four decades, mostly the last decade of my drinking and the last decade plus, consisting of being in and out of rehab three times, two visits to Father Martin's Ashley (in Havre de Grace, Maryland), for two weeks and three weeks, respectively, and one to Crossroads in Antigua (for the full recommended month). Since the year 2000, I also made numerous emergency room visits to detox from alcohol.

I also went in and out of Alcoholics Anonymous (AA). There are many sayings in AA. Most often, "one day at a time" is viewed as synonymous with the credo of AA. There are other "truisms," developed by members themselves. These truisms include "you can't be too dumb to get AA, but you can be too smart." I hold myself accountable for believing that one, that I was "too smart" to have to attend AA, or so I thought, and I was going to crack the code and figure out the whole program. I didn't care for the idea that if you took even one drink, you were "out" of AA. AA requires complete abstinence to maintain a time "track record" and be "in" AA. During my seventeen years in and out of AA, I compiled a broken track record of two years four times (for a total of eight years) and one year six times (for a total of six years), but that would not count as fourteen years of continuous sobriety, if you were truly honest, which is another requirement in AA—being completely honest, mostly with ourselves.

Another saying is "You can only drink on a lie," and that was usually lying to one's self. In my brilliance, I basically said "screw AA"; I was going to drink "my way." It would be very controlled, only good wines or Champagne, only in nice glasses. And in my last "hurrah," I did just that. It must have taken several weeks, living by myself, having alcohol delivered to my front door, on a pity pot, feeling bad about my relationship, that I got to a point after several days of Pinot Noir, where I fell down that steep flight of stairs (accidentally), broke my skull, suffered a traumatic brain injury, and changed my life forever! Obviously, my life needed changing, but importantly, I'm still alive! Looking at things positively, which I do now, every day, the possibilities are endless! My goal now is to make my new life worth having been saved in the first place. I need to share my message with others. Clearly, I made numerous mistakes, but my goal is to demonstrate that I've learned from them!

Debunking Conspiracy Theories

After my horrific accident that left me unrecognizable—my nose was sheared off my face, my eye sockets were broken, and my cheekbones were crushed—there were many questions about whether anyone had been there or knew what had happened to me. My family sought answers, terrified as they were, that their daughter, their sister, was going to die. The only person they thought might have some answers was Ron, my boyfriend and business partner at the time. As a result, Ron was called in to the Ramsey Police Department for questioning as a "person of interest," not a suspect. Ron had relayed to the police that I was an alcoholic and had been drinking heavily for several days (weeks), and that must have caused me to fall in the middle of the night. I was not pushed, or anything untoward. Because of the police questioning, people were reacting, speculating, and judging. Because Ron is Black and I am white, some people at the gym we both attended for years thought they were joking when they called Ron "O.J." (as in Orenthal James Simpson, a publicly presumed guilty man), as I was his blond girlfriend at the time (but not Nicole Brown Simpson). Ron must have been hurt and furious that anyone would have referred to his involvement with me at the accident scene as anything other than a friend finding me and calling 911. That led the Ramsey Police and a team of EMTs to come to my home and find me, lying face-down in a pool of blood, unconscious and unresponsive. On a Glasgow Coma Scale (GCS), I was a 3 (severe) out of a potential scale of 15.

I was furious when I'd heard about what people said to Ron at the gym. I even called the Ramsey Police and spoke with the detective (Detective Adam Szelag) who interviewed Ron, and informed him that Ron had nothing to do with my fall. I did! I even asked the detective if they'd call Ron to apologize, and he replied, "We don't do that." Click.

Ron was never violent with me! He never touched me in an angry way! Ever! Yes, I was present when Ron took his test for his black belt in November 1998, after he trained at Tiger Schulmann's Martial Arts in Ramsey. Watching him take his test was not easy, as many of the toughest-looking guys lined up to spar with Ron. As part of the test, the last part was fighting ten different spar partners for one minute each. If he was still standing after that, he passed the test. He passed the test and received his black belt, presented by his sensei, Vinny Gravina. When the contest was over, Ron was battered and bruised, but he was happy and proud of his accomplishment.

But to put together a tall, Black guy with a black belt and conclude it meant potentially violent behavior, specifically with me, is racist and wrong.

My family knew and loved Ron. They knew he'd always been against my drinking and, yes, he'd get upset when I'd relapse (which was all too frequent), but the man *never* hit me or slapped me, or pushed me down a flight of stairs! There were people who called me to say, "You don't remember the fall, but you have to keep trying to remember." They say "love is blind" and that I just "refused to see that he must have had something to do with my fall." Sorry guys, there was nothing more dramatic than a woman with too much alcohol in her system to *not* be able to break her fall or redirect the course of the fall.

I also believe that, knowing Ron, if he *had* pushed me down the stairs, he would have never come back the next morning to find me in a pool of blood, as he would have known he'd be a suspect. That just doesn't add up for me. To believe that he'd conveniently shown up at my townhouse the next morning, to find me in a pool of blood, and then ultimately call 911 and save my life, would not be like Ron, either. He'd be overwrought with fear with the knowledge that he would be a suspect. I think Ron thought, because he is Black, he knew where the suspicion would lie: on him! That's where his self-protective instinct kicked in, and why he called Karen Boaz before calling 911. When he found me, face-down in a pool of blood on the first-floor landing of my townhouse, he was genuinely shocked. He panicked and did not know what to do first. He called Karen Boaz, my good friend in AA (who was also called in as a person of interest), to alert her to what had happened, what he found when he got to my place, and she told him to call 911 right away. He did. That led to the Ramsey PD and a team of EMTs who came to my home, evaluated the situation, questioned Ron—who told them I was an alcoholic and had been drinking—and then Officer Rork and his team got me to Hackensack University Medical Center. There, the trauma surgeon told Officer Rork and his team that it didn't look good. When I called Officer Rork (in 2018, seven years after my accident, after reading his police report), he was genuinely surprised that (1) I was alive, and (2) I had called to thank him and his team for getting me to the hospital and saving my life.

In July 2020, almost nine years after my accident, I learned that my family, and more specifically, my father, who adored me but was also very protective, took issue with the fact that when Ron found me face-down in a pool of blood, he panicked and called my friend Karen Boaz before calling 911. It doesn't change that he did make the call to 911, but I know that contributed to my father's reaction to Ron, questioning that if he'd really cared about me and loved me, why did he call someone else first? My father also took issue with what he thought was Ron's influence on me, my decision-making process, and my moral upbringing, as we'd had an extra-marital affair. But I know that no one could make me do anything that I didn't want to do. I know it didn't make my dad happy, or proud, and along with my drinking, which almost resulted in my death, he wrongly directed his anger at Ron.

My dad told people that he had a restraining order against Ron, but after checking with my lawyer, I found out it was not true. It doesn't change that I'd remained perplexed, until now, about why I haven't heard a word, nor had a visit from the man who found me and eventually called 911, saving my life. Even after I had spoken to Officer Matthew Rork, he spoke of how fortunate I was that Ron had reason (our company, Veritas Partners) to come to my townhouse the morning of August 31, 2011, or I easily could have died. I thank Ron for that part of saving my life by getting help to me that morning. The self-protective instinct, while understandable, does not excuse that he hadn't demonstrated a scintilla of care and concern or love for me. I know he'd always been against me having alcohol in my life. That was a "deal-breaker." He was right about that, and now, finally, I saw the light, and have remained alcohol-free for over nine years. That's why every sentence with his name in it, and a reference that he was my boyfriend, is followed with "at that time." I wish the best for Ron in his life. I wish him love and success for his future. I will always remember what we shared because, thanks to God and Dr. Roy Vingan, my brain works very well again.

Officer Matthew Rork, Ramsey PD and EMT, and his team came to my rescue

For anyone who's been thinking, "Wait, this woman had a horrific accident because she relapsed on alcohol? She's lucky to be alive. She got what she deserved! What did she expect?" I hear you. That would have been me, too, before I was born again. As I became a born-again Christian, when I got baptized, I became a new (spiritual) creation. As a Christian, I do not judge anyone anymore. "Judge not; lest ye be judged" (Matthew 7:1).

Many people, even most people, wouldn't consider that they could come back from this near catastrophe. They'd be too embarrassed to show their face, let alone resume a normal life, socialize with people, write a book about their ordeal and be completely honest about the circumstances, start and fund a foundation for the type of injury sustained in the accident, become an advocate for people with all types of brain injuries, and, in promoting the book, go out and speak to people about their journey of recovery. Well, that's exactly what I plan—and hope—to do. As I mentioned, "to whom much is given, much will be required" (Luke 12:48).

Fortunately, my traumatic brain injury (TBI), while initially severe, has been largely resolved. I believe that my TBI recovery is the result of God (divine intervention) and an excellent neurosurgeon (Dr. Roy Vingan), as well as the Critical Care Nursing team who cared for me after my emergency surgeries. When I first became fully cognizant again, I was able to speak and understand commands and questions. It has been a nine-plus-year journey, and while difficult at many points along the way, I remain grateful for all that's been given me. I got my life back! That meant I was alive. But getting a "life back" will require that I rebuild one, from scratch, which will take time. As I'm very fortunate to have positive people in my life, I will draw upon them for help as needed. I'm not talking about money, in this instance, but rather their energy and positivity. Naysayers need not apply.

Since my accident, I've had to learn to walk again, but my bigger goal is to run independently again. You'll read in my story that I was a triathlete, including completing an Ironman distance triathlon (that requires swimming 2.4 miles, biking 112 miles, and then running 26.2 miles—a full marathon—for a total of 140.6 miles), which I completed on July 24, 2005. The next day, I was sore and stiff, but I was elated! It took me from 7 a.m. till just shy of 11 p.m., nearly sixteen hours, going the whole time, no sitting down for a breather—I just kept going. And I believe God gave me that ability to breathe while I swam, while I biked, and while I ran. I admit I did walk quite a bit during the marathon—but I kept on, keeping on. I kept on truckin'.

After a lengthy search, I finally found my 2005 Ironman results:

Swim: 1:22:15

Bike: 7:37:15

Run: 6:29:26

Total: 15:58:25

Under Ironman distance rules, a triathlete has 17:00 hours to complete the 2.4-mile swim, the 112-mile bike ride, and the 26.2-mile marathon.

I still had another hour to complete the race to qualify for the Ironman Finisher medal and T-shirt at the end. I came across several competitors that crossed at 17:00 or after and were not eligible for the Finisher designation. They were heartbroken. I can't imagine if that were me! To have been out there for all those hours, in the dark, wearing a glow-in-the-dark necklace to be spotted, it just seems unfair. But rules are rules, I suppose. I mean, they know they finished, as do their loved ones, but to not give them a medal and a Finisher T-shirt seems cruel to me!

Alyson Llerandi and Deb at the New Jersy Half Marathon, May 2009

After running and walking the last half of the marathon (the third leg of my Ironman in Lake Placid), it made me happy that I had a good adrenaline rush, while I ran (not walked) the oval at the high school in Lake Placid to the finish line. (It was almost like a runner's high, which I've experienced many times.). At this moment I'd been waiting for—crossing the finish line—I was able to put my arms up in a "V" for "Victory." After that, I saw my dad and my mom, who both hugged and kissed me, and some of my friends, who were up at Lake Placid to spectate. I was able to run across the finish line with Ashlyn Llerandi, my friend Alyson's daughter. Alyson is a very accomplished runner and triathlete, with a sub 1:30 half marathon time and I think the half is her sweet spot in racing. Her daughter Ashlyn was an accomplished pole vaulter, earning herself a "full ride" in her fourth year at Villanova. Also with me was Nicole Kincade, my friend Kirsten's daughter. Nicole was in high school in 2005 but subsequently went to Princeton, in New Jersey, for college, and had a stellar career in volleyball. Unlike me, Kirsten is an elite triathlete, who has done the World Championship Ironman in Kona, Hawaii, many times, including 2007. She was running it for the benefit of the Matthew Larson Foundation (see Ironmatt.org). Matt was diagnosed in 2002 with choroid plexus carcinoma, a rare but very deadly brain tumor cancer. Matt left this world April 2007 and is surely in heaven.

Kirsten Kincade, a world championship Ironman triathlete[1]

1. Fifteen years after my Ironman in Lake Placid, Ashlyn Llerandi married Joe D'Andrea on August 8, 2020, and Nicole Kincade just got engaged to her boyfriend, Mike.

Ashlyn & Joe, married on August 8, 2020,
first child, Joseph Michael, welcomed April 2021!

After the race, and after being so warmly greeted by my family and friends, it was time to bring this ol' horse home. I was able to maintain a deliberate pace for the distance from the finish line to where my bike had been stowed on the bike rack, with my number, and then back to the hotel and car (to put my bike on the bike rack for the ride home). Finally, when I got to my room, and bed, all the adrenaline that carried me across that finish line began to drain from my body, and soreness and stiffness began to replace the elation. I was tired!

It wasn't until the next morning that my stiffness really started to set in (it's called DOMS: delayed onset muscle soreness). But I was able to get my things together, load them in the car, and Gary, my parents, and I set on our way home. Gary had been great and supportive of me the whole time! Just as he had been at St. Croix the year prior. Who knew that one year later he'd be dead?

Troubling Signs I Didn't Heed: My Accident Was Coming!

The year of my accident, I was fortunate to chair a benefit casino night, in May 2011, to benefit the Matthew Larson Foundation, and it was a very successful event. During the planning process, I was exposed to the committee process of Matthew Larson's foundation, where a group of very bright, talented, articulate, and giving women did everything for the event—prize procurement, sponsor donations, casino invitation design, hiring a casino night vendor—everything necessary to put on a successful event. The event came off without a hitch, and I was grateful to have been a part of such a worthy cause.

Actually, there was a hitch. I ended up having to go to detox at Valley Hospital in Ridgewood, New Jersey, two weeks before the event, as I'd been drinking a lot for a few days, yet I wanted to make sure I got things back on track and go through with the event, which we had all worked so hard on. I was sheepish at our last team meeting, but nobody made me feel awkward (although inside, I was hugely embarrassed). In the end, the event was a huge success, and apparently they were happy with the job I did.

My friend Kirsten Kincade sent me a Facebook post after the event and after my accident. A couple of other friends chimed in.

Kirsten Kannengieser Kincade to Debbie Grosser
September 22, 2011

Found this picture of IronMatt Casino Night which you ran in May. What an amazing job you did. You blew us all away. Today is our NYC event that you have attended and supported every year since we started - you will be very missed at my table! Please know that even though we are not allowed to visit, we would be there, holding your hand and telling you we loved you every day if we could. As I told you the night of this picture, you are an amazing woman and I love you.

COMMENTS

Alyson Wheeler Llerandi Amen to that...

September 22, 2011 at 3:22 p.m.

Karen Finnerty

September 23, 2011 at 2:49 a.m.

I wish I could be there too Debbie. You have always been there to help me and get me through stuff. I hope you know that I too would do anything to help you now. Kirsten's right, you are an amazing person and friend. I love you too.

There was also a post from another good friend of mine, Alyson Llerandi, inviting people to her home to pray for me in a good, old-fashioned: prayer meeting. I didn't see this until I'd commenced writing my book, and it touched my heart.

Alyson Wheeler Llerandi to Debbie Grosser
September 15, 2011

Dear Friends of Debbie...please come to a gathering at my house this Sunday night from 7-9p.m.. We will be having a prayer/good karma session for Deb. Bring your thoughts and memories of Debbie, not to mention your collective positive mental energy! Please send me a message on FB if you can come. WE LOVE YOU DEBBIE!!!!!!!!!!!!!!!!!

These posts were from mid- and late September 2011. What has remained a mystery to me is how I got access to a computer at Hackensack University Medical Center, and at Kessler Rehabilitation Institute, while I was still in my coma. The truth is, the posts were written by others while I was in my coma, but I located them after I'd awakened, and started writing this book.

I finally fully awakened from my coma on October 7, 2011, when I arrived at Kessler Rehab in West Orange, New Jersey. I read the date on my admissions bracelet. It was my first cognizant moment! It would be some time before I was able to see anybody with any regularity. Contact, in any form, really lifted my spirits. During the writing of this book, I was reconnected with a critical care nurse practitioner (Lee Taylor-Vaughan, CCNP). He told me of the initial stages of my recovery, following my emergency surgeries. It was not a smooth path. He wrote me this on Facebook, in a series of comments about my post, as I marked my nine-year commemoration since my accident.

Lee Taylor-Vaughan

Lee Taylor-Vaughan, my life-saving CCNP; he and the team saved my life and my brain.

I remember the night your heart stopped in the corner room of the ICU. Your path for the last couple of days had not been promising at all. I looked at the fellow nurses, who were part of the "code" and we felt helpless. Then, your heart rate came back and was slow. From then on you kept us earning our paychecks. Lol. Your critical condition kept us very busy. We had no clue you would have everyone choked up and a tear in your eyes when you woke up a few days later. "Ironman is awake, was the text I received." Thank you for doing that. It reminds us to ALWAYS keep going, and we never know the outcome of many. I speak of your story to many of my attendees at my critical care seminars. Tens of thousands have heard the gist of your story and many are in awe of your amazing outcome. (I keep your name private, but I set the example to them and they are usually charged to go back to work.) Hang in there sister. We're very glad you're still with us.

Debbie Grosser

Lee Taylor-Vaughan, the story of you tending to me is a critical part of my memoir, post-accident! God blessed me with you, as my angel that night! Honestly, I never knew my heart had stopped! I was a FULL CODE?!!

Lee Taylor-Vaughan

Debbie Grosser, your heart slowed down. It stopped. I gave it a shot of Adrenalin (epi) and you came back. There was no "do not resuscitate order" (DNR) on your chart, so yes, you were a full code. Your heart likely did that because of the massive trauma you endured. We reckon that you were able to clear lactate quite efficiently due to your races and Ironman nature, and it's speculative that's why you survived.

He also informed me that I had very high fevers, sometimes spiking at 106 degrees. I was kept in an "Arctic Sun blanket," a mattress that had tubes running underneath my mattress with freezing-cold water, to keep my body temperature low, lest my brain get fried, and I could have suffered brain damage or death!

> **Lee Taylor-Vaughan**
> When someone has neurological injuries it is very common to see patients spike very high temps. Yours were some of the highest I've ever seen. The "artic sun" was wrapped around you to get you to defervesce. Otherwise the brain cooks (like frying an egg, all the proteins literally cook). It's horrid to see. Often the patient is unaware of it. If not treated quickly it results in brain death, or worsening neurological injuries. We broke your temp with the Arctic Sun.

All this dialogue reinforces for me that the critical care nurse practitioners and other team members who assist in the critical part of recovery (i.e., right after emergency surgeries) are so important to the ultimate outcome. Had I not received the Epi (when my heart stopped), or the Arctic Sun (when I was spiking temperatures of 106 or higher), I might likely have suffered significant brain damage (which is permanent brain injury), and it would certainly be unlikely that I ever would have been capable of writing a book about the whole ordeal. This should say to every critical care nurse practitioner and all the healthcare professionals who attended to me that I am eternally grateful to all of you for your extreme efforts in not only saving my life but saving my brain's cognitive capability, and that you should never give up in your efforts. Use every tool available to you to aid you in your attempts to save a life, save a brain, because you never know the result of the final outcome. A mind is a terrible thing to waste, and everything to save. I thank you all, forever.

Lee Taylor-Vaughan clarified for me that I came out of my initial coma after about my fourth or fifth day, post-accident, but was kept in a medically induced coma, as I continued to require more surgeries, frequently, during the first month after my accident.

Do you know the only good thing about a coma? The Coma Diet—painless food deprivation. For me, those six weeks melted about fifty pounds off my body, as all my nutrition was provided only through a "G" tube. Alyson Llerandi, who visited me, told me I was "thin as a pin." Since she is thin and muscular herself, I took that as a great compliment. But I don't recommend my "coma diet" for anyone, and as soon as I resumed eating normally, but not being able to exercise, the way I had, while I gained some muscle back, those pounds came right back.

Me and the girls from the gym: Jennifer Bottini, me (I am second from left, in yellow bikini), Lizabeth Cirillo, and Lisa Krug

I wasn't heavy-looking to begin with, but my flat, six-pack ab stomach is something I want back. With hard work, in time, it will eventually come back.

Scary thing is, I can picture a book, with that title: "The Coma Diet"—in the self-help section at Barnes & Noble, and wealthy people finding doctors who would medically induce a coma for a patient desiring significant weight loss. Hopefully, something like that would never come to pass.

Other Stories That Prove Life-Altering Experiences Bring about Change

In this book, I also plan to share some others' stories that inspire courage and gratitude. There are those who were in the military, and because of what they encountered, now suffer from PTSD, or post-traumatic stress disorder. Mostly, there are everyday folk who went through some of life's peaks and valleys, and have come out the other side stronger, while maintaining their faith and a healthy sense of gratitude. It does appear that life-changing or life-altering experiences are necessary to precipitate significant changes in perspective and attitude.

A case on PTSD. One of my best friends since high school, Robin Haushalter Guerire, has a son, Derek Giannola, who was deployed in Afghanistan in 2009–2010. It was during his deployment that the things he saw and experienced were cause for him to return home with symptoms of PTSD. Thunder and lightning storms were cause for him to scream out: "Incoming!" His life-altering experience there caused him to realize the importance of his family, and that the deep, lasting, and loyal relationships he had with his family were the most important things in his world.

Three generations of Giannolas: dad, Kirk; grandfather, Frank; and son and grandson, Derek

I started writing this book in my head, nearly nine years ago, when I became cognizant again, after coming out of my coma. After I became verbal again, and I described the story of my accident and my path back toward full recovery, most everyone I told commented that "everything happens for a reason, and yours must be very important." I agreed, and realized: *"God, you've got my full attention."* As I learned more about what had happened, came to grasp the severity of it, and understood that there would likely be residual effects for the rest of my life, I came to believe that something good had to come out of all of this!

Restoring My Relationship with God

As a former Catholic school girl, who severely deviated from my belief system with which I grew up (even being willing to consider atheism and Hinduism at different points), I have been working toward restoring my relationship with God, and it draws upon what I grew up believing: there is one God (a divine being) in three persons: God, the Father; God, the son (Jesus Christ); and God, the Holy Spirit. This conclusion did not come easily. While living at Gurwin, I had a variety of "teachers" to lead my way. Several years ago, I started studying the Bible with a couple of women who were Jehovah's Witnesses (JWs). They believe that Jehovah (God, the Father) is the one and only, almighty God. Jesus is a god (lower case *g*), but he is not almighty God. They do believe that Jesus (son of God) did die, but on a "torture stake" versus a "cross," but he did pay the ransom sacrifice that paid for all our sins. They taught me to "search for truth like hidden treasure," and so I took that literally, and began to explore the Bible more in depth. I also noted that the Bible used by the JWs was a New World Translation (NWT), which interestingly, only refers to Jehovah as God. Subsequently, I began reading the New King James Version of the Bible, with my sisters-in-Christ, reading the Gospel of John from beginning to end, and the differences between the religions became more apparent. Mind you, the women who came as JW representatives were perfectly lovely, and with that, I had no issue. Truth be told, when they first started to show up regularly (every Thursday at 2 p.m.), I, starved for intellectual stimulation, welcomed their visits, and came to care for them quite a bit. (And I still do.)

Quite honestly, because I was so starved to find the "One True God," I had to realize that I'd been looking in too many places and had not been resolved to figuring out just one answer. I was ready to automatically get baptized as a Jehovah's Witness (actually, I thought it was cool, because Prince was a Jehovah's Witness). This was a bold departure from having been born and baptized a Catholic (at three months old, as is custom), attending Catholic school, participating in all of the sacraments: communion, confirmation, and even marriage, and being taught the concept of the Holy Trinity (although the word "trinity" never appears in the Bible). Such a serious decision could not be made lightly. In came my sisters-in-Christ.

First, there was Donna Pennacchio, who showed up one day, unannounced. Donna is a longtime friend of my dearest sister-cousin, Gigi, and we spent the afternoon talking about her transformation to a born-again Christian, from a "sinner" (which we all are). She shared her own story of dependency on alcohol. She believes that it was her being saved by Jesus that released her from her obsession, the shackles of alcohol. Her heartfelt discussion with me opened my heart and eyes to a different possibility, and that maybe a transformation like hers was possible for me!

The story of my visiting sisters-in-Christ does not end there. Next comes Kerry Rohe, one of Donna's sisters-in-Christ, and Kerry and I started with the Gospel of John, and just kept reading, and we kept seeing, over and over, that Jesus is God! Next came Janis Mayors, sister-in-law of Kerry Rohe. Janis had a similar history as me. Born and raised Catholic, and also spent time studying with Jehovah's Witnesses, and she too came to the conclusion I did: Jesus Christ is God. God, in His bid to reconcile with us, and save us, came to the earth, was born a Man (incarnate), of the Virgin Mary, he suffered, died, and was buried, and was resurrected to the earth and then Ascended into heaven, where He is seated at the right hand of the Father. Through this process, Jesus (God) paid the ransom sacrifice for Man's original sin (disobeying God in the Garden of Eden; and eating fruit from the tree of the Knowledge of Good and Evil, making himself more like God, and therefore as good, and as smart as God). Through this ransom sacrifice, all of Man's sins were washed clean, our direct relationship with the Father was restored, and we had the prospect of eternal life.

Being at Gurwin Jewish Nursing & Rehabilitation Center for five of the last nine years, I've become witness to many things. The big question for me is: are nursing homes just a place to wait to die? When I arrived here in February 2016, I was fifty-six years old. It was certainly not an age, on my radar, for me to die. But I almost did, five years prior (2011), when, after a horrific fall down a steep flight of stairs, I broke my skull and suffered a traumatic brain injury. My odds of survival were dim. Thanks to God, an excellent neurosurgeon (Dr. Roy Vingan), and a superb Critical Care Nursing team, I did survive. Here I am, nearly ten years later, contemplating the next move in my life. My recovery has spanned more than nine years, during which I endured nineteen surgeries, and copious amounts of both physical and occupational therapy (which I have dubbed "optional torture") in between. There were fits and starts during my recovery for my living situation. After seven months at Kessler Institute for Rehabilitation, in West Orange, New Jersey, during which my physical therapists had me running again (with handheld assistance), I moved in with my brother John and his wife, Kelly. That was in April 2012. I went to another rehabilitation facility in Manhasset called Transitions, which also offered physical therapy, occupational therapy, and speech therapy. Fortunately, at every place I went, I did not end up requiring speech therapy. But I was witness to many who did. It's amazing to hear and see the impact of brain injuries on a human's capabilities: to speak, to eat, to do most anything. That is when I started formulating the basis for this book. I realized how much I'd taken for granted! Hence my book's title.

In the fall of 2012, I moved into a one-bedroom apartment with my new aide, Yolanda Miller, in Avalon Gardens, in Garden City, New York. Yolanda is a Jesus-loving, devout, Bible-reading woman, who was born in Jamaica. She wanted to work at a job that would allow her to read her Bible every day. Working with me allowed for that, and it was good for me, too. Living on Long Island is expensive. My one-bedroom apartment, albeit with granite countertops, stainless-steel appliances, a pool, and a fitness center, ran $3,200 per month. Yolanda was costly too. We agreed upon $1,000 per week. That brought the monthly total, excluding food, to $7,200 per month. As I'd initially had the proceeds from the sale of 17 Seminary, Gary's life insurance, and his pension, my nest egg sounded like a lot. But it wouldn't be long before that cash ran out. And it did.

In December 2013, I was facing eviction. In late December, I ended up in Nassau University Medical Center (NUMC), in East Meadow, New York. Apparently, I'd had a grand mal seizure. My aide at the time, Thelma, called 911 and an ambulance got me to the ER at NUMC. As it turned out, I hadn't taken my anti-seizure medication (common for brain injuries), Keppra, and that's what triggered my seizure. That really scared me, and I remember my lawyer, Arnie, showed up at the hospital, and we discussed whether I'd forgotten to take my anti-seizure medication. The light bulb went on—that had been the cause! Over the next two weeks, I was referred to yet another neurosurgeon, who ultimately performed another cranioplasty. My parents, who were both still alive, were there for me yet again! I was so blessed to have them every moment that I did.

Upon being discharged, on January 13, 2014, I moved to Oak Hollow Nursing & Rehabilitation Facility, in Middle Island, New York. I remember being there for two New Year's Eves, in 2015 and 2016. I was discharged, to move to Gurwin, in February 2016.

Because I survived my near-death accident, it didn't take too much time before I took that for granted, too. I'm not proud to say this, but it's my truth. I wanted to make sure that I wouldn't die if I drank just a little bit of alcohol.

(Clearly, it was not sensible or rational thinking, given my near-death experience.) I was able to procure one or more small bottles of wine, sold in four-packs (single-serving sized). All four combined would equal a 750 mL bottle of wine. I drank one. I didn't explode. All it did was make me tired. I did that several times. Imagine my sister-in-law Kelly's horror upon her discovery of my stash of empties. Imagine the horror and disgust when my brother John was contacted by Eddie Aiello, a neighbor from our old neighborhood. I'd seized upon the opportunity when Eddie told me he used to drink "two bottles of Pinot Noir a night." I suggested that when Eddie came to visit for lunch, that he bring some with him. Thankfully, Eddie called my brother to check if it was okay for me to drink, and my brother told him what had happened to me, and that in no uncertain terms, "*No*, she cannot drink!" Eddie never came for lunch.

Not surprisingly, my foolish request to Eddie caused a rift between me and my brother John, my other siblings, and even my parents, who were still alive at the time.

MY TRUE MOMENT OF CLARITY

In April 2013, after another small bottle of wine (single-serving size), and all it did was make me tired, that was *it*. The real "IT." Alcohol lost all its addictive appeal for me. I became apathetic to it. It's the way I believe that a non-alcoholic feels about alcohol. They can take it or leave it. They just don't think or care about it. I was done. And I did not want to lose my most precious siblings, their families, and my parents, who were still alive at the time. Stopping drinking this time was not going out with a bang (I'd done that already). I was exhausted at the prospect of getting back into that vicious cycle, never knowing how it would end. I became disgusted with myself and my seeming inability to just STOP. So, that was *it*. This all happened before I got baptized as a born-again Christian.

Finally, I was released from the horrific grip that alcohol had on me. It seems that I finally gained the sustained clarity and perspective to see all the negative effects that alcohol had in my life. As time went on, the reality of everything that had happened to me—the broken skull, the brain injury, the nineteen surgeries, the therapy—became crystal clear. Later, my faith factored into my newfound clarity. Previously, I'd been unable to do it alone, and now, I don't have to. This time, I had to rely on Jesus, my sisters-in-Christ, my family, and my friends to carry me through. That was April 6, 2013. I am very happy to say that on April 6, 2020, that after all I've been through, I was finally seven years completely free of alcohol. Hallelujah! As of this writing (2021), it's now nearly nine years, one day at a time.

I almost ruined the longest sobriety track record I ever had when I requested that Eddie Aiello bring some Pinot Noir with him when he visited. That was 2017. Fortunately, he never visited, I never drank, thus my nearly eight-year track record remains intact.

I prayed to Jesus to soften the hearts of my siblings. My parents had already forgiven me. That was while they were still here. After I was baptized, I had a discussion with my dad about my siblings and our rift. My dad simply said: "Debbie, you've got to ease up on them. They're hurt. They don't want to see you hurt yourself again," and "Debbie, Jesus forgave you, now you have to forgive yourself. Jesus remembers your sins no more. Give it time." He was right, as he always was with me.

It's a new decade. I'm interested to see what the new "roaring twenties" will bring. Since I've been at Gurwin, a long-term rehabilitation facility, I had a decision to make. It comes from my favorite movie, *The Shawshank Redemption*: I either get busy living, or get busy dying. Like James Whitmore, as Brooks Hatlen, in the movie, I've been institutionalized for most of the last ten years. I've become somewhat important here. In late 2019, I was elected president of the resident council here at Gurwin.

Now the global pandemic, the coronavirus, has put another roadblock in my path back to living a normal life. I've seized upon this time as the opportunity to finish my manuscript, once and for all! And that is a definite positive!

During 2018 and 2019, I competed in the "Golden Games" for Gurwin. In each year I've been a triple gold medal winner. I summed up my stellar performance: "I've cracked the code of winning gold medals: 'compete with people twice my age.'" In all honesty, some of my medal "wins" were as a team, such as volleyball and wheelchair relay. I must admit that I enjoyed all of our practices as much as the competition itself.

Another casualty of the coronavirus pandemic, the 2020 Golden Games have been cancelled and will resume in 2021. My hope is to be living independently by September 2021, a full decade since my near-death accident.

Sadly, on January 29, 2020, one of my teammates in the Golden Games, Angelo Cogliano, passed away at age ninety-three, after two bouts with sepsis, following a recurring UTI (urinary tract infection).

Angelo Cogliano in 1945

The Coglianos, who were present for virtually every Golden Games practice, were prepared but saddened by his loss. Thankfully, they, too, believe that their father is with our Lord, and all the other pre-deceased Coglianos, including Angelo's wife, Adelaide.

In mid-March 2020, the coronavirus pandemic hit, and the world stopped. I await the ultimate easing of restrictions for nursing care facilities. Gurwin must adhere to the New York State Department of Health and CDC guidelines, which will determine when it can open its doors to visitors, and residents can again use the facilities at Gurwin.

Part of the process has been testing. All Gurwin staff members are required to be tested for COVID-19. They're required to test twice a week. In early June, Gurwin started to test all the residents. Each of us was swabbed, and the results were due back within forty-eight hours. I'm happy to report that all of the tests on 3 East and 3 West came back negative. Hallelujah, and phew! Hopefully, that portends that an opening of Gurwin will ultimately happen.

Thankfully, in early June 2020, administration at Gurwin arranged that the recumbent bike would be moved to the family room on my unit, 3 East! Hallelujah for that, too! The return to my daily rides, the burning of hundreds of calories and the rush of endorphins, has truly been amazing! Thank you, Shua Sauer, Joanne Parisi, and Stuart Almer (Gurwin Administration) and Lynette Rutherford and Kim Thomas (Gurwin Nursing)! Your action on my behalf is something for which I will be forever grateful. It makes my life at Gurwin so much more of a place where I can feel happy about something again!

THE ORDER OF MY STORY

My story will progress in reverse. I begin with my most recent experiences at Gurwin Nursing & Rehabilitation Center first. I then get into my accident, which precipitated the sequence of events that occurred over the last eight years. I then go back to the beginning of my life and all the events that made me, me.

Chapter One

Kelly Dolan's Story

My Roommate at Gurwin. It Could Always Be Worse . . .

My roommate for two years (August 2016 to September 2018) at Gurwin was Kelly Elizabeth Dolan. Kelly had been in a serious auto accident as a passenger, at fifteen years old. Her boyfriend, Lance, then seventeen, was driving. They were going to make a quick stop home, as Kelly forgot her soccer cleats and she had a game. It was October 17, 1995. It was going to be a quick pit stop, but instead tragedy of the worst kind struck. Lance was speeding to get to Kelly's house quickly, but he lost control of the car, and it flipped over several times before coming to a stop on its roof, under which were Kelly's and Lance's heads. Kelly's parents, Tom and Karen, rushed to the hospital, after receiving a call from the police about what had happened. They were not given a positive prognosis and feared Kelly would die. Miraculously, Lance walked away from the horrific accident. There was never much contact between the Dolans and Lance's family, and Lance never came to find out what had happened to Kelly. Just a few months after the accident, it was Kelly's sixteenth birthday. I think Kelly's mom thought Lance might show up (she'd sent an invitation) for that, but he never did show.

Tom and Karen came and visited often at Gurwin, and every other place Kelly had been over the course of twenty-four years, as did her brothers, Matthew and Brian (the twins), Thomas (whom I've just met recently), and Michael (whom I've not met), but it must've been a heartbreak for them. Kelly had not spoken since the accident twenty-five years before. She was thirty-nine years old and had never really "lived" the bulk of her adult life thus far. She never got married, never had kids. Dependent on a "G" tube for her meals, she hadn't had the pleasure of a good meal, perhaps at a nice restaurant. The poor thing merely existed, for the last twenty-four years, in a minimally conscious state (the current term for vegetative state). There is a sad footnote to Kelly's story.

The Remembrance Store

eturnalmemorials.com/simple-store/1/products.html#store-start

Obituary for Kelly Elizabeth Dolan

Kelly Elizabeth Dolan, of Freeport, NY, on Thursday, May 30, 2019. Beloved daughter of Thomas P. and Karen E. Dolan. Revered sister of Tommy (Mindy), Brian (Cara), Matthew (Kim) and Michael (Meghan). Loving aunt of Aiden, Colin and Nate. In lieu of flowers donations to: The Kelly Dolan Memorial Nursing Scholarship, sent to: The Nassau Community College Foundation, 364 Rice Circle, Garden City, NY 11530 would be greatly appreciated.

A Mass of Christian burial will be held 10:45 a.m. on Monday, June 3rd at St. Anthony's RC Church, 110 Anchor Ave, Oceanside, NY.

I spoke to Kelly's mom, Karen, in late June. She said she was "still coming to grips with the fact that Kelly was really gone," and she wasn't ready to come back and see people at Gurwin, but she had nothing but good things to say about the care Kelly had received while at Gurwin, and said that one day when she was ready, she would come, "but not right now," as her voice broke off.

She did say that the family expected that one day the issue that would ultimately cause Kelly's demise would be respiratory, and Kelly died of pneumonia. It went from bad to worse, and she passed away. I said, "Kelly is now free, free from the body where she was held prisoner for twenty-four years, and that she's now in heaven, in the presence of Jesus, and she can run and play soccer, and jump hurdles again." Karen agreed with that belief, and it's her only comfort right now.

Interestingly, Kelly and I had the same diagnosis—traumatic brain injury—yet our current prognoses were vastly different. Why?

Traumatic brain injuries all seem to involve bleeding in the brain. Interestingly, wherever the bleeding is in the brain, the opposite side of the body is affected. In my case, since my brain bleed was on my right side, I suffered left side weakness. On the other hand, since I was lying on my right arm for several hours before being found, I required an emergency fasciotomy, resulting from something called compartment syndrome, which I will discuss later.

The Deb who was used to taking charge in her typical role had to take a back seat (and not a comfortable one), so as to allow my family to help me and protect me. This was not something I was comfortable with, or familiar. This was a whole new world for me.

Kelly's situation was so sad, and yet, rather than me wallowing in the sadness of it, I need to focus on getting better, walking better, walking independently. Instead, what's happened to Kelly makes me ever more grateful that I can talk, that I'm capable of writing a book, and have my wits about me, or so it seems, most days. There are deficits (mostly physical), but I can continue to work on them. It could be so much worse. I need to keep a positive attitude. And I need to keep up the gratitude. For the years we were roommates, I always prayed that one day, Kelly would "come to" and speak again, and laugh and talk with her parents and brothers . . . what a wonderful miracle that would have been! Her parents, knowing that I'm writing a book, have only asked that if the book were ever made into a movie, their actors of choice to play Tom and Karen would be Alec Baldwin (Tom) and Kim Basinger (Karen). If it happens, then I will see to it that their wishes are granted (if I have any say).

There was a picture on Kelly's bulletin board of Kelly jumping and clearing one of several hurdles (a feat requiring significant mental and physical coordination), so it seems we would have had a number of things in common. Her parents tell me that Kelly's prognosis was not good since the accident, yet her continued, multiple-decade existence defied the odds. In my humble opinion, Kelly performed her own Ironman and while not perfect, Kelly's family had derived much comfort that their little girl, their sister, was still alive and being taken care of at Gurwin.

During her stay at Gurwin, Kelly did come down to some of the musical performances in the afternoon and could at least listen to the music. She had big, beautiful blue eyes and long dark hair, which some of the certified nursing assistants (CNAs) braided into long, pretty braids in her beautiful, strong, just-washed-and-conditioned hair. I'm sure she would resemble her mom, Karen. But I could only pray for that miracle, and I did, every day.

After much meditating about Kelly's lot in life, I've come to another, more provocative view of Kelly's ultimate purpose. I believe Kelly became a great teacher. Anyone who came into contact with Kelly, heard her story, and made attempts to communicate with her, could not help but have great compassion, and sadness, about a life not yet realized. After twenty-four years, Kelly was unable to communicate anything about what she might feel or think. Actually, I take that back. One of her brothers, Thomas, said that if a family member had not visited in some time, and then they did, that Kelly's cheeks would turn red, she'd frown, and turn away from the offending family member. They got the message. Thus, she elicited true emotion. Her parents and her four brothers obviously loved her. They talked to her, read to her, and spoke about "what would Kelly think" regarding one situation or another, but what was her future? Kelly's immediate family became resolved to accept that this was the best Kelly was ever going to be. After twenty-four years, and thousands of visits over those twenty-four years (there are 8,760 days in twenty-four years, not all of them visits), there must have been a tremendous weight on the minds, souls, and bodies of her loving family. Thus, Kelly has taught them unconditional love and compassion in boatloads. They were always prompted by their pure, unconditional love for Kelly. And her condition taught them what unconditional love is all about. I'm sure it's become ingrained into their very souls and their characters. I imagine it's been carried into the rest of their lives and manifested into their own families.

Kelly's brother Matthew and his fiancé, Kimberly, came to visit to drop off Kelly's invitation to their wedding on November 17, 2017.

Unfortunately, on the day of the wedding, Kelly ran a fever and could not attend. Her family wanted her there, but not sick. I was very sad for her. She was their daughter, their sister, and now a sister-in-law, and an aunt, but unfortunately she couldn't really enjoy that, nor was she likely even aware.

In the past, Kelly had been to her brother Thomas's wedding and had pictures on the bulletin board to prove it.

Chapter Two

Other Types of Brain Injury

Anoxic Brain Injury: The Story of Philip Fantasia

During my time at Gurwin, I've observed other cases of traumatic brain injuries, from other causes. Most recently, I've come into contact with a woman named Susan Fantasia, whose husband, Philip Fantasia, suffered anoxic brain injury, from a lack of oxygen to the brain, while undergoing surgery to remove kidney stones in 2004 at a top-tier NYC hospital. It was a common and relatively simple procedure, or at least it was supposed to be. I've heard the saying, "the only time it's minor surgery is when it happens to somebody else." For Philip Fantasia, it was anything but minor. Apparently, his intubation tube was removed too quickly and his brain was deprived of oxygen for several minutes. His resulting condition has been catastrophic: he's had the complete loss of all of his cognitive and physical functions. He cannot speak, eat, write, walk, think, or function the way he once did. Susan and Philip were married for twelve years when this happened. It has been almost fourteen years in an acute care nursing facility (there are 5,110 days in fourteen years). They'll be married for twenty-eight years in August 2020.

Until COVID-19 restrictions, Susan came every day to visit Philip, her husband of 27 years. She's looked into, and tried, everything that can be done. She's tried hyperbaric oxygen chambers, and she's gone to the Dominican Republic for stem cell treatment. She says there have been recent developments in using stem cells from one's own skin cells. Stem cells by other means have been controversial, given the potential source is unborn fetuses. But Susan won't give up on Philip. Most of the funds for his treatments have been out-of-pocket. I don't know what limits there are on their funds, but I imagine the costs have been enormous. She's also had to pay all of the transportation costs, and the treatments are costly as well. Susan has been a fierce advocate for Philip; clearly, she has taken her wedding vow of "in sickness and in health" completely seriously. If Philip were ever to be restored to function the way he once was, it would truly be a miracle. I sense that Susan is both spiritual and religious, but I see this as another case of pure, unconditional love. She's not looking for kudos, praise, or adoration; she is just praying that the collective brains of medical science will yield a treatment or cure for Philip's condition. God bless her.

I've asked Susan what she misses most about Philip, and without missing a beat, she answers: "Everything. He was a great guy, one you wanted to be around." Before this tragedy, Philip had been a NYC corrections officer, many times supervising teams that retrieved prisoners who had escaped from prison.

One day, I saw Philip and Susan at a musical performance, in the 4 East dining room. I watched as Susan lovingly doted over Philip, kissing him on the cheek, and just looking at him adoringly, as a loving wife would. That is unconditional love in action. They don't care if people around them are watching (like I am); they are in their own unspoiled world, in love with each other. Unfortunately, only Susan is cognizant of her feelings at that moment.

In his dad's footsteps: Philip Fantasia and his son Philip Jr. at his son's graduation from the Rockland County Police & Public Safety Academy in 2002

Philip and Susan Fantasia on their wedding day, August 1991

Chapter Three

An Example of Courage and Bravery in the Face of Hardship: Scott Gingold

At Gurwin, I've come across many residents (patients) who are afflicted with progressive diseases and whose prognosis is not good. One such individual, aside from Kelly Dolan with TBI, is Scott Gingold. Scott is afflicted with ALS (also called Lou Gehrig's disease; see below). Scott is thirty-nine, and he is married to Marissa. He has a precocious eight-year-old girl named Darby. Her presence is always a day-brightener for the rest of us residents, and certainly for Scott. Scott was formally diagnosed in 2014, although he has said he had some symptoms in 2005. Darby was born in 2012, and Scott's family had been very hopeful that a new drug, recently approved by the FDA, may offer even further hope, as it may delay the progression of certain symptoms. Scott is an example of someone who has everything to live for—a young daughter and a wife—but how long will Scott survive? If Scott's early symptoms, in 2005, were in fact ALS, then Scott has outlived the usual life expectancy of ALS patients. Perhaps, the minds that have developed the recent drug may further the life expectancy, and finally find a cure. That would be another wonderful miracle, and I pray for that, also.

Scott and his dear daughter, Darby

Scott's love for his daughter, Darby, has prompted him to offer a father's advice to his young daughter, in the form of stories he writes for her to explain and assist in the everyday problems of an eight-year-old. I've heard some of them and they are quite good. Thus, in the face of an incurable illness, Scott still shows his love and hope for his daughter, as he can live vicariously through Darby, and the issues that his sweet eight-year-old confronts.

Scott has graciously approved my use of this story in my book. Thank you, Scott! I believe you could win much money on *Jeopardy!*

On Sunday, March 24, 2019, we attended Darby's seventh birthday party. It was a good time, with Darby in her princess dress, who, of course, noted that her actual birthday was Tuesday, March 13, 2019! See, precocious!

Animals Around the World

Giant Pandas are from China and they eat bamboo.

Spider monkeys are from Brazil and they fling their poo.

Bengal Tigers are from India and they have lots of stripes.

Squirrels live in the USA and they climb up pipes.

Kangaroos are from Australia and their young live in a pouch.

Bulldogs are from England and they pee on your couch.

Caribou are from Canada and their antlers are quite big.

Gophers live in Mexico and they like to dig.

Giraffes live in Kenya and their necks are very long.

Humpback whales live in the Atlantic Ocean and they sing a song.

Elephants live in Nepal and they have a very long trunk.

Raccoons live in the USA and like to go through junk.

The Apennine wolf is from Italy and they travel in packs.

Dromedary camels live in Egypt and have humps on their backs.

Brown bears live in Russia and are very strong.

Pythons live in Indonesia and these snakes grow so long.

Penguins live in Antarctica where it's very cold.

The giant tortoise lives on the Galapagos and they can be very old.

The great horned owl lives in America and can turn around its head.

The Penny and the Desmo like to sleep in Darby's bed.

– Scott Gingold

The passing of Stephen Hawking, on March 13, 2018, would be unremarkable were it not for the fact that Stephen outlived his diagnosis by fifty years, living until he was seventy-six years old. Stephen had been diagnosed with ALS at twenty-one years old.

I think that should offer Scott and his family some hope, given Scott's formal diagnosis did not occur until 2014. Certainly, there has been some progression of the disease for Scott physically, as he cannot move most of his muscles, nor walk, but notably, Scott's brain does think. A lot. And that is remarkable! I imagine it's both a blessing and a curse. Having all of your cognitive skills, yet realizing that you're trapped in a failing body, has got to be tough, if not torturous at times. God bless him.

Thus, despite his bleak prognosis, Scott was capable of having helpful legislation enacted so that others with ALS have access to the equipment that will allow those afflicted to communicate. God bless you, Scott!

Just think, if able-bodied people were to do good, as Scott is doing, how much better off the world could be in the present and future.

Chapter Three A

Joseph James Gallagher: An Example of "To Serve and Protect"

The Case for the Deborah F Grosser Foundation for TBI Research

Since the start of my stay at Gurwin, there's been no case clearer to demonstrate the need for more research into the causes and treatments for traumatic brain injury than that of New York State Trooper Joseph Gallagher. On December 18, 2017, Trooper Gallagher responded to a call related to a disabled motor vehicle on the overpass ramp to the Sagtikos State Parkway from the Long Island Expressway.

He parked behind two other disabled vehicles, with his lights flashing. He began setting up road flares. Two oncoming vehicles veered to the right to avoid Trooper Gallagher, but a third vehicle did not see him and struck him. Gallagher was propelled forward into the air and struck his head on the pavement, thereby suffering blows to both sides of his head. Trooper Gallagher sustained an extreme traumatic brain injury and required significant amounts of emergency surgery to save his life and treat the significant bleeding in his brain. He was treated and remained in the surgical intensive care unit, at Southside Hospital, in Bay Shore.

Thomas Mungeer, president of the New York State Police Benevolent Association, described Gallagher as a "reliable, dependable trooper…who does what the men and women who put on the great uniform do every day across New York State."

Gallagher served in the US Coast Guard before becoming a New York State Trooper in 2014. He is married and has two young children. Clearly, Joe is a smart guy with a tremendous motivation to help others. His injuries and resulting aftereffects have left him non-verbal. In December 2020, it was three years since the accident, and he's been unable to speak, as yet. Here's a really great guy, with great motivations and clearly a positive addition to the state police force, and he's unable, thus far, to return to his career as a trooper. Add to that, he's a loving husband and father to his two young children. He's also the son of his two loving parents, Mary Beth and James.

Trooper Joseph James Gallagher, 2017, pre-accident

A case like Joe Gallagher's is a primary motivation behind The Deborah F. Grosser Foundation for TBI research. There must be treatments and other therapies that can hopefully put Joe "back on the road" to recovery, to be able to speak, to walk, to do his job again. To return to being a loving husband and "Daddy" again. There have been advancements in the research into TBI, and much has been done regarding communication and cognitive difficulties following a TBI. Most improvements occur after a healing process for the brain. It remains unclear what his prognosis will be, the more time elapses without him being verbal. With the great minds in science that exist today, there must be additional treatments or therapies that can further his progress. Hyperbaric oxygen therapy has been found to help the brain to recover.

Given the circumstances surrounding my traumatic brain injury, I can't help but feel a bit guilty, having survived, and recovered from my brain injury, and I have recovered all of my cognitive and communication skills. Why me and not Joe?

Joe resided in the room next to mine, and often, he was seated by the doorway. I would attempt to get some response from him, calling out: "Trooper Gallagher, we need you!" But often, he remained unresponsive, but for some movement with his arms or hands. It was a tragedy that I hoped and prayed would improve soon.

I continued trying to elicit a response, and I kept him and his family in my prayers. Tragically, I received word in April of 2021 that he is no longer with us, more than three years after the accident. My deepest condolences are sent to his wife, his children, and his parents and siblings who will never get to see Joe "in action" again. My burden and great opportunity is to continue down my path: nearly 10 years sober, and working to fund my 501c3 foundation for TBI Research (part of which will be funded by the proceeds of my book).

Chapter Four

The Accident That Changed the Course of My Life

August 31, 2011

As you'll read soon, my loving husband, Gary, died, after twenty-five years of marriage, in 2006. He died in a shocking way, and one I can never forget. My recent Facebook post on June 27, 2020 (the fourteenth anniversary of his passage):

> Fourteen years ago, I lost my husband, Gary Steven Grosser. It was a tragic death; one that could have been avoided. In 1994, he had open-heart surgery that necessitated that he be placed on blood thinners for the rest of his life (it was an artificial heart valve). One requirement of that was he could never drink alcohol again. As Coumadin is notorious for causing severe bleeding incidents, Gary had many incidents with excessive bleeding in his body and eventually his brain. Most of these incidents were not his fault in any way. Sadly, the last incident

was exacerbated by me and my behavior. But never did I pour alcohol down Gary's throat. I was devastated on June 24, 2006, when he fell on our ceramic tub in our master bath. He woke up, angry, yelling at me, "Leave me alone, it's my day off, I just wanna sleep." He then got up and crawled on his hands and knees to the toilet attached to the master bath. It was there that he fell forward and hit his forehead on the rim of the toilet!

I screamed and immediately went to the phone to call 911, which dispatched an ambulance. Still, he refused to go, but eventually he relented, and off he went to Valley Hospital, in Ridgewood, New Jersey. The prognosis was terrible. He had extensive bleeding in his brain, and it was swollen, including the brain stem. Three days later, on June 27, after being declared brain dead, Gary left this world, at 2 p.m. on Wednesday, June 27, 2006. We were married twenty-five years, and while not a perfect marriage (as we were not perfect people, in any way), the one thing Gary did perfectly was to love me for me, with all my warts and foibles. Over the years, we had many great times, travels, and fun with friends. There were also times that were not perfect. For today, I want to celebrate and remember Gary Steven Grosser, who loved his family, his many friends, his dogs, our two golden retrievers, Samantha and Taylor. He was great at his job, a good friend to many, and yes, he loved me. We were both flawed in our love of alcohol, and it killed him, and nearly killed me. Fortunately, having survived, I now have the burden and great opportunity to prove I've learned from my mistakes, and now can live a life worth having been saved in the first place. Thanks to God and an excellent neurosurgeon (Dr. Roy Vingan), my brain remains fully cognitive and functional. It's been a nine-year journey, but I now can start

> my efforts of rebuilding my life from scratch. Sadly, Gary didn't get that chance. Gary, you are very missed by so many: your brother, Robbie, sisters, Lynn and Susan, and the multitudes of nephews and nieces and grand nieces and nephews. The family has grown! But you are with your mom, your dad, and all of the other pre-deceased Grossers, Rizzos, and the whole gang. You loved your goldens, you loved the children of our friends, and mostly, you loved me. Please watch over us all, as we live in this world of a pandemic, and many other issues which plague us. Rest easy, Gary. Know that we miss you, and we'll never forget your humor, the laughs you gave us, and your kind and caring ways.
>
> Love you,
> Debbie

Eerily similar to Gary's death in 2006, alcohol almost caused mine, five years later. My accident could have been avoided, also. On August 31, 2011, at I'm guessing 2 or 3 a.m., during a visit to the bathroom, I fell down a steep flight of stairs in the middle of the night, and in the process, I broke my skull and suffered a traumatic brain injury. I don't know if I tripped or lost my footing, and then the momentum of the fall took over, but from what I was told, I was found the next morning by my then-business partner and boyfriend, Ron, who called 911 (and that was the first step that saved my life). I have no memory of the fall, or the steps leading up to it, I just know (having obtained my medical records, all 5,000 pages of them) that my blood alcohol content (BAC) was 0.142 percent, nearly twice the legal limit to drive (of .08) in New York State! (Thankfully, I wasn't driving, nor would I have even been capable of even standing, as my fall demonstrated.)

Now, my BAC would be sufficient to put me in a coma (and near death) but it shows how high tolerance in an alcoholic can be. For instance, Princess

Diana had a driver, Henri Paul, in Paris, where he drove into the Place de l'Alma underpass, and at the entrance to the tunnel, Paul lost control. The car swerved to the left of the two-lane carriageway before colliding head-on with the thirteenth pillar supporting the roof of the tunnel, at an estimated speed of 105 km/h (65 mph, where the speed limit was 30 mph). It then spun and hit the stone wall of the tunnel backwards, finally coming to a stop. My point is that, according to the *New York Times*, Henri Paul had a BAC of between 0.173 and 0.187 percent, more than twice the legal limit to drive, yet he was at least functional enough to get in a car, and obviously drive, but in this case with devastating consequences.

I obtained this from a chart put together by BRAD (Be Responsible About Drinking). Since my BAC was .142, I wanted to see the physical effects at that level of intoxication:

> 0.13–0.15 BAC: Gross motor impairment and lack of physical control. Blurred vision, and major loss of balance. Euphoria is reduced and dysphoria (anxiety, restlessness) is beginning to appear. Judgment and perception are severely impaired.

Another interesting data point: I was born on May 6, 1959, which I learned was a Wednesday, and August 31, 2011, was also, you got it, a Wednesday. I think it would be a strange coincidence if my birthdate and the date of my death were both a Wednesday. Hmm.

I have no recollection of drinking the entire day and night before my fall, but I did learn that I'd agreed to go to Valley Hospital the next morning, with my good friend Karen Boaz and her husband Sam (who's no longer with us; RIP). It would have been the same as the many prior times (most recently, in May 2011, just prior to the IronMatt Casino Night Benefit), where I'd gone to Valley Hospital to detox from alcohol. But obviously, I fell instead, which resulted in my devastating consequences.

I do remember dreaming of a long, continuous fall on my back, sliding feet first, hitting my head on every step, and eventually landing at the base of several flights of steps. I do believe that my actual fall was much more violent, given my family's description of what I looked like afterwards—they said it looked like I'd been in a plane crash—my nose had been sheared off my face and there were two holes in my skull that used to be my nostrils. My eye sockets and cheekbones were crushed. I was unrecognizable. My nose had to be completely reconstructed. Another significant and serious injury was caused by something called compartment syndrome.

Finally, it's now clear to me that my accident could have been avoided. My new sustained clarity allows me to see that. It did happen, however, and now, how do I react in a positive way? Rather than wallowing in the wreckage of what has been lost, how can I move up and out from here? How do I rise from my ashes? Like every other thing I've accomplished in my lifetime, it can only start with one step at a time. That, I know how to do.

Chapter Five

My Extensive Emergency Surgeries (Right Out of *ER* and *Grey's Anatomy*)

My High-Caliber Surgical Team

I was fortunate to have had the surgical team that I did. It was all done without my input. There was no "surgeon shopping" while I was unconscious. And yet, for the most important surgeries, I ended up with some extremely qualified surgeons, the first two having specifically been trained in trauma units. Dr. Roy Vingan was the first surgeon to have said yes, when two others flat out said no. They'd said I was too far gone, and there was no way I was going to make it. Interestingly, it turns out that Dr. Roy was among a group that went out for our "long" training runs, leaving from Dunkin Donuts on MacArthur Boulevard in Mahwah. Our long runs could be anywhere from ten to fifteen miles. And Dr. Roy was part of that group (how fortuitous). Years into my recovery, a critical care nurse practitioner who cared for me while in my coma, Lee Taylor-Vaughan, said that I'd "proved a lot of people wrong." We reconnected during the writing of my book, and he came to visit me twice while at Gurwin, which really touched my heart, and provided good motivation for me (he was an Ironman Lake Placid guy, too).

The next surgeon who took on the responsibility of my survival was my orthopedic surgeon, Ylenia Giuffrida, who fortunately trained at the University of Miami Hospital, which is a Level One Trauma Center, one of the busiest in the nation. Thus, Dr. Giuffrida was well-prepared for what I came in looking like and was ready to perform the life-saving and limb-saving fasciotomy with which she was charged. Among all of my other ailments, I suffered acute compartment syndrome from lying on my right arm for several hours before I was found. Acute compartment syndrome can be life-threatening, or it could have resulted in the amputation of my right arm. Thankfully, those outcomes did not happen. Remember, I'm typing this, right?

Without question, I truly owe both my life and my cognition to God and Dr. Roy Vingan, and his exemplary skills and nerves of steel.

My Neurosurgeon: Dr. Roy D. Vingan, MD

Roy D. Vingan, MD

ROY D. VINGAN, MD

Dr. Vingan is a board certified neurosurgeon and founding member of the North Jersey Brain and Spine Center. He has been in practice since 1992 and received his medical education at the State University of New York in Brooklyn and his neurosurgical training at the Kings County Hospital-Downstate Medical Center. During training, he received extensive experience with neurotrauma and neurovascular work. He has served on the Medical Board and as President of the Medical Staff at Hackensack University Medical Center. He has been an early advocate of new technologies. He was the first, or among the first, to locally introduce the use of frameless cranial and spinal navigation systems, endoscopic cranial and spinal techniques and other minimally invasive surgical procedures to the brain and spine.

While developing the North Jersey Brain and Spine Center into its current sub-specialized team, his practice now focuses on patients with spinal conditions, and he strongly advocates conservative care. When surgery is appropriate, he uses state-of-the-art techniques in the operating room to improve outcomes, including a minimal access surgical procedure for fusion, which often reduces postoperative pain. He actively educates associates and other spinal surgeons in these more novel approaches.

MY ORTHOPEDIC SURGEON: DR. YLENIA GIUFFRIDA

Trained in one of the country's busiest Trauma Centers, Dr. Ylenia Giuffrida

(https://activeorthopedic.com/a-ylenia-giuffrida)

Dr. Giuffrida is a native of Bergen County, born in Hackensack Hospital. She attended Duke University, earning a degree in Biomedical and Electrical Engineering. Next, she continued on to the University of Medicine and Dentistry of New Jersey where she received her MD.

DR. YLENIA GIUFFRIDA'S TRAINING

Her Orthopedic Surgery Residency was completed at the University of Miami at Jackson Memorial Hospital, one of the busiest Level 1 Trauma Centers in the nation. She returned to the Northeast to complete her Fellowship Training in Hand, Upper Extremity, and Microvascular Surgery at the Hospital for Special Surgery in New York City where she trained in cutting edge surgical and nonsurgical treatment modalities for a myriad of hand and upper extremity disorders. She is board certified in orthopedics.

Dr. Giuffrida has privileges at Hackensack University Medical Center in Hackensack, Hackensack UMC (now Hackensack Meridian Health) at Pascack Valley in Westwood, Hackensack UMC at Mountainside in Montclair, Valley Hospital in Ridgewood and at Hudson Crossing Surgical Center in Fort Lee.

Apparently, after my fall, I'd been lying on my right arm, underneath my upper body, for five or six hours. I don't know exactly when I fell, but I believe I was found at some point, around 8 a.m. One of the primary causes of acute compartment syndrome, according to WebMD, is "prolonged compression of a limb during a period of unconsciousness."

What Happens in Compartment Syndrome?

Groups of organs or muscles are organized into areas called compartments. Strong webs of connective tissue called fascia form the walls of these compartments.

Compartment syndrome occurs when excessive pressure builds up inside an enclosed muscle space in the body. Compartment syndrome usually results from bleeding or swelling after an injury. The dangerously high pressure in compartment syndrome impedes the flow of blood to and from the affected tissues. It can be an emergency, requiring surgery to prevent permanent injury.

After an injury, blood or edema (fluid resulting from inflammation or injury) may accumulate in the compartment. The tough walls of fascia cannot easily expand, and compartment pressure rises, preventing adequate blood flow to tissues inside the compartment. Severe tissue damage can result, with loss of body function or even death. The legs, arms, and abdomen are most prone to developing compartment syndrome.

Source: WebMD. www.webmd.com, accessed 10/19/2020.

Added to the list of emergency surgeries performed on me that night was a fasciotomy. A fasciotomy is where the fibrous connective bands that hold muscle, veins, and other tissues connected into a compartment had to be cut to relieve the excessive pressure in my arm. Left untreated, I risked losing my whole arm to an amputation. I can't even imagine the difficulties I would have faced had that happened.

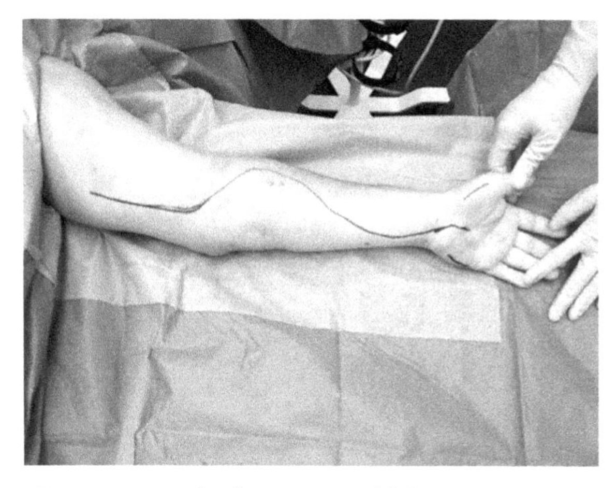

Fasciotomy: a limb-saving and life-saving surgery
(Source: Shutterstock.com)

My main surgery included a craniotomy, where roughly one-third of my skull had to be removed to relieve the excess pressure caused by the bleeding from my fractured skull.

Craniotomy: Procedure Overview A craniotomy is the surgical removal of part of the bone from the skull to expose the brain. Specialized tools are used to remove the section of bone called the bone flap. The bone flap is temporarily removed, then replaced after the brain surgery has been done.

Craniectomy is a similar procedure during which a portion of the skull is permanently removed or replaced later during a second surgery after the swelling has gone down.

Source: Craniotomy. Johns Hopkins Medicine. hopkinsmedicine.org, accessed 12/20/2018.

Example of a Craniotomy Procedure

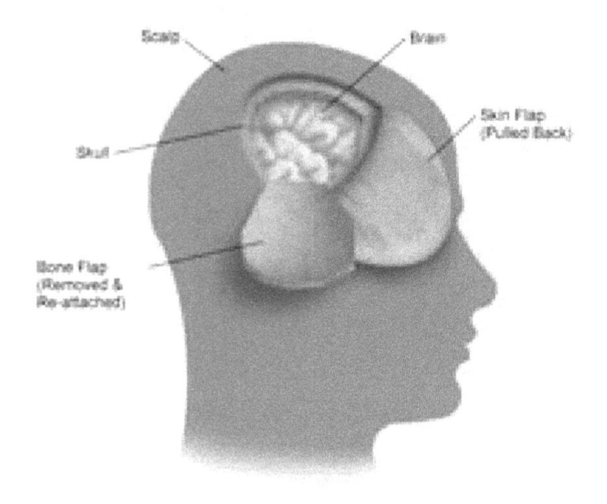

TRACHEOTOMY

A tracheotomy or a tracheostomy is an opening surgically created through the neck into the trachea (windpipe) to allow direct access to the breathing tube and is commonly done in an operating room under general anesthesia. A tube is usually placed through this opening to provide an airway and to remove secretions from the lungs. Breathing is done through the tracheostomy tube rather than through the nose and mouth. The term "tracheotomy" refers to the incision into the trachea (windpipe) that forms a temporary or permanent opening, which is called a "tracheostomy," however; the terms are sometimes used interchangeably.

Source: Craniotomy. Johns Hopkins Medicine. hopkinsmedicine.org, accessed 12/20/2018.

CHAPTER FIVE A

MY NEED FOR CORRECTIVE PLASTIC SURGERY

THE DR. ARMEN KASABIAN ERA, 2014–2020

Over the last six years, my primary plastic surgeon has been Dr. Armen Kasabian. As time has gone on, and he's performed the last seven surgeries on me, I've learned some things about the status of my recovery. He repeats that when he first met me, I hardly "said a word," which is hard for me to imagine, yet I'm unable to dispute his portrayal. Clearly, I've made up for not talking at the time, but I'm still perplexed. This must be the nature of a traumatic brain injury, in recovery mode. In this regard, I remain truly grateful that I never lost the ability to speak.

My cognitive skills remained intact. My ability to think, process information, and make mental calculations are all still there. Those things which most make me, me, are all still there!

Dr. Armen Kasabian
https://www.northwell.edu/dr-armen-kevork-kasabian-md-11351128

Dr. Kasabian's office assistant is Dea Butsi. She has arranged for several of my surgery details and logistics over the last several years/seven surgeries. She's been with Dr. Kasabian for nearly two decades.

Since my brain injury, I've read about neuroplasticity: the ability of the brain to re-wire into new synaptic connections to perform previously learned functions. The brain is an amazing organ in our body, as part of our nervous system, which is comprised of the brain, the spinal cord, and nerves. Previously, brain injury was mistakenly thought to be brain damage. But they are not the same thing. Because of the capacity of the brain to re-wire itself, brain function can remain intact, albeit with slightly different wiring.

Dr. Armen Kasabian is a very capable surgeon, the chief of surgery at Northwell Health, in Great Neck, and my plastic surgeon for a number of procedures in the last six years.

In 2014, Dr. Kasabian performed several debridements (to remove wound debris), and along with another neurosurgeon, Dr. Ashesh Mehta, placed a titanium mesh in my skull. These also necessitated additional cranioplasties to close up my skull, and subsequently rebuild my scalp.

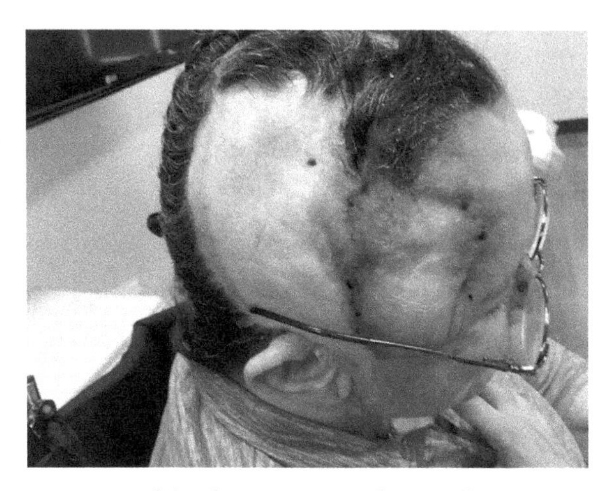

Post-debridement; pre-scalp installation

Dr. Kasabian performed the thirty-two-hour surgery (as measured from intubation at 7 a.m. on August 15 to extubation at 3 p.m. on August 16), in 2016. A herculean feat for him to perform, for me to endure.

During that surgery, Dr. Kasabian used a large skin flap from my inner left thigh and a saphenous vein from my right calf. He used those pieces to build a new scalp for me. It took careful coordination from the grafting process to combine the skin graft with the vascular harvest from my right calf. It needed to be monitored throughout the process to see if the graft tissue was "taking." This monitoring is called a Doppler ultrasound. It makes a swishing sound. It indicates that the grafted tissue is connected properly with the saphenous vein, and thus receiving an oxygen supply so that the tissue remains alive.

Maria Ametrano is Dr. Kasabian's PA, or physician assistant. She has been present for several of my last surgeries and has assisted with certain aspects. I also see Maria for a number of post-op visits, particularly on my hand, post my nineteenth surgery. She's very smart, sweet, kind, and pretty, and I think she's a positive addition to the Dr. Kasabian team.

A PA is a trained medical professional who works with a doctor to provide care and treatment to patients. PAs receive similar training to doctors, often taking many of the same classes. However, they do not attend medical school; instead, they obtain an undergraduate degree and graduate (Master's and PhD level from a nationally accredited physician assistant program), which usually takes about two years, pass a certification test and become licensed by the state in which they wish to work.

Obtaining a degree as a PA usually requires six years of advanced education.

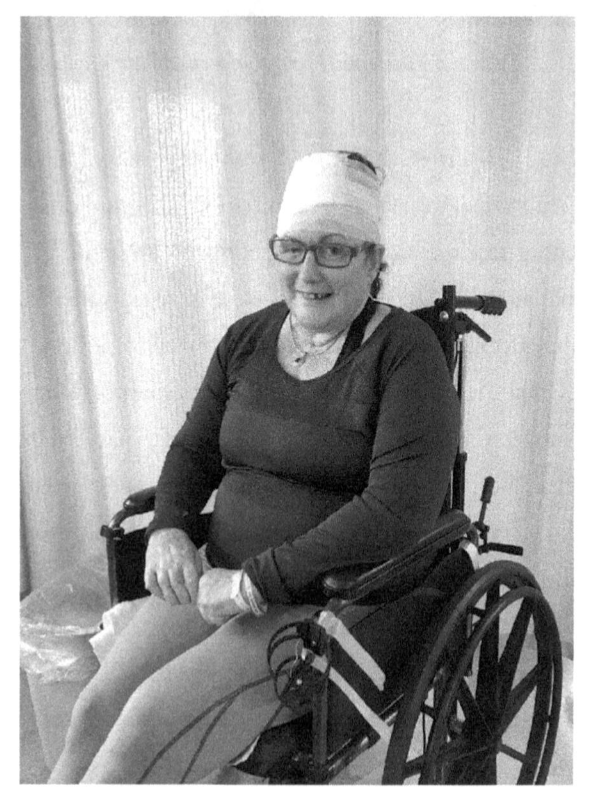

Post-scalp installation; bandaged while healing

After three years of being largely bald-headed, then bandaged-headed, my hair started to grow with a vengeance. The picture below was taken in April 2019, right after my father's memorial. I was with Donna Pennacchio, on the left, my dear sister-in-Christ. It was just three years after my new scalp was installed. My new scalp grows hair quickly!

2019; Post my scalp installation—
a brand-new full head of hair

Chapter Six

My Operating Room Experience

To my surgeons: I can't thank you enough, or write a check big enough, to compensate you for saving my life. Some of you (surgeons) might be thinking, "Why not try seven figures?" Your impressive backgrounds and ability to coordinate with each other to perform so many emergency procedures (not necessarily at the same time or together on a team) was amazing to learn about in hindsight. Your coordinated effort and near seamless results were nothing short of miraculous to me and my family.

With nineteen surgeries under my belt, I guess that qualifies me as somewhat of an expert on what to expect during the surgical experience. Not my goal when I went to college, but I am definitely speaking from experience.

So, here goes: When you arrive at the hospital for surgical prep, you are first directed to the surgical waiting room. Over the next few hours, you'll be directed to speak with a series of individuals with whom you'll become acquainted as they'll be assisting with your surgery. First, there will be a nurse or surgical resident, who will get you into a surgical gown and hat (which will be worn throughout surgery). Next, you might wait in a chair, or in a bed, as you wait for the anesthesiologist, the surgeon, and the nurse or nurses that will be part of the "team" performing your surgery. You will be asked several times what seems like the same questions: How long has it been since you've had anything to eat or drink? Did you fast since 11 p.m. or midnight (for precautions against aspiration while under general anesthesia)? Are you allergic to any medications? Have you ever had any adverse reactions to anesthesia? And this is before you've even met with the actual anesthesiologist, when you'll be asked the same questions all over again. When you finally meet with the anesthesiologist and have been asked the same questions, the first part of the surgical process will be to start an IV.

Years ago, I remember having been described as a "phlebotomist's dream," but now I have become known as a "hard stick," as it usually takes several sticks, or tries, before finding the right vein. Once in, the IV is ready to go.

I'd like to interject for a moment, to mention the phlebotomist at Gurwin. Her name is Eliana Lujan. She has incredible success is getting my veins to yield blood in her first try, every time! She is done in minutes versus other occasions when I've been "stuck" what seems like a gazillion times! Ouch!

Next, you'll meet with a team of surgical nurses, who will assist the doctors during the surgery.

Once ready and on the gurney, you'll be wheeled down a labyrinth of hallways, eventually leading to the entrance to the operating room (aka OR). This is it. There is no turning back. And who knows how long before it will be over!

When I was wheeled into the OR, it was bright, and it was bigger than I imagined. It appeared that there were several other teams awaiting their next "project." The OR was also very cold, and I was provided heated "warming" blankets. Thus, I never felt physically uncomfortable during the actual surgical part of the process. All of the pain comes during the "recovery" process, when the anesthesia wears off!

When the anesthesiologist starts, he or she starts me off with something to "relax" me, many times propofol or fentanyl. My anesthesiologist used propofol (also known as the Michael Jackson drug).

For my fourteen-hour surgery, after my "relaxing" agent was administered, I could briefly feel (a few seconds) as it entered my veins, and then "lights out." Immediately, I was intubated (when the intubation tube was put down my throat to assist with my breathing).

In this long surgery, a skin flap was harvested from my inner left thigh. A saphenous vein was harvested from my right calf (from my lower inner right calf, down to my ankle). The next step was to prepare them for use in my surgery. They basically put them together and then built me a new scalp. In retrospect, it was an amazing feat! And it was good that the doctor used the skin flap from my inner left thigh, because, importantly, it has hair follicles, and it grows hair! As I sit here writing this book, I now have a full head of hair, which was just recently blown dry and able to be styled!

WHAT IS PROPOFOL?

Propofol (Diprivan) slows the activity of your brain and nervous system.

Propofol is used to help you relax before and during general anesthesia for surgery or other medical procedures.

Propofol is also used to sedate a patient who is under critical care and needs a mechanical ventilator (breathing machine).

Source: https://www.uofmhealth.org/health-library/d00933a1#:~:text=What%20is%20propofol%3F,mechanical%20ventilator%20(breathing%20machine)

My Nineteenth Surgery

On June 27, 2019, I had my nineteenth surgery. I'd hoped that number sixteen would be "sweet sixteen," and the last, but contractures in three fingers on my left hand dictated otherwise. Left as it was my left hand was essentially non-usable. And I have other plans for my left hand and its use. This surgery was a rather delicate procedure. Tendons from my left forearm would be used to lengthen the tendons in the third, fourth, and fifth fingers on my left hand. Following that, the doctor performed a "closed" capsulotomy, which was essentially breaking my knuckles. Finally, the doctor placed pins in those fingers, in order to keep the fingers "open" (straight). The next step was performed by Maria Armetrano, Dr. Kasabian's PA. After my arm and fingers were all sutured up, my forearm and hand were splinted and wrapped with an ACE bandage to keep the fingers in an open position, and wrapped safely with Xeroform gauze to protect the pins and keep them in place until my post-op visit, which was on Thursday, July 5, 2019.

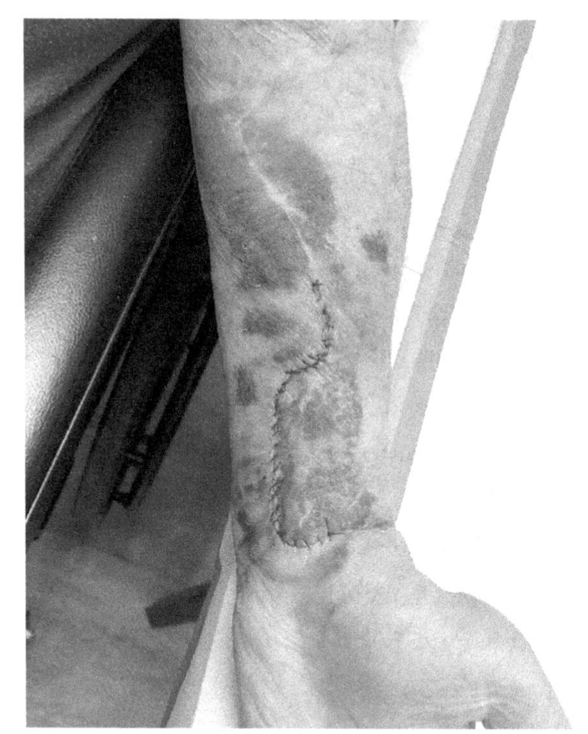

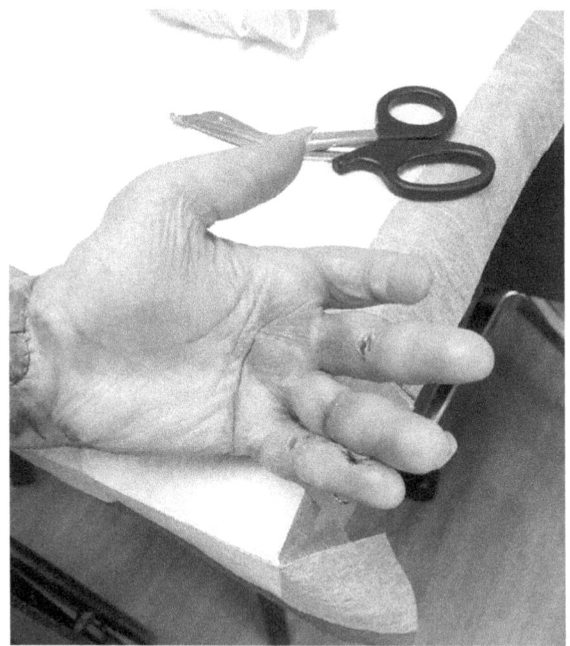

Post-op pictures on July 5, 2019, after Surgery 19, June 27, 2019

By July 27, 2019, my hand and arm look much better than these photos from three weeks earlier, I can still feel the remnants of the procedure. But I'm moving forward, as I started occupational therapy on Monday, July 30, with Anita, the OT therapist in charge of my case.

The true test will come with occupational therapy, to determine the level of functionality that can be restored to my fingers and my left hand. Since I was left-handed my whole life, my hope is that I will possibly be able to write with my left hand again. Only time and OT will tell. I missed my beautiful cursive writing from my Catholic school days! Perhaps I can produce that again! All of this was caused by some bad decisions of almost nine years ago. But I am moving forward and will only have positive people in my life. Not to be "Pollyannaish," but just to maintain positive influences in my life, as I have so much to do! Finishing my manuscript is key! And the finish line is almost in sight. My wonderful family, my dearest friends, and just all-around positive people are in my life, and I'm going to keep them there. I can only demonstrate to them that I've learned from my very hard lessons! All nineteen of them.

Chapter Seven

The Rest of My Story

The rest of this book is my story, a memoir—all of it—the good, the bad, and the embarrassingly ugly. Spoiler alert: there is no happy ending, because my story isn't over and won't be for some time (God willing). There will, however, be many, many, happy points along the way. Happiness is in the eyes of the beholder (or in this case, reader). There have been times filled with laughter. Times filled with the knowledge that God loves me, that my family loves me (unconditionally, like Jesus Christ), and maybe one day again, I'll find someone special with whom to share things. Times free of worry and anxiety, which, for me, border on euphoria.

In my career, I did extremely well as a Wall Street industry analyst. It offered a substantial financial upside, beyond anything I'd ever imagined was possible for me, and it came with power, prestige, and intellectual stimulation, but it was very hard work, long hours, and it was pressure-filled.

I turned to alcohol for relief (they call it "self-medicating"), which, in turn, "self-medi-cratered" (I think I just coined a new term) my Wall Street career. All the big money I made is gone, all the material things are no more, but I am still rich in God and family. I pray that my physical abilities return. I know that will take much hard work, but I believe it will happen, because I have the determination and dedication to do so. Also, one big obstacle, alcohol, has finally been eliminated, with lots of help and God's grace for me.

Because of my deep love of my family, I need to make sure I am doing things according to God's will, not my will. In 2017, I had some critical errors in judgment, and it was made known to me that I risked losing parts of my family if I made those same errors again. I couldn't bear the loss of my precious siblings, nor their offspring, and quite honestly, I couldn't blame them. I mean, how many times can I do the same thing, expecting different results (the definition of insanity, according to Einstein)? I couldn't blame them because I also judged myself, watching myself over and over, and not only were the results the same, but they got worse and worse! Between my near-fatal accident and DUIs at various points, the consequences were increasingly bad, embarrassing, and lengthy—such as my ten-year loss of license for my third DUI in ten years (the last one being in the year of my accident, in July 2011). My license will finally be eligible for reinstatement in 2021!

Fortunately, none of my DUIs ever resulted in an accident, or death or harm to another human being; mostly, I was found asleep at the wheel, unable to communicate, and with odors of alcohol present to the arresting officers. On the last occasion, I even had my sweet baby Kayla (my golden retriever) with me, and the officers had to watch her and worry about her while I was being "booked."

Sweet baby Kayla, Semper fi

Fortunately for me, I still had money and was able to hire an attorney for a couple of my DUIs, Michael Beatrice, who was able to at least put up a defense on technical reasons, such as dismissing the evidence of my Breathalyzer analysis because of improper calibration by testers of the equipment, which occurs on a regular basis.

Making Restitution

Thus, while the case was made that equipment had not been tested properly, that defense never held up in court. Nor did it hold up with the prosecuting attorneys during the period between arrest and going to court, an attempt to suppress evidence. In two of my DUIs, we were able to get the charges dropped, as my keys were in the back seat while I was asleep in the driver's seat. It doesn't absolve the fact that my BAC was legally impaired, but the charges were dropped. After my second DUI where I was charged, my license was suspended for two years and I was required to perform 180 hours of community service.

In April 2007, I was contacted by Jim Dougherty, the head of the Saddle River Building Department. He asked if I would come and help them get their filing system in order. I chose this option for my community service, as organization is a key skill I'd used in just about every job I'd ever had. As I had no license, Jim Dougherty offered to pick me up, and I accepted. Upon arrival, while everyone there knew why I was there (including the borough administrator, Ted Preusch), everyone treated me well and were kind and courteous to me, as someone who made a mistake. I was now making up for it, in part, through community service, not like a convicted drunk driver. Ted, who learned I'd done an Ironman, spoke to me about his regular biking (the longest leg of an Ironman). Ted spoke of his many bike rides into Manhattan over the George Washington Bridge and down the West Side Highway, and he suggested we might try it some time. As I had no license, I had to secure rides each way, or walk partway to the community service "job." I made the best of it, devising a better way to keep track of open construction permits and ultimate approvals. Upon completion of my service, Jim Dougherty indicated that my new filing system would remain in place going forward.

Chapter Eight

Back to the Beginning of My "Paved Paradise"

I had it all. I really did. But like in the lyrics to Joni Mitchell's song "Big Yellow Taxi," "Don't it always seem to go, you don't know what you've got till it's gone, they paved paradise and put up a parking lot." Well, my paradise done got paved on me and I didn't know what I had, and no, it's gone. Please read my story and let me know what you think.

I was born in Bay Ridge, Brooklyn, on May 6, 1959, at 10:54 in the morning at Methodist Hospital, in Park Slope, Brooklyn. I was six pounds, eight ounces and nineteen inches long. Up until 2018, my mother still called me on every birthday to recount the story, including how my dad was sure her pain was "just gas" because she had eaten sausage the night before.

In April 1961, my mother had a baby girl named Donna Marie. She was five pounds, fifteen ounces, and legend has it that Donna was a little underweight because one night I hid my dad's license and credit cards under the doorsill to the kitchen between the kitchen and foyer. My dad was sure I had flushed them down the toilet and was so mad, and while completely unrelated, my mother's placenta ruptured, and Donna wasn't getting enough nutrition.

They found the wallet contents when they moved out to Long Island in mid-1964.

I was just shy of two years old at the time Donna was born but my memory still spans back even to eighteen months old, when I was already potty-trained (because I was anal retentive and afraid to "go" number two in public). I also remember that one night I'd woken up crying and my mom took me into the living room and plopped my butt down and shook me, hoping not to wake up my dad. (Yes, I remember these things.)

The Overdose Episode: A Foreboding Precursor of My Future Dependency on Alcohol?

I also remember an episode where my mom took two-week-old Donna (which happened to be the day before my second birthday, Friday May 5, 1961) to the pediatrician and then went food shopping. After getting home, I told my mom, "I have a cold, so I took a couple of aspirin." Alarmed, she checked the newly bought bottle of St. Joseph's baby aspirin, and deduced that I didn't take two aspirin, but rather twenty-eight out of fifty-two that are in a full bottle (or 54 percent). Then she went into panic mode and called the doctor and hospital and was told to "get her over to the hospital right away, and don't let her fall asleep." Imagine, not even two years old and I was risking death by an overdose of baby aspirin (there was no such thing as childproof caps back then, and I ate them like candy). Well, my mother called my grandmother, who called Aunt Margie (no familial relation but we called her "Aunt" for as long as we knew her), and Aunt Margie had a car, and the three of them got me to the Maimonides Medical Center, in Borough Park, Brooklyn.

I remember the whole hospital episode, except for the stomach pumping part, but I was absolutely convinced that the doctor attending to me was Dr. Kildare of TV show fame, played by Richard Chamberlain. I also remember that during the night, there were two little boys in the ward who kept falling back into their beds, while appearing as if they were falling off a ledge from the building. Finally, the next morning, I remember having pancakes with syrup for breakfast, while I played with Cecil, the stuffed "sea serpent" animal character from the show *Beany and Cecil.* Overall, I remember liking all the attention that was bestowed upon me, so I can see there being a dangerous connection that I made. (Noted for future reference.)

THE PARK ALONG SHORE ROAD

The fab four, in reverse age order: my sister Donna, my cousin John, me, and my sister-cousin Gigi, circa 1963

Living in the same building at 1-74th Street, my sister Donna and I, along with my cousins Gigi and John, spent much time together. We were more like siblings than cousins. We were all exactly one year apart, so the order went Gigi, short for Georgia Anne (she was named for her father, George, who passed in November 2019), who was born May 8, 1958; Debbie, short for Deborah Anne (or Debba, as my grandmother called me), born May 6, 1959; John Joseph (or the mad Russian, as my grandfather dubbed him while bowling), born April 5, 1960; and then Donna Marie (or Don-dons, as my grandmother called her and "twiddle ass," as my grandfather called her while bowling), born April 20, 1961. We always found a reason to be together and would always be disappointed if we could not. Their apartment was always a "new" adventure for us, and our apartment was the same for them. I loved to go over and play with Gigi's large collection of Madame Alexander dolls, and we would also like when our Aunt Joan would allow us to make strawberry Nestle Quik shakes in their built-into-the-counter blender (fancy for the '50s/early '60s).

One of our favorite places to go was the park along Shore Road. Driving west along the Belt Parkway, just under the Verrazano Bridge, down to 68th Street, one could view the long stretch of parks, baseball fields, and playgrounds. And our parks were not deemed "child safe," as many are today, as there was no cushioned or rubber flooring, just rock-hard pavement or asphalt beneath the swing sets, the monkey bars, and the slides. And on that subject, there didn't seem to be a day hot enough for us not to go down the metal slides, with metal probably well into the skin-burning/scorching range. The plants and foliage, which also spanned each park, were great "hiding" spots from each other, and from our parents. Outside the park at several locations (usually near various apartment buildings, like ours) were sandboxes, built into the brick-pavers that made up the Shore Road sidewalk. The sandboxes were little havens for us kids. I have one distinct memory of my dad coming over to the sandbox (probably coming from work) and giving me a ride on his shoulders. Boy, did I feel special.

THE CORONAVIRUS OF THE 1960S: THE CHICKEN POX

Before we ever heard of the coronavirus, in the 1960s, there was another equally contagious virus, called varicella, commonly known as chicken pox. If one lived in close quarters, or spent time with one who had the virus, chances are that within a few days, you would have it, too. As me, my sister, Gigi, and John all lived in the same building, and spent as much time as possible together, we all contracted it at the same time!

Varicella chicken pox is a member of the herpes family of viruses. It often starts with a rash and burning pain but ultimately it develops into small blisters that crust over and finally heal. This evolves over a two- to three-week period, during which the rash of "pox" can drive anyone crazy. And the ability to not touch it and let it heal was unheard of as a three-, four-, or five-year-old! So, pick, pick, pick, we did, as the annoying blisters continued to cover our torso and arms and legs and head. Of course, each pick continued the virus spread. The only treatment was calamine lotion, and the relief was only temporary. But it was something.

To distract us from our chicken pox, we decided to do something to occupy our time of "agony." We decided to play with Play-Doh. We did that at our Aunt Joan's apartment at 6R. We played with the Play-Doh in the living room. We utilized our Aunt Joanie's mosaic-tiled table. It was round and perfect to spread out that Play-Doh, all over the table, into every groove where there was grout between each tile! We wondered why Aunt Joanie was so upset upon seeing our "creation." She was horrified! She yelled at us and told us, "You need to fix this, and fix it now." And so we fixed it. It took quite a while, but we scraped out every inch of that Play-Doh, so "Aunt Joanie won't be mad at us anymore."

Smells That Will Always Remind Me of 1-74th Street in Bay Ridge

I can distinctly remember the smell of rain on the sidewalk and pavement in the spring and summer (I can even picture the checkered capris and white cropped cardigan I was apt to be wearing when I was two to five years old—my mother always made sure we were presentable). I can also recall the wafting smell of incinerators at dinner time (still permitted for use up until 1989, when a law to ban them was signed by Mayor Ed Koch). It was a mix of roast leg of lamb, meat loaf, roast pork, and various sauces for pasta. You could smell it, even in the lobby, mixed in with the amalgam of laundry room smells like sheets in the dryer and Bounce dryer sheets. I also remember the clothes lines on the roof with hanging towels and sheets, and the smell of clean laundry hanging in the breeze.

GRAMPS: THE STORY WOULDN'T BE COMPLETE WITHOUT HIM

My grandfather John Peter Feltman, Sr., was an amazing man, with an amazing story. He could have written his own book if he were still alive. Born in 1901, he would be 120 years old if he were still here! And through our memories of him, he is alive. He was a wonderful grandfather, many times over, with eight grandchildren, and ten great-grandchildren, so far. Gramps would have loved all of his sprouting legacies, and probably developed nicknames for each of them.

Gramps was born March 6, 1901, apparently in the field on the farm on which his family lived at the time. He was the youngest of nine children born alive. Three sets of twins did not survive. Of the nine born alive, my grandfather was my great-grandmother's favorite. There was only one girl, Anna, who we knew as "Tante Anna." My great-grandmother, Marie, or Mutter (in German), also emigrated to the United States shortly after my great-grandfather Hermann Feltman. Apparently, they were so in love that the slight difference in perceived class stature did not matter to Marie Dietz and Hermann Feltman.

John Peter Feltman, Sr., in Saudi Arabian garb while working in the Middle East. Despite his eighth-grade education, he spoke twelve languages.

My grandfather enlisted in the Navy during WWI after lying about his age (he was seventeen). He served in World War I. He received a Purple Heart for saving a French sailor, who nearly drowned falling off his ship.

After WWI, he met and married my grandmother, Dorothy C. LeStrange, on June 30, 1925. They had a daughter, Joan Mary, my aunt, born in 1926, and a son, John Peter, my father, born in 1930. My grandfather worked as a NYC Detective with the NYPD for several years during the 1930s. He had a storied career in that field as well. In the early 1940s, after not having much luck finding a job in the United States, he found work in the Middle East, doing things like building roads and other infrastructure projects. Because of his ability to speak twelve languages, he was able to communicate in many arenas. One was to sell snake skins. There were stories he told us, his grandchildren, that he learned how to kill a boa constrictor: "You had to let the boa wrap itself around your body, and when it got high enough, say up to your chest, and before it would 'constrict' or tighten around you, you could slice its head off with a fine wire that you would wrap around the boa's head." (Sounds easy enough.)

My Grandfather John Peter Feltman, Sr.: His Beginning

My great-grandparents owned a large farm, named the Feltman Farm, in the area where the Roosevelt Field Mall in East Garden City, New York, is located today. Roosevelt Field Mall, and previously Roosevelt Raceway, was named for President Theodore Roosevelt's son Quentin, who was killed in air combat during World War I. Given its proximity to the Feltman Farm, Teddy used to ride his horse over to the farm, where they hunted rabbits. The twenty-sixth president of the United States had his house at Sagamore Hill, near Oyster Bay. He lived there until his death in 1919.

As the story goes, Hermann Feltman, my great-grandfather, was killed by the Long Island Railroad while taking produce to market, in 1925. His wife, Marie, was forced to sell the farm, which garnered about $50,000. That sounded like a lot of money in the 1920s, but one could only imagine the price that the real estate of the farm (about 420 acres) would fetch in today's Long Island real estate market!

Roosevelt Field was the takeoff point for many historic flights in the early history of aviation including Charles Lindbergh's 1927 solo trans-Atlantic flight. It was also used by other pioneering aviators, including Amelia Earhart and Wiley Post. Source: https://en.wikipedia.org/wiki/Roosevelt_Field_(airport)

ROOSEVELT FIELD (AIRPORT)

Roosevelt Field
Hempstead Plains Aerodrome

Nearly a thousand people assembled at Roosevelt Field to see Charles Lindbergh take off in the* Spirit of St. Louis*, May 20, 1927

In use	1916–1951
Commander	Training Section, Air Service (1916–1920)
Occupants	Air Service, United States Army World War I (1916–1920)

Source: Wikipedia

Charles Feltman, Inventor of the Hot Dog

John Peter Feltman, Sr. (my grandfather) was a cousin of Charles Feltman, the man who invented the hot dog.

Charles Feltman (November 8, 1841–September 20, 1910) was a German-American baker who invented the hot dog in 1867 at Coney Island, New York.

Feltman was born in 1841 in Germany and emigrated to America in 1856, at the age of fifteen.[1] He was familiar with the frankfurter, named for Frankfurt-am-Main in his native land. Feltman's operation began by operating a pushcart pie wagon at the Coney Island beach in 1867, selling food to beachgoers. In 1869 he came up with the idea of inserting a frankfurter in a specially made elongated roll which could conveniently be held and eaten on the street or at the beach. Feltman called his 1869 creation the Coney Island red hot, and it was soon the eating rage.

Henry Collins Brown, a New York historian, explained its attraction: "It could be carried on the march, eaten on the sands between baths, consumed on a carousel, used as a baby's nipple to quiet an obstreperous infant, and had other economic appeals to the summer pleasure seeker." However, it took some time for the public to decide what to call Feltman's creation. Frankfurter, sausage, Coney Island red hot—none of them really captured the public's imagination. Coney Island chicken and weenie (from the Austrian wienerwurst) both had their proponents. But it was popular uncertainty about exactly what kind of meat was in these casings that ultimately determined that it would be called "hot dog." In 1871, Feltman leased land and began building his restaurant complex. It achieved its heyday in the 1920s, serving nearly 5,250,000 people a year, being a large restaurant complex with several restaurants, two bars, a beer garden, a famous carousel, and other attractions, and offering many types of food beyond hot dogs.

Feltman's restaurant in Coney Island
Source: https://www.6sqft.com/before-nathans-there-was-feltmans-the-history-of-the-coney-island-hot-dog/

Nathan Handwerker was working at Feltman's as a roll slicer when he quit to found rival Nathan's. Handwerker undersold Feltman (hot dogs for ten cents instead of five) and ran a more downscale operation than Feltman's, but eventually Nathan's became the most successful and iconic Coney Island hot dog purveyor and a nationwide brand which thrived into the 21st century. Feltman died in 1910 (he is interred at Green-Wood Cemetery in Brooklyn, New York) after which his family ran the business. Feltman's sons Charles L. Feltman and Alfred F. Feltman and grandson Charles A. Feltman, who had been operating the restaurant, sold the operation in 1946 to Alvan Kallman and others. The restaurant closed in 1954. The land was later used to construct the Astroland amusement park which opened in 1962 and closed in 2008, subsequently replaced by a new Luna Park. The last remnant of Feltman's—the building that had housed the kitchen—was demolished in 2010.

Charles Feltman's grandson Charles A. Feltman invented the Shooting Star Tommy Gun, a pneumatic BB machine gun used in fair and amusement park stalls for many decades and continuing well into the 21st century (the device is used by players to shoot out all traces of a red star on a paper target). Shooting Star Games was founded by Charles A. Feltman and continues to manufacture the device in the 21st century. There was for years a shooting gallery on the original Feltman's site.

"In the 2010s, entrepreneur Michael Quinn opened a hot dog emporium named Feltman's of Coney Island in New York's East Village, in homage to the original Feltman's and on Memorial Day, 2017, he cut the ribbon on a Coney Island location in the very structure where the aforementioned shooting gallery had been located, on the original Feltman's site." (*Source:* Wikipedia - https://en.wikipedia.org/wiki/Charles_Feltman/)

Charles Feltman's final resting place: Green-Wood Cemetery

Charles Feltman, Inventor of the Hot Dog

Source: Wikipedia

Chapter Nine

The Rest of the Feltman Siblings

Born Deborah Anne Feltman, I was the eldest of five children. My sister, Donna Marie, was next in the lineup. The two girls were then followed by three boys, in fairly rapid succession. Here's a little recap of the boys of the Feltman family.

John Peter arrived on December 27, 1964, two days after Christmas. He was the first boy—a redhead like my dad—and they named him John Peter, after my father and grandfather. He was John Peter the third. He was a beautiful boy, an early riser, and a roamer. One morning, at about 5 a.m., he was awakened by the sound of the garbage truck, and in his pajamas and robe (he called it his karate robe), he decided to follow the garbagemen (now called sanitation workers) around the neighborhood (at about 5:30 in the morning). I was awakened by my mother coming into my room, panicked because "we don't know where John is." They got a call from one of the neighbors that John was there. They drove around the block and luckily, they found him, safe and sound. John was always independent; he had his group of friends from the neighborhood, who he always called "you's guys." He remained close to them, despite the different paths in life they have all taken.

Robert William arrived just eighteen months later, on July 18, 1966, and it was a tough job getting my mom to the hospital in time to have the baby. Here was another boy and now another brunette to join me. Robert and I have always had a special bond, being the only brunettes in the family, and the only two of us whose skin pigment would allow us to tan and not just burn, like our three redheaded siblings. When my grandparents, whom we called Nanny and Poppy, also known as Bubby and Zawhny, were visiting, Robert made the mistake of using John's "you's guys" term to answer the question, "Who had clogged the toilet?" As my grandfather thought Robert was blaming them, poor Robert got a quick smack upside the head. He wound up crying and thinking Poppy hated him and certainly rethinking the use of the term "you's guys" ever again. Robert is very family oriented. I like to say that he has a heart the size of a roast beef. Robert always remembers that I used to chase him down when he was in the kitchen taking a big jar of peanut butter, with a large tablespoon, from the corner cabinet. (I was his unwelcome food police.)

Finally, there was Michael Joseph, the third boy and final redheaded sibling, who joined us on June 12, 1971. The fifth time, however, they didn't make it to the hospital in time. My mom went into labor precisely at dinner time, yet she had to take a shower and shave her legs and underarms (she had to look good for childbirth, right?). And she had to make sure we all had our dinners. According to my parents, my mom was starting heavy labor in the car on the way to the hospital, and as they exited off the parkway from Robert Moses Causeway, to Montauk Highway, and to the hospital, my mom let out a huge scream and said she didn't think she was going to make it in time. Just as they pulled into the ER entrance, all the fathers, having just seen their own new babies, were exiting because visiting hours were over. My dad parked the car and was going over to my mom in the back seat, but he wasn't prepared for what he was about to see—Michael was crowning as he was forcibly coming out of my mother's uterus and vagina. My dad called out to anyone within earshot, as my mom took hold of his throat: "HELP, my wife is having the baby!"

With that, the doctors, nurses, and the police came out of the hospital and jumped into action, all in the back seat of the station wagon! They delivered my brother Michael, placed him on my mom's stomach, and pushed them into the OR to cut the umbilical cord. So all went well—Michael and my mom were fine, but what a story they had to tell! And we do tell! Years later, when we were selling or getting rid of the "old 66 squire," we were all sad as we watched a piece of Feltman history go down the street for the last time, but we would never forget!

A piece of Feltman history:
Our 1966 Ford Country Squire

WE MOVED OUT TO "THE BURBS": WE MOVED TO "LAWN GUYLAND"

We lived at 1-74th Street, which was a lovely building and a great location on Shore Road, in Bay Ridge, but we were outgrowing our apartment in 5H (we'd moved to 5H from 2L when Donna was born), as my mom was pregnant with their third child. My dad went out looking for houses and found 100 Powell Court, in North Babylon, which was a three-bedroom, one-bath house in Suffolk County. It is exit 39 on the Southern State Parkway, about fifty miles from NYC. To think that seven adults survived in a one-bath house is amazing to me. Our one bath had a separate stall shower and a shower over tub, and I can remember having to blow dry my hair while one of us was showering and one bathing in completely humid conditions, and one of us kids knocking on the bathroom door, having to use the toilet. Ah, memories.

On the day we moved into Powell Court, my cousin John Joseph (see, John) somehow became involved in my sister Donna falling down the basement steps and breaking her arm. Still, she somehow managed to shift the 1966 Ford Country Squire station wagon (think Chevy Chase in *Vacation*) parked in the driveway into reverse and backed into the street. When she got out, she was crying and telling people who came to help that she "wasn't allowed to cross the street" (but backing out of the driveway at three years old? No problem.)

I also remember that, on the rare occasion my poor mom got to take somewhat of a relaxing bath, Donna and I would play "Big Man." Donna would get on my shoulders and she would put on one of my dad's overcoats, which was long enough to hang down to my knees, and we would barge into the bathroom, saying, "Hello, Mrs. Feltman," in a deep voice, completely scaring my mother, and her "relaxing" bath came to an end.

I was also guilty of putting ketchup on my forehead and my chest/Carter's undershirt and falling down in front of the upright vacuum while my mom was vacuuming the living room, feigning that I'd been shot or stabbed (you know, the normal things to happen to a suburban kid, living on a cul-de-sac). There were "real" bleeding episodes over the course of the more than twenty years all five siblings were living in the same house, but most of them involved my brothers. John and Robert, in particular, had many fights and disagreements, where Robert would lock John out of the house while John was mad, and Robert watched in horror as John removed the slats to a jalousie window in our basement, and proceeded to slide through that narrow window opening, to "get at Robert" and "kill" him.

I also remember my brother John driving my Toyota Celica, and, seeing me driving with my mom in the Ford Country Squire on the next block, made a quick right turn in front of me, drove home, and high-tailed it into the house, making believe that "it wasn't me driving your car . . . musta been someone else."

Then there was the morning that my brother Robert, acting on impulse after being badgered by my mom because "the pool liner wasn't straight, and can't you fix it" on a morning that was 95 degrees, threw a rake like a spear, hitting the back dining room bay window, and causing broken glass to fly into my brother John's Captain Crunch cereal, all while the rest of us were conjuring up stories of "what really happened," as my father was due home from the supermarket, "up on the Avenue," so we had to think quickly. Unfortunately, my dad thought more quickly than we did and figured out that "a ladder had not fallen into the side window" (our conjured-up story) of the large bay window that made up our dining room window.

When confronted, Robert became all flustered and stammered, "I did it! I need help! If Mommy hadn't frustrated me while I was trying to fix the pool lining." Yes, that was a story for the books (at least this book). I can't remember if John ever finished eating that cereal, but he seemed to be enjoying it before the rake came careening through the window like a spear.

It was my family's home until August 15, 2019, some fifty-five years later, albeit until both my parents passing, but it will never destroy our many great memories over the years. There were family vacations and day trips with our cousins, but I won't bore you with the details of all of those adventures, and there were many—Howe Caverns, Ice Caves, and the Catskill Game Farm, to name a few. My dad was like Francis Ford Coppola with a Bell & Howell movie camera. We loved the finished product of the movies, but I do remember our semi-annoyance with having to continuously come out from behind a pine tree, waving, no matter what we were doing, as there was no sound from movie cameras in the sixties era. And the spotlight that was employed during that time was blinding. Everyone always looked like they were tearing up, because they were!

CAPE COD, A FAMILY VACATION WORTH MENTIONING

In the summer of 1969, my dad and mom, Aunt Joan and Uncle George, and Nanny and Poppy all decided that we would take a multi-family vacation in Cape Cod, Massachusetts. It was a wonderful idea from all of us kids' perspective! Two weeks, for me and Donna, to be spent at the beach with our favorite cousins in the world, Gigi, John, and Scott (who was still a toddler, at two years old). John and Robert, four and three, respectively were also there. I was ten, Gigi was eleven, John was nine, and Donna was eight. This was the perfect environment for my grandfather and my dad, as both loved the beach, the water, and the sound of the pounding surf. Cape Cod was magic for us. It was at Cape Cod that my grandfather, who'd been in the Navy in World War I, taught us to dive and swim! As we waded and then walked into the surf, once we got to shoulder height in the water, my grandfather would dunk, and we then managed to stand on his shoulders. He took our hands, and he stood up, creating the perfect perch from which we would learn to dive! As we got our bearings, we then got into diving position, hands together above our heads. We then bent forward, and naturally were able to dive into the surf! After that, it was time to swim. We didn't freestyle but we placed our arms down by our sides, leaned face-forward into the water, and flutter-kicked our legs, our faces in the water, turning our heads to breathe as necessary. As each of us did this, Gramps encouraged our performance: "And how, you betta believe it! Bravo." Those were my Gramps's words to encourage us. We repeated this exercise several times that day, and for the rest of the two weeks. He had successfully taught his four eldest grandchildren to swim! Thank you, Grandpa! (That was the way we expressed our gratitude.) He loved it, and he was glowing with pride!

In a slightly different story, it was decided that our families would enjoy "fresh lobster from Cape Cod." This meant going into town to the market and buying the live lobsters to be consumed that evening. There were about a dozen large (three- to five-pound) lobsters purchased and transferred back to our vacation rental. Upon our arrival "home," it was decided that it was best to store the lobsters in the bathtub. As the afternoon wore on, dinner preparations began. My mom, Grace, and Aunt Joanie teamed up to start the process. Aunt Joanie was tending to a large pot of clam chowder to accompany our lobsters. My mom started to make baked potatoes, rolling them up in tin foil to place on the grill. She also made a salad, as our final entree accompaniment.

Fresh lobsters for dinner, or would they go on the attack?

Getting closer to mealtime, Nanny decided to get cleaned up. She wanted to take a shower. It was then that a near riot broke out. Nanny went into the bathroom to shower but was unaware that the lobsters were being stored in there. As she drew back the shower curtain, the lobsters rose up, along with their claws. Naturally, Nanny was shocked and horrified and decided to flee to safety! Using the only coverup she could find, she wrapped a towel around the front of her body, holding it closed at the back with her one free hand, she then burst out of the bathroom, across the living room, and out of the front door! All the while, she was screaming in horror that the lobsters were out to kill her! "Jackie, Zawhny, HELP! Gigi, Debba, HELP! Don-Dons, John, HELP!"

She was genuinely frightened and almost naked in the outdoors at Cape Cod. It was quite a sight. Ultimately, there was no lobster murder of our Nanny. Instead, the lobsters met their demise in the large pot of boiling water. A delicious lobster dinner ensued. Everyone had their fill, and more, and the night's adventure became family legend forever!

BEING A "MOM" AT TWELVE: TIME TO HAVE "THE TALK"

When my mom was pregnant with my brother Michael, I remember one day, while we were folding the cathedral window drapes (a pretty big task), my mom told me she was "expecting." At the time, I assumed it was like a FedEx package, so I asked, "Expecting what?" She replied, "A baby." There was no obvious baby bump, but it was time to have "the talk." She explained that when two people are married and love each other, and want to have a baby, that the husband puts his penis inside the woman's vagina, "and nine months later, a baby is born." I asked, "Where do you do this?" And she replied, "In a chair." And that was the extent of our "talk." I got dribs and drabs of some other information in the ensuing years, but there are still questions I have about that original discussion. I was happy, though, that a new baby was coming, and I was determined to be part of the process. I became my mother's helper. I helped my mother when she went shopping to pick up a bag to pack for when she would go to the hospital. Powder, deodorant, toothpaste, toothbrush, body lotion, pajamas, and slippers, all went into the bag to be packed and ready for when it was "time."

I DIDN'T HAVE KIDS . . . BUT I DID . . .

While my mom made babies easily, I was never fortunate enough to have my own children, yet I always thought I would have three or four if I did. When I was in my late twenties/early thirties, I first went to see a doctor that my high school BFF, Robin Haushalter Giannola, referred me to. She was at the University of Michigan Hospital, and the doctor's name was Sue Ellen Sauder. Gary and I went to stay with Robin and Kirk Giannola at their apartment in Ann Arbor, Michigan. This was a new experience for us. While in Ann Arbor, Kirk was kind enough to take us to Detroit—Motor City. We went to The Towers Center Mall and took the opportunity to take in the sights, as well as the shopping. The next day, I was taken to University of Michigan Hospital to see Dr. Sauder. Dr. Sauder did a tremendous amount of bloodwork, and after the results came back, it was discovered that I had a significant thyroid deficiency. The official term was hypothyroidism. That would explain my history of abnormal period length, my dry skin, and what I believed was a slight weight gain (at 107 pounds). A-ha! I was prescribed Synthroid to be taken daily, without interruption, and I'd need periodic re-testing to determine if my Synthroid dosage needed any readjusting. I started out on 125 mg. In the first month, my cycles, which could run anywhere from thirty-five to forty-two days, suddenly became the normal twenty-eight days! I was amazed about the immediate impact of having my hormones normalized. Now, if Gary and I were ready to get pregnant, we could, or so it seemed. Then I got involved with my new job on Wall Street.

My priorities shifted to moving up the corporate ladder, making more money, business travel, learning all about the industry I followed—electric utilities—and the one in which I worked, Wall Street. Getting pregnant would come later.

In my mid-to-late thirties, having not gotten pregnant, I decided to consult with another doctor about my fertility, or lack thereof. A good friend of mine, Joyce Timko Becker, referred me to her former neighbor in Haworth, New Jersey, Dr. Jamie Grifo, so I made an appointment at his office. After filling out a ton of paperwork, and submitting to several blood tests, I finally got to see Dr. Grifo. He was nice, and very good-looking. We decided that rather than start me immediately with more invasive treatments, like IVF, he'd start me with a course of Clomid, which is notorious for producing multiple births.

I had several IUIs (intrauterine inseminations) (I always called it the turkey baster method) and a number of miscarriages, some planned and others unplanned. When I took Clomid, I ended up with twenty-four or more stimulated eggs and a bad and very painful case of peritonitis, where the entire peritoneum (the inside abdominal lining) becomes inflamed. I had to sleep on my side with a belly pillow and it hurt so bad. The last miscarriage, in 1998, was the worst, since I conceived naturally, after years of trying. I was thirty-eight years old. I was going to have this baby (I thought God was sending me a message, but maybe not). My family was happy, and some friends even sent me congratulatory cards when they'd heard the news, including my husband, Gary, who called the baby "secret traveler" in a card he gave me to thank me, saying how happy he was, along with some roses. My friend Isabelle Madonia also used the term in her card to congratulate me. It is memories like these that make me regret my transgressions in my marriage.

I need to interject something. When Gary and I were separated from June 1983 to June 1985, I still maintained contact with his family (in part, to find out what Gary was doing at the time), and in year two (1984), I was invited to the Grosser family Christmas party at the beginning of December. It was a great party, as it always was at the Grosser household, and everyone seemed friendly and glad to see me. Of course, everyone was there, including Gary, and we got along well that night. So much so that I ended up staying the night, and Gary and I slept together, and as a surprise for both of us, I ended up getting pregnant. Given that we were separated, and I was just finishing school, and our marriage was in question, Gary agreed with me that I should terminate the pregnancy. After all, I was only twenty-five, and we'd have plenty of years to have children, once our marriage was on solid ground, and we were both settled in our careers and our finances would be in good shape. Never did we think that I'd not be able to get pregnant and carry a baby full-term again. But that was the case for us, and for me. As it turns out, my blood type is O-negative (for the Rh factor), and that likely was the cause of my inability to carry a pregnancy full-term. Or, perhaps God knew that I was too selfish to rent space in my body for nine to ten months, thereby getting fat and unattractive, or that I would become an alcoholic and potentially be a bad mother. Those are hard facts to swallow, but they are the truth. I do have much regret that I didn't have children, and despite my alcoholism, I think could have been a good mother, but after menopause, I'll never get to know.

Thankfully, I have four nephews and one niece: John Gregory, Matthew Thomas, Natalie Grace, Nicholas Michael, and James Philip. I love them all as if they were my own and I try and do special things with them, as time and money allow. For instance, I've taken my brother Michael and his boys, Nick and James (my cubby bear), with me to Lake Placid. We went in 2008 and 2010. I volunteered for the bike transition area and even signed up for another Ironman the morning right after the race. But I didn't have it in me again (at that time), so I wasted my money—the race fee alone was more than $750. I'm also "Aunt Deb" to my cousin Gigi's two daughters, Lorianne and Jackie, and their offspring, which entails one grandniece and four grandnephews: Frank Jr., Jack Thomas, Lucas Vito (Lorianne and Frank's three boys), and Zachary Joseph and Sophia Grace (Jackie and Zachary Brethauer's two children).

GODPARENTS ARE KIND OF PARENTS, AREN'T THEY?

I was also a godmother to four children (now adults): my youngest brother, Michael Joseph Feltman, my cousin Gigi's daughter Lorianne Marchiano, my high school BFF Robin Haushalter Guerire's daughter Kelsey Mesarina, and my sister Donna's daughter, Natalie Grace Maida, who just graduated from my alma mater State University of New York (SUNY) Stony Brook with a degree in psychology. Due to the pandemic, they were forced to have the ceremony virtually. Being a godmother has been my blessing as a "mother," as I get to spoil them, and then send them home, to their parents.

Lorianne Diana, my 2nd goddaughter

My niece and goddaughter, Natalie Grace Maida

Kelsey Mesarina, my goddaughter, daughter of my high school BFF, Robin Haushalter Guerire

Chapter Ten

My Formal Education Years

Parliament Place Elementary School: The Very Beginning

When we moved to 100 Powell Court, in June 1964, I was already five years old, and it was time for kindergarten. The school in the North Babylon Public School district that I would attend in September 1964 would be Parliament Place Elementary School. I entered into kindergarten, and my teacher was Mrs. Naomi Feldman. Because our names were so similar-sounding, people assumed she was my mother. But the T versus the D in our last names made all the difference in the world. Traditionally, Feldman was a Jewish name, while Feltman was a name of German descent. I'd learned that, when emigrating from Germany, our last name, Feltman, was pronounced "Fielt" man, or fieldman which, loosely translated, meant "farmer."

AT PARLIAMENT PLACE, I MET MY FOREVER FRIEND

Parliament Place Elementary School in North Babylon, New York

Since 1964, in Parliament Place Elementary School, two little girls, admonished for talking during the Pledge of Allegiance, have been best friends! Her name was Jeanne Patrice Cusack. We moved on to be the inaugural attendees at Our Lady of Lourdes Roman Catholic Church and School (OLL) in 1965. Ours were the first tiny butts to grace the newly installed toilets at the school. The classrooms were brimming with over fifty students per class, more than one hundred per grade! In 2018, OLL closed due to lack of enrollment! Only forty-five people were scheduled to be enrolled in the entire school! Back in the mid-1960s, Catholic schools were viewed as a premier education, harder to get into, yet there I was, as was Jeanne Patrice Cusack, new attendees as a brand-new student body! The ensuing years were filled with a great education, as we and the school morphed into the formative years of our lives: we made friendships with others in the classes, and we diligently studied the subject matter taught to us at OLL. Many fun experiences were had, as we developed into young girls and young women. One funny story: at the time we were young women, we viewed the movie *Growing Up and Liking It*, which discussed the ultimate onset of menstruation. It depicted a young, attractive woman going out in the rain (with the proper umbrella, of course), riding horses (which Jeanne went on to do), and generally leading fun, normal lives, despite the onset of this change in our bodies. We were going to be okay, better than okay—we were going to have a great ol' time! Flash forward to 2019 when the movie *Period, End of Sentence* won an Oscar for Best Documentary Short.

ON THE TOPIC OF BOYS

In kindergarten through third grade, boys and girls were friends. We liked each other in an innocent, friendly way. Then, there was an abrupt shutdown. We started to like boys again in the fifth grade (after we squelched the semi-nauseous feelings in our stomachs). Finally, there was actual "kissing" that went on, out of sight from Sister Ruth or any of the other nuns or lay teachers. My first public kiss, at OLL, was with Chris McCormick, in fifth grade, in the back of math class, taught by Mr. Troy (also our basketball coach). Chris and I moved into the cubby area at the back of the class, and that's where it happened: my first kiss. It wasn't a French kiss, just lips touching lips, and it didn't last long. But what it did do was to cause a warm feeling from my head, down my neck, and it was a strange sensation—but I liked it! I imagined I would do it again. Likely *not* in the back of a classroom, but somewhere more conducive to maybe French kissing, or maybe not. I was eleven, and not ready for primetime, *yet*! Time would tell. I would grow up. Jeanne and I would remain friends for fifty-five more years, with marriages, children, living abroad, and so many other life events that brought new circumstances into our lives. But me and Jeanne, we'd always be friends. And I'd always love her! She's been my BFF for all these years, and I can't wait to see her again! Praise God!

My BFF's Exotic and International Life

Jeanne Patrice Cusack ended up having the most international and exotic life of anyone I've ever known. During her college years she went to Northeastern in Boston, and it was there that she met Anthony (Tony) Placido, a dark-haired, good-looking guy with a big family of boys. He also attended Northeastern. Ultimately, Jeanne and Tony fell in love and got married in 1983. Tony studied criminal justice and set his sights on a career with the FBI. Ultimately, Tony was inducted by the US Drug Enforcement Agency (DEA), under President Reagan. Jeanne, Tony, and their girls, Megan and Molly, ended up living in Lima, Peru, and La Paz, Bolivia. After each international stint, Tony, Jeanne, and the girls would spend time stateside, usually in Washington, DC (headquarters for the DEA), the field office in New York (Manhattan), or south Florida (close to Miami), where there was a significant level of trafficking in the drug trade. In each country they lived, it became quite useful to be fluent in Spanish. Tony was fluent, and Jeanne knew enough to get her point across, and later became conversant. Megan and Molly both became fluent over time. In each country where they lived, they also were entitled to live in areas of diplomatic immunity, and they were somewhat protected.

Jeanne & Tony Placido and daughters Megan and Molly, and Megan's husband, Scott

OUR LADY OF LOURDES, IN WEST ISLIP: FEELING CLOSE TO GOD

Our Lady of Lourdes, in West Islip, New York

In 1965, my parents decided that I would attend parochial school, after I passed the entrance exam to do so. I became part of the inaugural class of Our Lady of Lourdes, in West Islip, the first-ever to sit at the new desks and first to use the newly installed toilet seats in the school. Being a Catholic school, all of the teachers were nuns or lay teachers. We had a very strict principal, Sister Ruth Francis, whom, in my six-year-old's eyes, stood about six foot three and had big dark circles under her eyes. Scary. No messing around with her. Follow the rules. Be a good girl. Years later, when Sister Ruth was celebrating her fifty-year "Golden Jubilee," my six-year-old view was sharply adjusted: in reality, Sister Ruth stood about five foot two, and she was sweet as pie!

It was interesting to me to remember that I never learned to view people of different color as being any different than me. No one was any better, or worse, than me. Attending Catholic school, it was part of the curriculum to require our attendance at church every Sunday morning. This was not new to me, as my family had been attending Sunday mass since I was a toddler. My mother described an occasion of our attendance at mass at Our Lady of Angels, in Bay Ridge, Brooklyn. The time came, during mass, when collections were made. Ushers (usually men) passed long-handled baskets through each pew, and each attendee dutifully gave either paper or coin into the baskets. On this occasion, my mother had given me some coins to put into the basket, and she was mortified when I bent over and the skirt of my dress flipped up, revealing that I had no underwear on! No mother of that era (late fifties/early sixties) wanted to be viewed as a parent that would allow her children to "go out like that," especially in church! I remember her walking me out of church very quickly, and scolding me all the way home, until we returned home so she could rectify the situation.

Our Lady of Lourdes provided a good education for me. In my first year, we had Sister Mary Emily. She was our teacher for every subject. In second grade, we had Sister Ann Immaculate, also our teacher for every subject. In third grade, we had Miss Marie DiFiore, who was very pretty and we all liked her very much.

Sister Rosalie was our teacher for fourth grade, and Mrs. Fairchild was our teacher for fifth grade. Sister Paul Miriam (my personal favorite) was our teacher for sixth grade. I liked her specifically because she gave her own personal example of how God forgives. Growing up in Brooklyn in a large Irish family (her given name was Patricia Sullivan, later becoming Sister Paul Miriam when she took her vows, then later she went back to being Sister Pat Sullivan), the children were always getting into trouble for one reason or another. On one occasion, Sister Paul Miriam detailed an episode when she was pulling her brother around the neighborhood while he was in a wagon, unconscious because he had fallen and had gotten the wind knocked out of him. She couldn't imagine how to tell her mother that her brother appeared to be dead. Upon arriving home, her brother had miraculously come back to life, thus her confession to murder was unnecessary. Phew. The moral of the story was that God forgave her, as He knew that no harm was done, yet her willingness to confess demonstrated her commitment to the truth. Number one, I liked that she shared her own example, and number two, God forgave her because she told the truth because all children are apt to lie on occasion. Footnote: I remained in contact with Sister Pat over the years, up until she turned ninety, in 2010, and was living in Northport, New York. My parents and I went to visit her, and we enjoyed fresh lemonade out on the porch of the convent where she lived. Ultimately, I learned that Sister Pat Sullivan passed in late 2016. She had to be ninety-five or ninety-six at the time she passed. Not a surprise; Sister Pat had a zest for life that was infectious!

In third grade, while our homeroom teacher was Miss DiFiore, we started to rotate to different teachers for different subjects. For math, our new teacher was Mr. Troy. He was handsome. He was my first-ever school-girl crush. He had dark hair, neatly combed back, and he had the most beautiful blue eyes. He smelled good, and he looked good. And he was smart.

Cheering for the Trojans

Being limber and coordinated, I tried out for the cheerleading squad, and I made it! Cute uniforms, pom-poms; cheerleading, here I come!

In OLL, the school didn't have a football team, but they did have a decent basketball team. As Mr. Gere Troy became coach of the team, it was only fitting that the name of the team was the Trojan (from Greek mythology about the ancient city of Troy, and their soldiers were called Trojans). At the time, I was not aware, and I don't think it was known among the other kids in my grade, that Trojans was also the name of a popular brand of condoms.

Imagine, Catholic school girls, cheering for the Trojans, which must have sounded odd to anyone who knew the dual meaning of the name of the team. Thus, our cheer: "Trojans, Trojans, can't be beat," was probably more an advertisement for the condom brand!

ROBERT MOSES JUNIOR HIGH SCHOOL: THE NEW GIRL IN THE SAME TOWN, WITH DIFFERENT CLIQUES

One night, in the middle of the night, I had an epiphany: I wanted to go back to public school! In my neighborhood, the kids I hung out with went to public school. By thirteen, I had already become enamored with certain boys, and I knew many of them were already in the public school system. Thus, I wanted in! I summoned my parents, and told them of my decision, and they agreed that I could go.

Robert Moses Junior High School,
North Babylon, New York

For eighth grade, I started public school again, at Robert Moses Junior High School, which covered grades seven to nine. For me, having been out of the loop at parochial school, I felt a bit like the new kid on the block. Suddenly, the same kids that were from my neighborhood were already entrenched in their own cliques!

Sports Night was a big event at Robert Moses. There was a tremendous amount of planning, decorating, and training for events. My forte turned out to be the obstacle course. To excel, one needed to be fast, relatively small, limber, and have lightning-fast reflexes to change course! The race started with a quick, running burst, then we had to navigate around orange cones, crawl under some rope netting, emerge and run toward a rope, and then spring (on a springboard) over a bar with a wrestling mat flung over it for padding, and then finally, a short sprint to the finish! I forget my exact time, but it was under a couple of minutes! I remember during Sports Night preparation that I thought one boy was very cute. His name was Chris Burke. I was at the phase when if I liked a boy and thought he was cute, I'd get a little nauseated every time I'd see him!

So, back to Chris Burke at Robert Moses. Our grade, eighth grade, won over ninth grade in Sports Night. We were so excited and happy! Chris Burke asked if I would go outside with him for "just a little while." Well, we found a place out in the back field and, surprisingly, Chris had a blanket for us to lay upon, and so we did. Immediately, Chris laid on top of me, and we started tongue-kissing! Madly! It was so exciting. He was so cute. Man, did I love doing this!

Drinking was not part of this night, but I had already started experimenting with alcohol, at about thirteen years old. My Aunt Joanie introduced us to drinking politely, at about age fifteen for me, like the time we went to the Chinese restaurant and ordered "grasshoppers" and "pink ladies," which were made with grenadine, half and half, egg whites, and gin in a very pretty glass. A typical grasshopper cocktail consists of equal parts green crème de menthe, white crème de cacao, and cream—shaken with ice and strained into a chilled cocktail glass.

But prior to this, it became a rite of passage when the neighborhood kids got into a wide variety of mischief, like "I'll show you mine, if you show me yours," and there was the drinking "sampler": find a mayonnaise-sized jar; pour in whatever variety of alcohol your parents had in their liquor cabinets. I can only remember that some of the jars were creamy and sweet, but others were like pure, high-octane gin or vodka, and tasted awful. But it wasn't the taste we were after but rather the effect! My head and face started getting warm and I remember feeling woozy and not liking that. But I couldn't wait to do it again. The idea of becoming an alcoholic never entered my mind. Drinking was something that adults did during parties, or at dinner, or at home with friends. I glamorized alcohol from the first time I came into contact with it. Later, I learned that this was called "romanticizing or romancing" alcohol. I only thought of the positives of what alcohol could do for me: the social lubricant, the relaxer, the "special night out, with someone I loved." I never envisioned drinking so much, over a period of days, leading to a fall down a flight of stairs, so hard, and with such force, that my nose got sheared off my face! I could never have foreseen that outcome and all the attendant consequences. But here I am. Now, what to do?

NORTH BABYLON HIGH SCHOOL: MY SPRINGBOARD TO THE FUTURE

North Babylon High School

In September 1974, I entered North Babylon High School. In the photo above, the Flying W provided overhead coverage in the event of inclement weather. I later learned that it was a trade-off, instead of getting an Olympic-sized pool. What a bad trade! At NBHS, now I was with the big kids! The cute guys, the football games, the cheerleaders, the soccer games, the cute guys (did I say that already?). My future brother-in-law, Bobby Grosser, was on the soccer team. He had ripped abs and kind of long hair (popular in the

'70s), and strong, muscular legs. I immediately thought he was cute, and we became friendly during my tenth grade (sophomore) year and his senior year. He would graduate in June 1975, headed for the US Air Force.

I had many great teachers at NBHS. Mr. Wayne Panarese was a favorite, for biology. It was while taking bio with him that I decided to take AP Biology. Mr. Panarese liked when I wore my beige corduroy pants, regularly making comments about how good my butt (booty) looked in them. He referred to them when he signed my high school yearbook (which I've kept). There was Rich Meyers for physics, and I took an AP course in that as well. Finally, we had Mr. Harris for chemistry.

Fortunately, I did extremely well academically at NBHS. I worked hard to excel in the sciences: biology, chemistry, and physics. Ultimately, I took Advanced Placement courses in each of them, thus graduating with a full year of college credits in those subjects. I graduated in the top 10 percent of a class of more than 750 students. That qualified me for high honors, which meant I had to wear an additional yellow collar on my graduation gown. My family had a nice party at our home. I felt special that day. Thank you, Mom and Dad, for all you did to celebrate my big day!

It was during my high school years that my friends and I sought some more excitement. We wanted to be older than our years. We wanted to go to places that held excitement. We wanted to go to the clubs and bars. In the mid-1970s, NY State driver's licenses were not photo IDs, as they are today. Once licensed, all it took was the swipe of a black Sharpie, and our date of birth could be miraculously altered. On the DL, as long as the month and the date of birth were constant, all we had to know was our astrological sign. With that completed, where to go? There was a place on Deer Park Avenue. It was called Cheers. It's where we went first. On a Thursday night, we went to Cheers. It was Ladies Night! We presented our IDs to the guys at the door (the bouncers), we passed, and we were in! Our group that night consisted of me, Jeanne Cusack, Susan Miesemer, Susan Wojnarowski, and Louise Perrotta. We heard the loud reverberating music inside the club. I looked over by the bar and saw Jeanne ordering something. In short succession, once she got hers, it was time for me and the rest of us. I think my first drink at the bar was a Madras: cranberry, pineapple, and vodka. It seemed like a reasonably innocent type of drink to order, first time out. As we started to act more like we belonged there, we looked at each other with a smile of satisfaction. Here we were in a bar, with music playing for the first time! We were so cool! As the beat of the music picked up, so did our choice of drink. We quickly graduated to doing shots. Why not? Let's try Bacardi 151 rum? Sounds good to me.

The music playing was by Foreigner. I loved the song "Feels Like the First Time" (which was apt since this was our first time in a club/bar). As the tempo and percussion of the song blended with the words, we swayed to the music. I don't know who initiated it, but the next thing we knew, we were standing on the barstools around the bar! Feeling triumphant, we all got up there, one after the other! I made eye contact with Sue, and then Jeanne, as if silently saying, "How cool are we?!" Shot glasses in hand, we each did our shots, which quickly had an effect. This was 151 proof, after all. There we were, standing on the barstools, shots in hand (or done already), and then we were singing at the top of our lungs: "It feels like the first time. Feels like the very first time, it feels like the first time, it feels like the very first time." It was 1976. We were all seventeen, but this night, we were eighteen-plus!

In June 1978, Robbie (as we called him, among the family), Gary Grosser's younger brother, was headed for Germany to play soccer in the Air Force! It was Robbie who called me at the last minute to invite me to an impromptu going-away party at the Oak Beach Inn in Oak Beach, New York. It was to occur on June 9, 1978, which turned out to be the night I met his brother, Gary, who eventually became my husband for twenty-five years.

Also along for the party were friends Charlie Gunkle and Jeff Schoedler, longtime friends of both Gary and Robbie.

THE STONY BROOK YEARS

Stony Brook University; a sprawling campus

In June 1977, I graduated from North Babylon High School. I graduated with high honors. My SAT scores were high as well, so going to an Ivy League school might have been possible, on an academic basis, but not for my parents or our finances at the time. Mostly, they depended on me to take care of my siblings at night while my mom worked in retail. She first worked at Gertz, which later became Sterns, and then went on to Ann Taylor Loft. My mom always seemed to be assigned to work in the domestics department. It's where they sold the sheets, towels, and bedding. As a result, my mom taught me how to fold towels and fitted sheets the "right" way (that came in handy when I got married). Since going away to college was not an option for me, either practically or financially, I eventually decided I would go to the SUNY, at Stony Brook (aka SUNY Stony Brook). It was about forty-five minutes away from my parents' home, and not far from either of my jobs, at Dr. Jaffe's office and NY Telephone, in Babylon, New York. So, I could go to Stony Brook as a commuter student. For instance, NY Telephone paid for college tuition, contingent on maintaining a "C" average (which I didn't think would be a problem). During the first year at Stony Brook, I realized that the pre-med curriculum was going to be super hard, despite having a full year of college credits in biology, chemistry, and physics. I started to think of other options. I decided that economics might be the way to go. My father's career took off while working for then–Merrill, Lynch, Pierce, Fenner & Smith (put that on a bumper sticker), and he suggested that I consider becoming an industry analyst at a Wall Street firm, maybe covering pharmaceutical companies. And that's exactly what I ended up doing. Except the industry that I covered was utilities, not pharmaceutical companies. Different industries but both required many of the same analytical tools to analyze an industry as well as the companies that comprised it.

Chapter Eleven

On Norwich Pond

It is here, on Norwich Pond, that my life began to take parallel and divergent paths. My first boyfriend was John Clasen, whom I met in my junior year of high school, and to whom I lost my virginity. With him, I was introduced to his family's lovely summer home in Connecticut, on Norwich Pond, in Old Lyme. It was beautiful, and I was introduced to the beauty of summer life on a lake. I loved diving off the dock and racing toward a bottle of Suave strawberry shampoo, thrown off the dock; both John and I raced to see who could get there first. Despite John having nearly a foot of length over me, I often won that race, and John's father, Hal, seemed to get a kick out of me beating John in that race. I loved the echoing sounds of voices, as the occupants called between cabins, and the lovely *On Golden Pond* look of the whole scene. We could often hear the voices across the water as we played board games and cards at night. There were gas-powered lamps, and the refrigerator was powered by natural gas, as was the stove. Who knew that I would learn all about the power and natural gas pipeline industries in my life to come on Wall Street?

Me at 19 years old, in June 1978

During the years I went there, I got to meet Aunt Janet (Janet Samaha and Mary Clasen, John's mom, had both grown up as MacRostie) and Uncle Sam Samaha, who owned several McDonald's restaurants in the Tri-State area. I met their kids, Lynn, Peter, Amy, and Steven. We'd gone to their home, in Armonk, New York, which was very nice. Uncle Sam was very affectionate with his children, and we enjoyed the various stories they told.

John was the first boy to break my heart. I was a year behind him in high school, and he went off to college, at SUNY Brockport (eight hours away), and I was naïve to think that he would remain faithful for four years. I remember, as he was about to leave for school, he came over and we both cried so much, and we blew our mucus-filled noses so much, and I saved those napkins, and because he came home after three weeks away at school, I thought that maybe we would defy the unfaithful odds. But he was indeed unfaithful, meeting a girl named Sue Lawrence (and she had a boyfriend at home already, as well), and I believed John (in his silence) that he was remaining true to me. It wasn't until his sophomore year, and after I'd made the 400-mile trip to Brockport, that John stepped away from "us," and in the summer of 1977, we finally broke up. Naturally, it was "his" time of life to explore new paths, and new people. It was his time to be free. It was at this time that the song "Free Bird" by Lynyrd Skynyrd came out and we dubbed it John's song, as his friends called him "Claybird." I was torn up for several months, but then I met Gary in June 1978, who later became my husband, in 1981. As the saying goes: "One door closed, another one opened." And so it did.

John Henry Clasen, 1976 yearbook photo

Chapter Twelve

The Gary Years

Another Door Opened: Meeting Gary at the OBI

Gary and I met on June 9, 1978, on a Friday night at the Oak Beach Inn (OBI). I was invited last-minute by his brother Robbie, whom I was friends with (and to whom I was attracted, but I don't think it was mutual). He was more interested in me keeping tabs on his ample-busted, cheerleader girlfriend, Marlene Miano (she was a popular cheerleader, and yes, I was envious of all the attention she garnered). After two years in the Air Force, Robbie was going to Germany, and while there, he wrote to me regularly. I loved getting his letters and kept them all in a shoe box under my bed.

Gary was cute, I thought, and we made some small talk to break the ice. I'd brought my friend Carol Latva with me. We went to high school together and I worked with her at Dr. Jaffe's office. Dr. Jaffe was an orthodontist who had a penchant for a few mothers of his patients. I was glad she was there in case things weren't going well, but so far, they seemed to be. Much later, I heard the story that my mom was worried until I got home, since I broke curfew and I never had before—I ultimately got home after 2:30 in the morning. Gary made up a story that someone had taken his car and he needed a ride home. Naturally, I said "yes"—I was already smitten—but in reality, his car was parked right out front (I had no idea he was driving a Mercury Cougar XR7). The next day, my mom told me she had called Carol Latva's mom, and Carol wasn't home just yet either, so two moms were worried. I couldn't tell you what music was being played, but OBI usually had some good stuff. I think there was an Eagles song on, and Gary leaned in and kissed me. Full-on, open-mouth. Good kisser. Nice. It felt good. We went out back and took a little walk on the beach in the OBI's backyard. We'd walk a little and then stop and kiss for a while. It felt exciting. I hadn't kissed anyone since John Clasen broke up with me, and that really broke my heart. So, it was nice to be back in the game. Still, caution was warranted. Take it slow, Deb.

JAMAICA MON: "WAH GWON?"

Years later, I found the pages from a journal I was keeping back then, and my entries said: "Met Gary last night at OBI, tall, green/blue eyes. He's cute, good-looking. I think there's something there." A few months later I wrote: "He told me he loved me." What happened in the intervening period? I went to Jamaica with Jeanne Cusack (now Jeanne Cusack Placido). This would be my first-ever vacation on my own.

I found Liberty Travel and booked a one-week trip to Negril Beach Village, including flights on Air Jamaica. I remember feeling so empowered as I went to Liberty each week to pay more of our deposit money. I loved the folders they put together with information about the hotel, the island of Jamaica, and information about boat trips (including some nudity, which scared the bejesus out of me and we never did go). This vacation was an "all-inclusive" (as Kelly Ripa says on her show every morning at the "travel trivia" segment, "all-inclusive means it includes *all*"—emphasis added). As we found out, we would get a shark's teeth necklace, and they would pay for drinks, and so on, with teeth from our necklaces.

As previously discussed, I've known Jeanne since kindergarten. We got in trouble for talking during the Pledge of Allegiance. We're now celebrating our fifty-six-year "golden jubilee" (like nuns celebrate fifty years after taking their vows). We had a great time in Jamaica, and we made some interesting connections while there. We met a family where the parents had just gotten married, and there were three boys and three girls, so we called them "The Brady Bunch." The boys were cute, too. We got stuck in Montego Bay due to an Air Jamaica strike and Gary missed me. I guess absence and independence do make the heart grow fonder. From the first time I ever asked him how tall he was, Gary would always answer: "Three feet, thirty-seven inches," instead of just saying six foot one. I guess he was trying to be clever and funny at the same time.

History of OBI and Controversy

In 1969, Robert Matherson bought what was then a waterfront barrier island restaurant and converted it into an enormously popular (and controversial) nightclub. He later opened four more OBI night clubs and named them according to their geographic location. Per Wikipedia, the OBI North was in Smithtown, New York; the OBI East near the Shinnecock Canal, en route to the Hamptons; and two OBI West locations were in Island Park, New York. All five clubs were located on Long Island and were wildly successful for many years, bringing people in from all over Long Island, New York City, Westchester, southern Connecticut, and New Jersey, and hosting acts such as Twisted Sister and The Good Rats. In 1979, Matherson sued the town to lease him more land for additional parking, which the town granted. However, two years later, new officials disagreed, which caused Matherson to sue again, and when the court favored Matherson, the town granted him $3 million and the nine acres. In 1993, an unhappy Matherson actually started a "Move Out of New York Before It's Too Late" campaign complete with a hearse, banners, and TV ads. A 1993 New York Times article provided more details about his campaign, including that the NY State Division of Alcoholic Beverage Control raided the club one year earlier, in 1992. One of the OBI West locations burned down after only a couple of years of packing in thousands on the weekends. Arson involving organized crime figures referred to in the movie *Goodfellas* was alleged but never substantiated.

Over the years, the OBI was involved in many disputes with the local community over issues such as noise, parking, and traffic. Finally, in 1999, Matherson sold the property to developer Ross Cassata, who planned to build condominiums, and moved to Key West, Florida, to open a new club of the same name. When it closed, the inn's two-ton statues of whales and dolphins, which were commonly touched by clubgoers, were moved to Danfords on the Sound in Port Jefferson, Long Island. However, Cassata then sold the nine acres to Suffolk County for $7.95 million. The original property was torn down in 2003 and was replaced with a town-operated park, with later plans of adding a bed and breakfast, an upscale restaurant, boardwalk, water-sport area, and boat ramp. The park now hosts activities such as car racing and has caused controversy in itself. At the time of demolition, the Suffolk County Legislator commented that the park agreement avoided "an enormous tax increase in Babylon, which would have had to pay a court judgment of as much as $20 million or watch its coastline be forever scarred by high-rise development," and the money came from the county's greenway program. Source: https://en.wikipedia.org/wiki/Oak_Beach_Inn

The Day After OBI

Gary Steven Grosser, at his favorite spot, the beach, all three feet, thirty-seven inches of him!

The morning after my first meeting with Gary, I went to the beach, as usual (probably with Jeanne and Sue Miesemer and others who would already be there). We went to Robert Moses, an extension of Jones Beach on the barrier island of Fire Island. We went to Field 5—it was less crowded and a bit quieter. It was a really nice day—sunny and hot, with a nice breeze. There was the sea of bodies lying on blankets (which we surveyed from the boardwalk), a mishmash of boom boxes, playing the radio or cassette tapes, and (I loved this part) the wafting smell of Coppertone, Hawaiian Tropic, and Bain de Soleil, all mixed together. Periodically, on the radios, we'd hear WABC's disc jockey say: "time to roll your bod," in a deep baritone voice—a reminder to turn over to make the tan lines even. Ahhh, the beach. Oh, and the background sound of waves crashing. Time to lay out, then get in the water and body surf. Yee-hah!

Not long after being there, I spied Gary arriving at Field 5. He was about fifty feet away. He spread out a blanket and then lay down. It looked like he was in good shape, but I really couldn't see. After laying out for a while and going in the surf a couple of times, I went over to say hi. The first thing Gary said to me was "See my fat stomach?" as he lightly smacked his stomach, which was not fat at all, and which I really didn't see, and then he waved me over and said, "Come and sit down."

I did, and then I asked, "So how's everything?"

He said, "Well the beach is great, but I have to work later."

"Oh really? Where do you work?" I asked.

"I work at the Roosevelt Raceway, near Roosevelt Field Mall," he replied. "I park cars there. My Uncle Gus got me in last year."

I said, "That's good. How do you make out there?"

He said, "It works out pretty well, as long as there's not too many guys to split with. And if I work the entry booths, it's even better, and the best part is it's all cash." Gary added, "And I have a day job too, at Western Electric." Western Electric was the precursor company to AT&T.

I said, "Oh and what do you do there?"

Gary said, "Mostly, right now, I make a lot of copies, but this is all about breaking up Ma Bell, it's anti-trust litigation. I got my paralegal certification last year, and this job required it."

I said, "Nice, are you going to be a lawyer?"

He said, "No, but this is the next closest thing."

I said, "Sounds interesting, I guess you have to wear suits every day?"

Gary said, "Well, that's my least favorite part, especially the ties."

We continued to talk for a while, and finally he said, "How'd ya like to grab a bite tomorrow night?"

I said, "Sure, where would you like to go?"

He said, "Beefsteak Charlie's okay?"

I said, "Sure, I like their surf and turf platter."

He said, "Sounds like a plan to me. When should I pick you up?"

I said, "Seven's good."

He said, "Robbie told me you live on Powell Court, right across Deer Park Avenue from our block, 'Magro.'"

I said, "We're at number 100 Powell Court, which is on the second part of the street after you fork left onto Powell at Taylor, it's about six houses on the right side after you pass the 'Dead End' sign. It's red, with white bricks around the cathedral window and white shutters on the rest of the house." I leaned down to his head on the towel and gave him a little kiss on the lips. I was excited. It was a good day at the beach, and I had a dinner date for the next day! Way to go, Deb!

FUNNY GARY STORIES

While dating, Gary and I had our usual assortment of good times and bad, and sometimes very funny. I can recall one of Gary's conversations with my mom. Ever the gracious hostess, when Gary arrived at my parents' house one afternoon my mom asked Gary, "Can I get you anything?"

Gary replied, "Sure, Gracie, I'll have a beer."

She returned shortly afterward, only to say, "Gary, I don't have a beer, how about a chocolate pudding?"

Gary replied, "Gracie, equally enjoyable, but hardly interchangeable!" He never had that beer, nor the chocolate pudding. A classic conversation within our family that has been passed down many times!

HEADING FOR A WEDDING

Gary and I dated for about eighteen months, after which we got engaged. We had talked about it and gone shopping for rings, so I knew where we were headed. We went to Banta's Steak and Stein for dinner, with my sister Donna and her boyfriend, and when they went to the restrooms, Gary asked me to marry him, and I said yes. Nothing fancier than that, but the wheels were now in motion.

I was working at NY Telephone in 1979 as a directory assistance operator. I also started catering waitressing at the Manor East, a catering hall in Massapequa, New York, where Gary and I were married on June 28, 1981. We got a nice discount, but the joke was, they put me on the schedule to work the day of my wedding.

THE WEDDING: A GRAND AFFAIR

We had a large wedding party: seven bridesmaids and seven groomsmen. Of course, I wanted to choose the bridesmaid dresses so that they could be used again. I chose something I thought was pretty, and the girls seemed to like them. In my bridal party, I had my sister Donna (maid of honor), my cousin Gigi (matron of honor), and the bridesmaids were Jeanne Cusack (my BFF), Robin Haushalter, Susan Miesemer, Carol Latva, and Gary's sister Susan. I also had Jennifer and Michelle Celeste, Gary's nieces, as flower girls. Gary's best man was his brother, Robbie, and his groomsmen were Dennis Reilly, Ronald Main, Bud Fee, Kevin Herron, Donard Reilly, and Keith Lambrecht. My brother Michael accompanied Jennifer and Michelle down the aisle.

Having our wedding at the place where I worked was a little strange, but I knew we'd be treated well. The cocktail hour was as much the wedding dinner as the actual wedding dinner! Everyone enjoyed themselves very much. My mom and my dad were both proud of the party we'd thrown. Gary and I both danced with our parents, Gary with his mom, and me with my dad. All in all, it was a great party. After the reception, we both went back to our respective parents' houses to party some more! I ended up staying up well into the next morning, going through my wedding cards, and adding up the checks we'd received.

My bridal party, June 28, 1981

The next morning, we got a ride from my parents to JFK, where we boarded a flight to Bermuda for our week's honeymoon. We were staying at the Southampton Princess, which looked like a beautiful place; definitely a honeymoon haven. Curbside, before we even entered the airport, I kissed my mom as I handed her an envelope, with cash, checks, and a deposit slip to drop off at our bank branch in North Babylon. Consequently, several of our gift checks bounced, as the givers never expected that we'd get to the bank so quickly. Oops. On our flight to Bermuda, we met another couple, also just married, named Barbara and Doug Joseph. They were married two days before us, on June 26. They were staying at a different hotel, called the Sonesta Beach Hotel, and suggested we hook up when we got there. Our first day in Bermuda was pretty mellow, and after our whirlwind wedding weekend, I was tired for sure. Since we got married on Sunday, June 28, we were bumping up to the Fourth of July weekend. There was a welcome reception at the hotel, where we got to meet other guests. We met one couple, who I'll just call the Tall Couple: she was six foot three, and he was a full seven feet! I remember looking at a few pictures we took, as we were heading to dinner together, and both Gary and I looked like dwarves compared to them!

The next night, we connected with Barbara and Doug Joseph. We clicked immediately, and Barbara effervesced about the multitude of friends she'd grown up with, while Doug spoke of his job, which involved engineering for television broadcasts, and all of the aspects necessary to bring programs to the small screen—television. Doug was a smart guy, on the quiet side, but he and Gary got on well, while Barbara piqued both of our interests. She was an assistant principal at a school in Brooklyn. She spoke in great detail of her friendships with various girlfriends, her long-term prior relationship with her ex-boyfriend, Kevin O'Brien, who seemingly abruptly met, and married Sue, thus making it sound like Doug was a rebound relationship of short duration that also turned into marriage.

Barbara and Doug described a weekend out in the Hamptons, where they'd met a couple of women, who, as Barbara recounted, were quite forward with their overtures toward Barbara, but "nothing ever happened"; the story was just for illustrative purposes only.

CHAPTER THIRTEEN

MARRIED LIFE

91 FRIENDLY COURT

After returning from Bermuda, Gary and I went about setting up our new apartment. It was in Babylon Village, at 91 Friendly Court. (It sounded nice enough.) It was part of a garden apartment complex, within walking distance to the Long Island Rail Road (LIRR). This was great news, as Gary would be commuting to NYC every day. And I was very close to my job at NY Telephone, at the Babylon Directory Assistance Bureau, or DAB. We were the people who answered the phones live, not the way it is now, which drives me crazy! When you worked a shift, you would get plugged-in and pick up calls as they came in. We had pencils, with specially attached flat spatulas, that could locate a number in our "books," which were actually microfiche strips, magnified onto a screen, that pulled up pages according to the first several letters of the last name of the person they were looking for. Once located, we recited the number (live) to the person who was waiting on the other end of the phone.

It was during my time at NY Tel's Directory Assistance Bureau that I met another decades-long friend. Her name is Linda Susan Cudahy. She was friendly toward me at the get-go. On breaks, she was the first to be friendly to me, as I was the new employee. We struck up a conversation easily. She told me of a boyfriend, Bob Purcell, who had a horrific car accident. He survived but Linda was unable to see him.

It was just around that time that I took up running on a regular basis. Linda and I got into working out at a gym called Rainbow Racquet Ball. There was exercise equipment, most of it Nautilus, and that was my first exposure to weight-based exercise. We started working out with some of the personal trainers there, and they gave us the nickname "Hulk" and "Bulk." I forget which one was which but I developed muscles pretty easily, while Linda was fairly vascular, and more "cut." But we liked that the trainers referred to us that way. They were cute, too.

Linda and I became very close starting with our years at NY Tel. While I left after I got married, Linda stayed with NY Tel until it became Verizon, and she ended up retiring from there a number of years ago.

Lovely Linda Cudahy

What I'm most happy about is that Linda ended up having twins, with her boyfriend/husband, Kevin Shaunnessy, utilizing IVF. The twins were named Hailey and Spencer. They are sixteen now! The twins went to my Catholic grammar school, Our Lady of Lourdes, in West Islip, and graduated from there in 2015. As they live on Oak Island, the kids became beach kids—always outdoors, by the water, on the dock, or in the boat. Hailey became involved with a dance troupe, and they competed all over.

Hailey Shaughnessy, at 16

Spencer Shaughnessy, at 16

At NY Tel, even though our office was located in Babylon, Long Island, we were in charge of Manhattan Directory Assistance. It was purposely done like that for emergency reasons. If someone in Manhattan was looking for someone or a place of business in Manhattan, they didn't realize it, but they were calling fifty miles away from Manhattan.

In 1979, at Manhattan DAB, it was the first job where I learned all about the locations of different department stores, salons, hotels, restaurants, and doctors' offices. I was also educated on the various government bureaus that handled school issues, health and human services, the Federal Reserve, where all the Wall Street firms were located (and most were *not* on Wall Street). This became all useful information later, after I graduated college and worked on Wall Street (but not "on" Wall Street, just in the vicinity!). We also learned the cross streets of different addresses on the avenues. See the "key" to calculate the cross street.

FINDING AN ADDRESS

A useful formula has been devised to help pinpoint any avenue address. By dropping the last digit of the address, dividing the remainder by 2, then adding or subtracting the key number given here, you will discover the nearest cross street. For example: to find No. 826 Lexington Avenue, you have to drop the 6; divide 82 by 2, which is 41; then add 22 (the key number). Therefore, the nearest cross street is 63rd Street.

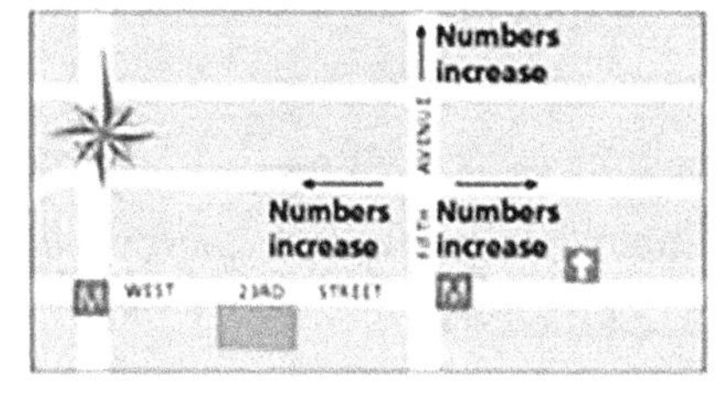

Avenue Address	Key Number	Avenue Address	Key Number
1st Ave	+3	9th Ave	+13
2nd Ave	+3	10th Ave	+14
3rd Ave	+10	Amsterdam Ave	+60
4th Ave	+8	Audubon Ave	+165
5th Ave, up to 200	+13	Broadway above 23rd St	-30
5th Ave, up to 400	+16	Central Park W, divide full number by 10	+60
5th Ave, up to 600	+18	Columbus Ave	+60
5th Ave, up to 775	+20	Convent Ave	+127z
5th Ave 775–1286, do not divide by 2	-18	Lenox Ave	+110
5th Ave, up to 1500	+45	Lexington Ave	+22
5th Ave, up to 2000	+24	Madison Ave	+26
(6th) Ave of the Americas	-12	Park Ave	+35
7th Ave below 110th St	+12	Park Ave South	+8
7th Ave above 110th St	+20	Riverside Drive, divide full number by 10	+72
8th Ave	+10	St Nicholas Ave	+110
		West End Ave	+60

Source: BusinessInsider.com

To get unplugged from our phone "tether," we had to "make busy," so our calls would be routed to the next available operator. Alternately, there was a book we'd line up to sign each week (on Thursdays) that would place us in a queue to receive non-paid time off. It was called the "AE" book, for Absence Excused. There would be a long line to get our names in that book, and God forbid you cut in line ahead of someone so that you could be entitled to not get paid! That was how much everyone "loved" that job! Since the worst part of my job was sitting for eight hours on my butt, I quickly learned a way to be able to get up and out of that seat, by learning how to replace the daily microfiche in each of the machines. Every day, there would be address changes, phone number changes, and other items that required changing the whole page or pages that covered various parts of the phone listings. So this microfiche needed to be changed just about every day! It wasn't rocket science, but you needed to be dexterous and nimble-fingered to replace the microfiche in a quick transaction. When making the switch, the person changing the microfiche had to "make busy" the person whose microfiche was being changed, pull the old microfiche out, put in the new, and then remove the "make busy." This all had to be accomplished fairly seamlessly, so as not to disrupt the perceived service by the customer on the other end of the phone. Replacing the microfiche on all of the available machines could take an entire shift, or about four hours. But I'd be up, walking around, and out of that seat. Phew! As I've heard recently (that's 2018, nearly forty years later), sitting is the new smoking, and I believe that. Sitting for long periods just makes one feel sluggish. It was good to be up and about, and I'd found a way to be free of my "tether"!

As I was going to college at the same time (at Stony Brook), I opted to work on the split shift. It would be eight hours in a day, but the hours would be split; for example, from 7 to 10 a.m., and then 4 p.m. to 9 p.m.

In between, I had to figure out what class offerings were available at Stony Brook in my chosen field of study. By 1979, I'd already figured out that pre-med was not going to be my major. Instead, I made the bold move to switch to economics, which I did, commencing in the 1980–1981 school year. The year 1981 would also be when I would get married to Gary Grosser, having gotten engaged in November 1979. Everything seemed to be fitting together nicely.

Chapter Thirteen A

Mid-1983 to Mid-1985: The Separation Years

After just two years of marriage, Gary and I had a two-year separation, after fighting because of his increasing absences on weekends. He was a partner, building a club to be called Scarlett's. We separated in June 1983. It was also the time when I'd accepted a position of office manager for a periodontist named Dr. Jack Goetz. His office was on Deer Park Avenue, in Dix Hills.

Dr. Goetz had a sizeable practice and was a good-looking man. He was divorced but had primary physical custody of his daughter, Randi. He had several US Marine recruiting posters (in which he was featured). When framed, these became the artwork in our office. He thought well of himself, and so did a number of his female patients. In fact, his office hours facilitated quite a bit of "off campus, under-the-covers activity," which could be scheduled before and after Monday's 4 p.m. to 9 p.m. office hours, and many other days when office hours could be "blocked out."

I took the place of Jill Cordell—who was leaving for a new job—as office manager in Dr. Goetz's office, and it was a newly created position for me. I got to do all sorts of things, including planning Dr. Goetz's wedding to Jan Bell, in the late summer of 1984 (too bad, Jack and Jill would've been a fun wedding party to plan). But Jan was beautiful girl, daughter of Doty and Eli Bell, and a prima ballerina too! (The first real one I ever met.)

The Young and the Jewish

Working for Dr. Goetz, I got to learn about the young and affluent Jewish culture in Dix Hills. It could have been the back story of many a soap opera: think of *The Young and the Restless*, *The Bold and the Beautiful*, *Days of our Lives*, and *General Hospital*. They had tons of money, ran successful businesses (like "Stewie Rah," who ran Kinray and then sold the company to Big Pharma [Cardinal Health] and, even prior to that, became a billionaire), and, above all, they knew how to make beautiful parties for their children's bar and bat mitzvahs. No expenses were spared, no party favors too extravagant, no band or other music too expensive. The more over-the-top the ingredient in their affair, the more likely it was to be replicated in someone else's event (imitation is the sincerest form of flattery, I'd always heard). They drove Ferraris, Lamborghinis, Maseratis, Porsches, and all sorts of Mercedes (C-, E-, and S-Class to AMGs). There was Judith Ripka, famous jewelry designer, who dropped off a basket of warm rugelachs for Dr. Goetz, "just because." (Thank you, Judith, they were divine.)

CHAPTER THIRTEEN B

WAITRESSING: CATERING, WICKER'S, AND THE BONWIT INN

Prior to graduating college, one of the best means I had to make money was waitressing. In 1979, I did catering waitressing at the Manor East in Massapequa (where Gary and I were married in 1981). I also worked at North Star, also in Massapequa, and a few other places. I mostly worked the weekends: Friday, Saturday, and Sunday. I could do doubles or even triples, but those were exhausting. Remember, I was also working a day job at NY Telephone as a directory assistance operator. In any event, waitressing was good, continuous work, all cash, and it was very physically demanding, which I liked very much. It was boys and girls, working as a team, and I learned much from that field. Believe it or not, it prepared me well for Wall Street. Case in point, it was a job that constantly had lots of people needing lots of different things from me, all at the same time! I came to learn later that it was just like a trading floor.

One event that conjures up memories at North Star is when we worked a party for Tony Danza's grandmother. We all had crushes on Tony, and he was kind to us that night. He volunteered to take pictures with us. He was on the TV show *Taxi* at the time. The show had just debuted in 1978, and it was already a big hit!

In 1983, I worked at Wicker's, in Hicksville. Funny, I found Wicker's when I was still working for Dr. Jaffe, and I used to go there for lunch. Dr. Jaffe's office had expanded, moving into a brand-new office, called Orthodontics Only. It was on Old Country Road, in Hicksville. It was one big room, with about eighteen chairs, and, like the name said, all we did was work on kids with braces (this time, the metal ones on teeth). Working both there and at Wicker's filled both my days and nights (and the nights were long). It was a bit of a dark time in my life, as both drinking and, more recently, cocaine became an ever-increasing part of my life. The one benefit was I lost weight, dropping at one point to 102 pounds. At five foot five, I thought I looked great. My family saw another picture and was worried about me. Looking back at pictures from that time, I saw how thin I was, but I still liked it. I eventually dropped Wicker's and cocaine, and started another waitressing job, at the Bonwit Inn, in Commack, not far from where I eventually lived (thirty-plus years later, in 2016) at Gurwin.

We separated exactly on our two-year anniversary, June 28. Our apartment lease was up at that time as well. During the separation, I found a place to live, at first for free, with Pamela Parker, formerly Rava, after living at her parents' home, in East Northport, on Woodrise Court, which had already been sold. Later, in 1984, we found a place in Commack (funny how things come full circle in our lives). We rented a house on Hedgerow Lane, and then one on West Farms Lane. The rent was reasonable, and we got some extra cash help from a very wealthy individual (thank you, Stewart). The house on Hedgerow must have been built in the 1970s. At least it was decorated in that style: shag carpeting throughout the place and foil wallpaper in many places. We found a use for one of the walls, this time in the living room. We used it to play a paddle game called Kadima. The balls used were small, called "smashballs." You could play Kadima at the beach, hitting the ball back and forth like tennis, but we played it against the living room wall, hitting it as many times as we could without missing a shot. Friends of Pam's came over to watch us play. They were Mike Menafra and Martin Venezia. We had many laughs together.

THE BONWIT INN, 1984 AND 1985

After Wicker's, I interviewed for a waitressing job at the Bonwit Inn. The Bonwit was owned by Greeks, Charlie and Jimmy Tsunis. I got the job and started the next weekend. I started on a lunch shift, did okay, and then went right to the dinner shift (bigger checks, bigger tips). I finally got to work in the bar room, which featured more tables, higher turnover, and you had to be a really good waitress to work in there. You could have eight two-tops (the number of people a table could seat was two), and if they all sat down at the same time, that meant eight consecutive drink orders, stop in the kitchen for bread and Greek salad, deliver them, eight entree orders (stop in the kitchen and deliver), eight dessert orders (same as salad and bread), eight checks, eight collect checks, eight reset tables, and so on. And there were times that those eight two-tops turned over three times. Phew! But I went home with a lot of cash! About this time, I got to work with Joyce Timko—she went by "Joy" and had vanity plates on her car that said: "FULAJOY." I liked that. Joyce was to be my "trailer," and like it sounds, she got to follow me around, doing what I was doing, and me explaining every step, including, at the end of the night, "marrying" the ketchup bottles, where you could consolidate the ketchup stored in the hundreds of bottles we had. She did a good job and could follow direction, and I gave her good marks on my "trailer" report. Joy had a roommate named Pam, and together they got into a bit of a pickle, when they called in, unable to make it to work. They were stuck on Block Island, because the plane had to gas up, before flying back to Long Island—Pam's boyfriend was Richard Caracella, and I guess it was nice to have a plane, except when you had friends who needed to get to work.

Joyce with her dad, Alan, and her mom, Camille

THE LONG ISLAND JEWISH DIALECT

While waitressing at the Bonwit, I waited on many customers who had what I call the Long Island Jewish dialect. Long Islanders have their own particular accent to begin with, but this was slightly different. I noticed that there was a tendency to take a one-syllable word and make it into three. For example: "I'll have the filet mignon, but make sure its cook-kuh-da properly." Or, "I'll have the ba-kuh-da potato, please." They could also do it in reverse, making a two- or three-syllable word into one: "You shouln't do that to yourself," or "I couln't help myself."

After I got my first job on Wall Street in September 1985, I had to give notice at the Bonwit. My last week at the Bonwit, one of the waiters working on my shift barged into the kitchen and yelled: "Eighty-six Debbie," restaurant lingo, indicating that "something" or, in my case, "someone," was no longer available on the menu. I had a great time working at the Bonwit. I made good money, all cash, and there was great chemistry and camaraderie among the crews that worked the various shifts. I worked all shifts—lunch, dinner, Sunday brunch, and special parties as well. It was a very physically demanding job, as we had to tray-carry all dinners out of the kitchen on large oval trays. On that point, I had one notable episode where I had a party of ten and had to stack all the dinner plates very carefully. I had two levels of dinner plates with covers and managed to get eight on the tray, but I had a five-pound lobster to add on the top of eight dinner plates already there. I knew it was going to be heavy. I squatted and lifted the tray on my shoulder, and I started to walk toward the stairs. When I went forward, the lobster tray slid back, the plate crashing to the floor! The loud and bustling kitchen fell silent. Everyone waited to see what Alberto, the Bonwit's Peruvian chef with a hot temper—who sported a gold front tooth with a diamond in it and terrified most of the wait staff—would do. Alberto was always walking around the kitchen, with a large, meat-carving knife, periodically slamming it down on the stainless-steel countertop. When Alberto walked toward me, I was initially scared, but he always had a sweet spot for me. When we got eye-to-eye, he deflected his orders to the dishwashing staff, and barked, "pick it up"! (pronounced "peek it up"!) Without a blink, the kitchen occupants went from stunned silence to laughter, resuming their ongoing tasks, and breathing a big sigh of relief. Crisis averted.

There was also a night when Joyce and I went out with Jimmy Olafankas and George Tsunis, a nephew of one of the owners and a busboy, and Joyce had an incident later in the night, where, in Jimmy's car, she burped and "fluffed" (really farting), and was mortified when it happened (and again, when she reads it, in print). Joyce is still in my life, today, some thirty-five years later, and we've both been through plenty. We look back at the Bonwit days fondly.

Chapter Thirteen C

Back to Bay Ridge, Brooklyn

September 1985 to June 1988

Gary and I reconciled at Christmas 1984 and moved back in together in the fall of 1985, right about the time I started my first Wall Street job at Donaldson, Lufkin & Jenrette (DLJ). In May of that year, I both graduated from Stony Brook and I did the Long Island half marathon. We stayed briefly at an apartment (Gary's old room) in his mom's home, but I was anxious to be back in our own place. We moved back to my place of birth, in Bay Ridge, Brooklyn, to 9901 Fort Hamilton Parkway. We lived on the top floor of a two-family home. Get this: the apartment had three bedrooms, a living room, a dining room, and one and a half baths for $750! In Bay Ridge today, it would probably cost at least three times that amount. Our landlords were Teddy and Athena Lambrakis (I felt comfortable with the Greeks, after working for them.). They had a son, Peter, who went to Poly Prep, a prestigious high school in Bay Ridge. Athena was a true Greek, a meticulous housekeeper, always cleaning and banging carpets out of doors or windows, against the brick façade, to get the dirt out. I got a kick out of her shrill voice, as she yelled out for "Peter, Peter," (pronounced Pita, Pita) "is your homework done?" That was toward her son, Peter. She had a similar shrill voice for her husband, Teddy, who owned a diner in Bay Ridge, called the Bay Shore. She ran a tight ship. Most Greek women do.

9901 Fort Hamilton Parkway,
in Bay Ridge, Brooklyn

GARY'S SIT AND SPIN

I remembered another funny Gary story that I'm going to include here. On Fourth Avenue, Bay Ridge, Gary and I used to go to the laundromat. Gary and I had an idea of a combo laundromat and bar, and we'd call it "Gary's Sit and Spin." We thought it could be a sitcom, people meeting at the laundromat/bar. It seemed to makes sense; you sit around waiting for your clothes being washed and dried, why not have a drink and talk to a girl or a guy? We even thought of having the window into the washer be the camera lens for the "June Taylor Dancers" like on Jackie Gleason (kinda like the Rockettes, lying on the floor but kicking up their legs).

It was during one of our many laundromat visits on 4th Avenue that we met Mabel Lee, an attractive Asian girl, also living in Bay Ridge. On one of these occasions, I mentioned to Mabel that I knew someone at work that she ought to meet. I was working at DLJ at the time, and the person I'd thought would be a good fit for Mabel was an investment banker at DLJ named David Chow (pronounced Cho, long "o," not chow, as in chow-down). David was a very hard-working, very smart banker at DLJ (he was number one in his class at Amos Tuck Business School at Dartmouth), and I observed that he worked so hard all the time, he probably got paid very well and would be a good catch, but he had no girlfriend. He admitted that he was socially awkward, and said, "Who would want to date a 'geek' like me?" I thought Mabel would be a perfect fit. Next time we saw each other at the laundromat, I mentioned David and suggested that she meet him sometime. I asked for her number so that David could give her a call. She provided me with her number, which I promptly gave to David the next time I saw him at the office. Eventually, David did call Mabel, and they met somewhere in the World Financial Center. Not long after, I heard that they had a good time on their first meeting. Not long after that, I heard from David that things were going well and they were thinking about getting married! You can add matchmaker to my resume!

After some thinking and joking about it, my friends at work thought it would be cool to "brand" my matchmaking services as "Get Closer with Grosser"! Kind of catchy, eh? Long story short, David and Mabel did get married, and after a couple of years they gave birth to their first son, Daniel. Gary and I went to visit them at their new home in Westport, Connecticut. It was in the West Farms section. They found a lovely home there and were settling in comfortably. We were happy to meet Daniel, who'd received a teddy bear who was bigger than him. The Chow family was very kind to Gary and me when we visited. We had a very enjoyable time together. I was happy that I had a tiny hand in bringing them together! A couple of other matchmaking efforts were not as successful; one led to a bit of an awkward break-up. Oh well, keep the career options open in other fields! The next word I heard from David was that the Chow family would be adding another baby to the mix, making their family complete! This baby turned out to be a girl, named Courtney. Perfect!

CHAPTER FOURTEEN

HERE TODAY, GONE TO MAHWAH

71 MALCOLM ROAD AND 17 SEMINARY DRIVE

Mahwah Assembly was a Ford Motor Company manufacturing plant in Mahwah, New Jersey, thirty miles from New York City. It was located behind the Sheraton Mahwah and occupied over 172 acres when it was open. The factory began operations in 1950, building the 1949 Ford Thunderbird, and was closed in 1980. It was one of three manufacturing facilities in New Jersey. It was built two years after the Edison Assembly (built in Edison, New Jersey).

Mahwah Assembly produced six million cars in the twenty-five years it operated before the last car rolled off the line on June 20, 1980. At the time of its completion, it was the largest motor vehicle assembly plant in the United States. The Ford plant, along with other businesses such as American Brake Shoe and Foundry Company, helped contribute to the economic development of the town and its reputation for low home property taxes. The Mahwah town sports teams remain named Thunderbirds in honor of the Ford plant. A portion of the plant site is presently the US headquarters of Sharp Corporation.

Source: https://en.wikipedia.org/wiki/Mahwah_Assembly

Chapter Fourteen A

71 Malcolm Road, 1988–1994

We got connected with a Realtor named Judy Miller through Paul and Cathy Parshley, who lived in Allendale, in a lovely home on Oak Street. They then sold their home and had a brand new one built on East Orchard Street. We followed the Parshley model: we bought and sold our first house on Malcolm Road, and our next house, on Seminary Drive, required blueprints. We first moved into a section of town called Cragmere. We'd heard that the prices in Mahwah were reasonable and the property taxes were low due to some larger corporations that housed headquarters there. We went looking at many houses in the area, and finally found 71 Malcolm Road. It was up on the north side of the street and had a very steep driveway. It also had an in-ground pool. We were sold, and so was the house! We brought our parents up to see it, and they liked it, too. We were approved for a mortgage, and soon we were in the house. Just before we moved in, we went to the Catskills, to the Villa Roma, in Callicoon, New York, for a family reunion with the Grossers and the Rizzos. Gary's dad had a sister, Arlene, and a brother, Fred. Arlene was married to Richard (Dick) Rizzo; thus, the group included Uncle Dick and Aunt Arlene, and Uncle Fred and Aunt Shirley. Gary's cousin Greg's son Gregory came along with his grandparents.

Along with the group also came Richard (Ricky) Rizzo and his wife Debbie, Jody Rizzo and her husband Fred Lopez, and their daughter Samantha, and Diane Rizzo and her husband Bill Roth, and their children Jessica and Bill Jr. Finally, there was Laura Rizzo and Tom Lindner. We arranged for a block of rooms, and we had a great time! The movie *Dirty Dancing* (set in the Catskills) had just been out, and one night, my brother-in-law Robbie and I re-enacted "the lift" scene in the movie, and we did it! Robbie also won a bikini contest, with a little help from balloon "implants" and one of my tiny bikinis. It was hysterical! We didn't "put baby in the corner," and a good time was had by all. Gary and I came back to Malcolm Road and ate McDonald's on the living room floor. We had a big task at hand. But first, we had our meal, and went to sleep. The next day, we were to tear up the orange shag living room carpet and quickly order new carpeting.

We found Huffman Koos, our first-ever furniture store in New Jersey. There was a nice man named Peter who helped us sort through hundreds of Oriental carpets, flipping them back, one by one, to show us the lot. We ordered wall-to-wall in the bedrooms and hallway, and floor rugs for the living room, dining room, and one for a room that was yet-to-be decided. We'd also ordered a couch, coffee table, end tables, and a wing chair for the living room. And a dining room set with a table, six chairs, and a breakfront. Oh, and a grandfather's clock, which I still have today.

Judy Miller referred us to a painter named David Raimondi. David ended up painting virtually every interior of every home I've lived in over more than twenty years. David's pricing was always more than fair. As we paid him for the paint, the labor was pretty much free of charge. The only other requirement for David was that he liked when I made my chocolate protein shakes. I'd always make an extra-large batch for both us, and that worked out well. David was a die-hard Miami Dolphins fan. He loved their team color, a vivid aqua blue. Thus, David's car was that color, and he often wore aqua blue shirts or anything aqua blue. David was a skilled painter, he cleaned up his workspace well, and his paint jobs always turned out well.

I began to see how my tastes in color changed in each place we lived. At Malcolm Road, I went with more pastel colors, except for the kitchen. In that room, I went with a bright pink, almost Pepto-Bismol pink. In the living room, we went with a pale blue color, and same in the dining room. In the spare bedroom, we went with an aqua blue color (which David loved to paint). In the master bedroom, we chose a brighter peach color.

We loved our new neighbors. Two doors down there was the Duffy family. Sean and Fiona (born in Ireland) had three children: Megan, Sean Jr., and Ciara, when we moved in, and they went on to have a fourth, Catherine. That was 1988. We also loved our across-the-street neighbors: Howard Weisman and Pamela Foss. They had a daughter, Hannah, and ultimately, a son, Joshua. We enjoyed each other's company and had many fun dinners together. When we built our deck around our pool, Sean livened up one afternoon by introducing us to George Thorogood: "One Bourbon, One Scotch, One Beer" and "Bad to the Bone" were favorites while backyard work was being done! Thanks, Sean! It was a momentous time.

Gary and Sean, enjoying George Thorogood

At Malcolm Road, we had some great celebrations. In 1988, we had a great Halloween party, at which some friends from Wall Street came out: Barbara Germain, Peter Petas, Tim Foxe, and Paul and Cathy Parshley were in attendance. Peter's costume was "medical waste on the beach," with tampons, syringes, and a rubber rat. For the backdrop, he wore medical scrubs.

Paul and Cathy Parshley came dressed as Dan and Marilyn Quayle, given Quayle's 1988 vice presidential bid. They arrived carrying golf bags, ready to tee off!

In May 1989, Gary threw me a surprise thirtieth birthday party. He invited all our friends from our Breezy Point/Belle Harbor days. Barbara and Doug Joseph, Kevin and Sue O'Brien, Mary Ellen and Robert Fett, plus Marguerite and Paul Scherpf, and Peggy and Peter Frontera. My friend Joyce corralled me for a "day of shopping" as a ploy to keep me busy and not suspicious that anything was up even though it was my birthday, May 6. Gary did a great job buying and preparing food. It ended up being quite a party. While it was only May, we opted to use our gas pool heater, so the gang could go swimming in our in-ground rectangular liner pool. It was quite a scene, for an evening in May 1989. I remember one scene where Kevin O'Brien dove off the diving board with a Swiss Army knife in his teeth, only to stab the Inflatable Shark, rendering it "harmless." Ha-ha.

In 1990, we hosted my dad's sixtieth birthday party, which was attended by the Grosser family, the Feltman family, and some neighbors and friends who lived locally. The Rizzo family, who were always up for a party, made it completely festive. There was a conga line that went around the pool and deck in our yard. My dad's birthday is August 11, and it was certainly a day perfect for pool usage (without the heater).

Dad, at his sixtieth birthday at 71 Malcolm Road; a great party!

In 1992, Paul and Cathy and Gary and I added to our families. We went to Cold Spring, New York, to see Tom Cusack (my friend Jeanne's younger brother) about the golden retrievers to which he had just helped to give birth. They were all adorable (as goldens are), but we met our beautiful new girl, Samantha, and we fell in love with her instantly. Paul and Cathy met their new golden, sister Molly, who they would bring home in another several weeks.

The Parshley kids and our new puppies in 1992

There was another aspect to our relationship that ultimately had a big impact with huge consequences. Along with alcohol, Gary and I got into using cocaine. At first, we used it at parties, along with many others who were there. I can only describe the feeling it gave me—a very heightened sense of awareness—and it provided the ability to speak rapidly, seemingly able to connect all the dots, which included ideas, sometimes complex, and it would seem as if we reached the right conclusion, as if we found the cure for cancer! This was different than the effect of marijuana, which was all "love, peace, and bell-bottoms." The cocaine became a bad addition to our lives and our relationship, but we didn't see it at the time. There were several episodes that are difficult for me to dredge up. But there were encounters, when I'd invite my girlfriends over, and we'd all partake in the amalgam of cocaine and alcohol, so why not throw in sex? It happened several times. And worse yet, I encouraged it and I watched, all of it. In the twisted mechanics of my mind, I rationalized that it would be a turn-on. Instead, it was a visual assault, something I couldn't un-see, and it caused much damage to me emotionally. (Wasn't I good enough?) It shook us to the core. But I was unable to hold Gary truly accountable. (After all, I encouraged it.) If I did, maybe he'd leave me for good. So, as we had done in the past, it just got swept under the rug.

Clearly, there was no exercise of good judgment. If ever there was a display of why we shouldn't do drugs of any kind, this was it. It doesn't justify what I did, by having an affair, but it was me acting out, in my contempt for Gary's actions. I went to therapy for years. Intertwined with my dependency on alcohol, my unresolved issues became a ticking time bomb.

From 1990 to 2000, Gary and I made many trips to Sanibel Island, Florida, as Paul and Cathy Parshley invited us to stay at their condo, at Pointe Santo de Sanibel. Sanibel is on the west coast of Florida, just off Fort Myers on the mainland. We'd fly into Fort Myers, rent a car, and drive over the causeway to Sanibel. It was a beautiful island, and we loved going there whenever possible. Paul and Cathy were very gracious in allowing us to rent there, at a very reasonable weekly rate. Thank you, Paul and Cathy! Theirs was a beautiful three-bedroom unit on the ground floor. It had sliding glass doors everywhere and was an oceanfront unit! As soon as we arrived, we checked the place out and immediately set to get settled in. That meant making sure there was food in the place. Gary always took pleasure in heading out to the local grocery market, Bailey's. We could get anything we needed there: lunch fixings, dinner for the evening, salad and produce items, ice cream, key lime pie and beverages, and breakfast items for the next day. The food was high quality: fresh, healthy, nutritious, and delicious. We also stocked up with generous amounts of beer and wine.

While in Sanibel, we found out it wasn't far from another beautiful island, right next door. It was called Captiva. There were several recommended restaurants over there, to which we availed ourselves. The first, and favorite, was called The Mucky Duck. The restaurant's location provided for the most incredible sunset views! Arriving around sunset time, we could get some great shots of the sun setting, as well as pictures of us, and many times, our friends: Robin and Kirk Giannola drove over from their home in Fort Lauderdale on the east coast to Sanibel. The owner of The Mucky Duck always had a window, frame and all, on wheels. Thus, he could wheel the window around the restaurant, always being able to offer "a table by the window." (It was funny for the first several times.)

My high school BFF Robin Haushalter Guerire

We spent a couple of New Year's Eves in Sanibel, dining in Captiva. We had begun to dub ourselves "the Party Starters," as we could liven up a group of others and get the party started! At one place we went, the music being played by the DJ was the Al Green song "Ride Sally Ride." Paul's sister Sara, or "Sally," was along that year, and we had the whole place up for dancing! The Party Starters were a success that year!

In 1993, we'd been touring the other areas in Mahwah and came upon Rio Vista. In late November 1993, we contracted on building a new home with Atillio (Artie) Bett. He was a mason by trade, but he was kind to us, and we warmed up to him right away when he said, "I'm going to build you a nice, comfortable house that you'll love."

I remember that our Realtor, Judy Miller, met us at Aldo's Restaurant, in Wyckoff (a popular spot in Bergen County, often featured in *BC Magazine*).

She handed us the rolled-up blueprints and said, "Hello, darlings! Thank you!" We were with Paul and Cathy Parshley, and Judy was their Realtor for both of their homes in Allendale, New Jersey, one on Oak Street, and the second on East Orchard, just miles away from our house in Mahwah.

In winter 1993–1994, we put 71 Malcolm Road on the market, and of course, all it did was snow, multiple feet of snow. Our steep driveway became an issue for prospective buyers, but in the end, we sold our home to another young couple. We closed in June 1994. As a result, Gary's brother, Robbie, was kind and invited us to "stay at his place" (also in Mahwah) for the summer. Thus, on the day of closing on 71 Malcolm Road, we moved into an upstairs bedroom at 1098 Devon Court. It was during that summer that Gary went to the cardiologist. It was determined that he had a congenital defect in his aortic valve and it would require valve replacement surgery. After discussions with the long-tenured cardiothoracic surgeon Dr. Randall Griepp, Gary decided on using an artificial valve (called St. Jude's), as opposed to a tissue valve, as a tissue valve would require replacement in another eight years, as opposed to the St. Jude's valve, which could last more than twenty years. Gary was just forty when he had his open-heart surgery.

CHAPTER FOURTEEN B

17 SEMINARY DRIVE, OUR TIME AT RIO VISTA, 1994–2009

Our time at 17 Seminary began, just six days after moving in, with Gary's open-heart surgery, on November 4, 1994. I'll always remember that date because Cathy Parshley gave Gary a heart-shaped keychain with the date inscribed on it. I will also remember that date because, as we waited for Gary to be taken into surgery, Cathy received a call from her brother, Mike O'Meara (who was a good friend of Gary's and an on-air radio personality, with his friend Don Geronimo). Mike had heard from Gary while he was on his gurney and partially under the influence of anesthesia, and Mike thought, when he heard Gary was calling, it might be Gary calling "from the Great Beyond."

There were many memorable incidents while Gary was in Mount Sinai, such as the time the nurse was trying to take him in for a treatment of sorts, and the nurse mistakenly stopped into the bathroom, at which point Gary said: "No, don't hon, it's your funeral," given the noxious fumes she was about to confront. There were also times when Gary was not so nice, so annoyed at his family's attention to his plight that he called them "pole-sitters"!

17 Seminary Drive, in Rio Vista, our dream house

Shortly after our return home to Seminary, Gary experienced just some of the complications of taking Coumadin (the brand name for warfarin), and he began to have symptoms of internal bleeding. I was at work and Cathy Parshley was called in; she luckily called an ambulance to get Gary to the hospital. This time he went to Valley Hospital, in Ridgewood, New Jersey. I believe she had also called one of the Co brothers (two of the cardiologists attending to Gary), and explained Gary's symptoms (shortness of breath, chest pains, and pressure), and actions were taken to relieve what turned out to be cardiac tamponade, a serious and possibly fatal condition in the sac around the heart. I believe they had to insert a needle into Gary's chest cavity to suction the blood around his heart. Another huge, life-saving crisis averted.

There is a story that emanated from this incident. While all of this was going on, Paul Parshley (Cathy's husband, and my boss) received a note, handed to him at his desk, that "Cathy was in an ambulance, with Gary, heading to Valley Hospital." Thank God for Cathy Parshley. If one didn't believe in God then, they did shortly after hearing that story.

Gary's life-saver after his open-heart surgery,
Cathy Parshley

As things got settled down, post Gary's surgery and a second surgery to correct his subdural, bilateral brain bleed, it was finally time to start enjoying our beautiful, brand-new home. In 1996, we decided to host our first Christmas party at 17 Seminary Drive. First, we needed a great tree. For that, we went to Secor's Farm, on Airmount Road (right near our friends Cindy and Tom Quinn's house). As the family room had a cathedral ceiling, height was not a big issue. We ultimately purchased an eight-foot balsam fir, with a wide and generous body. The tree had to be "topped" for placement in our tree stand. Then it had to be wrapped in netting for transport home, on the roof rack of our Lexus GX470. Tree in tow, we anxiously headed back to 17 Seminary to place our new tree in its stand. Getting it home, we had to open the front door (fortunately it was wide enough to accommodate this big tree). Gary was able to lift it off the roof rack, and I waited until he brought the top of the tree to me. I helped him carry it through the foyer, into the dining room, and finally into the corner of the family room. Phew.

But the work had just begun. Getting the tree into the stand that would hold it straight for many weeks was our next big task. We had a rather flimsy metal stand with four legs, spread out evenly, to bolster and balance this heavy tree. With a strong "heave-ho," Gary was able to position the tree in an upright stance, into the hole in the stand, and it seemed to be holding. Our next task was to screw keyhole bolts into the bark of the trunk to stabilize the tree and prevent it from falling over. That set, our next and biggest task would be the ultimate decoration of it. That would take many hours and usually lasted an evening and the next morning. I preferred all white lights, with colored ornaments. We had a collection of ornaments that were given to us in years prior. Those were stored in their own special box. As we'd place each one on our tree, we'd remember who gave us the ornament, and in what year. And, I wonder, how they're doing now? The rest of the ornaments were silver and red balls. We'd also use some garland, sparingly, but alternating the opposite of the red or silver ornaments. When it was all completed, time for "lights on"! It wasn't the tree at Rockefeller Center, but it felt like it was, and we were satisfied that we'd done it ourselves.

The actual tree at Rockefeller Center in 2019

CINDY AND TOM: TRULY WONDERFUL PEOPLE AND DEAR FRIENDS

Cindy and Tom Quinn have always been a couple to be admired. Married for over forty years, until Tom's untimely passage in 2012, they had a relationship that one could only aspire to. Cindy is stunning, and Tom was handsome.

Most importantly, they were the first friends to arrive at Hackensack University Medical Center (HUMC) after my arrival via the EMTs from the Ramsey PD, following my near-death accident.

Tom and Cindy were the first to meet with Dr. Vingan after my initial emergency surgery. As my family was coming from Long Island, Cindy and

Tom stayed till late at night until my family could arrive that fateful day. Cindy and Tom visited every day and prayed constantly. They are the very definition of true friends. I am very blessed to have had them as my friends. Thank you, Jesus.

Cindy and Tom Quinn—
truly wonderful people and dear friends

Chapter Fourteen C

Church of the Presentation, Angel's Wings, Soup Kitchen

Faith without Works Is Dead

In the early 1990s, Gary and I began attending Church of the Presentation, in Upper Saddle River, New Jersey. The pastor was Father Jack McDermott, who coincidentally attended and graduated from the Immaculate Conception Seminary, which had been on the grounds of where Rio Vista, our former neighborhood, exists today. To think that he might have been swimming in that large pool on the grounds of the seminary back in the 1950s is just amazing. Presentation was one of the cornerstones along my path back to God. Just an odd coincidence? No. Just God's careful planning. I spent about ten years at the Church of the Presentation. Ultimately, I became a lector at church, and Gary became a Eucharistic minister. I was encouraged to participate in something called "Cornerstone" weekend, which I did in 1995. It was a weekend of reflection and prayer, and it usually resulted in some very strong bonds with the other women who attended. That was the case for me. I started as a newbie to Presentation, and relatively new to Bergen County. By the end of the weekend, our newly created group, which we called "Angel's Wings," was elected to sponsor the next year's Cornerstone weekend (1996), and that meant creating the schedule, activities, prayers, scriptures, and everything for the weekend. One thing we underestimated for the weekend was the amount of tissues we'd need, as crying equals spiritual cleansing, and boy, were our spirits clean by the end of that weekend.

Our group went on to other ministries. For instance, Angel's Wings started to volunteer for soup kitchen delivery, in Harlem, New York. Every Sunday, there would be a team that would transport about ten large trays of food, previously prepared by the soup kitchen cooking team, and they would be assisted by confirmation students. These students would come with us, help set up the dining room, serve the food, clean up the dining room and kitchen, mop the dining room floor, wash all the dishes and trays, stack them for transport back to Presentation, get everyone in the car or van, and go back to Upper Saddle River in time for 11 a.m. mass at Presentation. The kids we brought always said they enjoyed the experience. These kids came from relatively affluent but down-to-earth families. One time, there was a boy who could not operate the mop bucket—it was foreign to him. He'd never seen one before.

It was during both our 1995 and 1996 Cornerstone weekends that our Angel's Wings group did forge some very strong bonds. So much so, that twenty-five years later, when I needed a visit from my dear friends, we arranged for a group of them to come out for a lunch. Carol Sileo, Marsha Simchera, and Eileen Collier Geraghty made the ninety-minute trip to Gurwin. There, we shared a sushi lunch and shared multiple memories of our experiences together over many years. I'd found a photo album filled with pictures of our Angel's Wings weekends, down at Long Beach Island (courtesy of Amy McLennon Marklin). We also had another weekend retreat, which was much more spiritual in nature. It brought back memories of the strong friendships between Carol Sileo and Jane Connors, Ginger Maher and Isabelle Madonia, and me. There was the precious Grace Pichardo, Cheryl Hermansen, Jo Williams, Ruth Harrison, and Jan Mansley (many of whom I send Daily Devotional emails to). Many of them showed up in April 2019 for my dad's memorial at Faith Church. Thank you, my Angel's Wings!

My friendship with Eileen Geraghty has always been a jewel to me. Our Cornerstone weekend was always a treasure. That first weekend, we named ourselves "Angel's Wings," and it was a hit from the get-go. Our group branched out, agreeing to help with other ministries, so we chose soup kitchen. We started out with another existing transport group as their helpers, but soon, we branched off on our own, splitting the weekends among me and Eileen. In doing this, we knew we'd be agreeing to get up early on Sunday mornings (like 6:30 a.m.), having to go to the church to pick up food trays and confirmation students, who would be our team that day. Once in tow, we'd set off to Harlem, with a stop on either Route 17 South or Route 4 West for bagels or whatever else our team members wanted. From there, we'd head back on Route 4 East, across the George Washington Bridge (GWB), south on the West Side Highway, or on the Harlem River Drive, to the 125th Street exit.

Arriving at the Missionaries of Charity Convent, the real work began. We'd transport the trays inside, get them set into the oven for heating, and assess how much we'd need to do before first seating.

We'd make sure the dining room was ready for each seating. Each place had a plate and a cup for water. Water pitchers were filled for continuous refills. As each group came in, we'd be prepared for the continuous flow of people. Each person was asked to present at the serving table, and it would be manned by either me or Eileen (if she were going) and one of the confirmation students. The flow was pretty constant, and we'd get into a rhythm, or a groove, so we could move through a seating pretty quickly. Many attendees would ask for extras and would provide an empty bread bag or cake box, and we'd reload it for someone's later feeding. There were usually two or three seatings. We'd end at 9:30 or 10 a.m. Then, clean-up commenced. And that meant to clean everything. We'd have to sweep the floors, mop the floors, and clean and wipe down the tables. Then we'd have to repeat the process for the kitchen, the bathroom, and the hallways leading in and out of the building. We had a good-sized group, yet it was easy to work up a sweat. One last push, and we'd be good to go. All the trays had to be washed and stacked for transport back to Presentation. Once we got the car loaded back up, we'd set forth back to the church. With any luck, we could make it back by 11 a.m., for Sunday mass. I love you, Eileen Collier Geraghty! We were a great soup kitchen team! I'll remember it always!

What Could I Possibly Have in Common with Princess Diana and Mother Teresa?

Feeling a bit like Forrest Gump, I find myself showing up in the middle of many historic moments. The question posed is a natural question to ask but, as it turns out, Princess Diana and I almost shared the same date of death, August 31, but mine would have been fourteen years after hers, in 2011. As for what I have in common with Mother Teresa, the icon of caring for the poor, sick, and destitute, I was fortunate to serve as a soup kitchen delivery team captain for ten years, 1996–2006. We served these meals at The Missionaries of Charities Convent, for homeless mothers and their children and many others in the Harlem area, who came weekly for their "meal of the day" (maybe the week). The Missionaries of Charities was founded by Mother Teresa in 1950. Mother Teresa and Princess Diana met for the first time in 1992. The world mourned both of their deaths in 1997, five days apart from each other: August 31 and September 5.

Yet, I was fortunate to have crossed the same paths that these iconic women once walked. No kidding. It's another reason I feel I have been blessed with a new life, to do good things.

Mother Teresa walks with Princess Diana in the Bronx

Photo credit: Michael Schwartz/New York Daily News

BACK TO ENTERTAINING AT 17 SEMINARY DRIVE

We hosted Christmas parties every year from 1996 to 2000. It was usually the first weekend in December. Rather than sending out formal invitations, I usually worked the phones. I had a fairly long list of names and numbers, and within a short time, I was on a roll and the number of guests was ticking up! I invited friends from work, friends from the neighborhood, and friends I'd had since forever. In the end, we usually drew a guest list of about seventy-five. No question: we'd need help. I'd remembered Monica L'Estrada, who'd helped us when we were on Malcolm Road, and I called her again. Monica was available and she had some additional help to provide us with extra support.

Our first party was on Saturday, December 7, 1996. We had a big crowd the first year. Thankfully, Monica and her crew were extra helpful throughout the event, helping with food setup, utensils (wrapping them, rolled up, in a basket near the serving table), making sure we had enough cups, plates, and napkins, checking on mixers, ice, wine bottles (in ice, outside in a plastic barrel), checking on the bar setup. Did we have enough of the usual? Vodka, gin, rum, Rémy Martin, tequila? One of Monica's team would be our bartender for the evening. Fortunately, neither Gary nor I were drinking at this time.

Monica and a couple of the other girls would take coats, hang them in our front closet, and they'd take drink orders and fill them. They'd set up hors d'oeuvres. They'd check on the cooking status of the main dishes (chicken FranÇaise, chicken marsala, stuffed shells, ravioli). To have as a snack, we'd also order a six-foot hero, both American and Italian (sliced into thin pieces). I'd preorder the main dishes and make the hors d'oeuvres, and potatoes and veggies, and have them all heated by dinnertime. From drinks and hors d'oeuvres to dinner and dessert and coffee, every other minute was spent talking, laughing, enjoying the festive atmosphere. And yes, there was music playing throughout the party.

Monica L'Estrada Shouten,
our extraordinary party helper

Throughout those five years at our Christmas parties, one of Gary's main tasks was keeping the fire going. He always did a great job at that. I don't know if there's something about guys and their fires, but one year, Gary had some blaze going! So much so that Danny Loughran (our friend and one of our guests) exclaimed, "Gary, I think your fire's on fire!" And so it was! Flames seemed to almost ride up the mantel wall.

Another year, our tree had a leaning problem. It almost seemed as if any moment the tree would be lying on the floor. That year, it was Chris and Trish Cellary with, "Gary, your tree is listing!"

In the year 2000, in the spring, Gary and I decided to undertake a big project: building our in-ground pool and focusing on our beautiful yard. We contracted with a pool company in Ramsey. We decided on a kidney-shaped pool with a built-in jacuzzi on one side. We wanted steps in one corner of the pool, so that Samantha, our first golden retriever, could easily walk into the pool. Interestingly, Samantha was the only golden retriever that didn't love the pool (she preferred the lake, over at the Ramapo Reservation!). Give it time, and she'd ultimately love it. The project required much ground clearing and dirt fill in order to make the backyard, and thus the pool, at a flat ground level. In order to do that, a big rock wall had to be taken down and fill put in its place. We ultimately got there, and it was time for the actual pool construction. The next week, the pool company showed up with the mold of the pool. They started to put the mold pieces together. The frame of the inside of the pool had to be laid. There were wooden 1- by 8-inch plywood pieces, with screening that was attached. This would become the surface upon which the gunite would be sprayed. Once hardened, the gunite would be spray-painted whatever color we chose (an aqua blue). And once fully installed, the water would become the color of the sprayed gunite. Also, in the midst of all of this, all the piping had to be laid underneath the pool; the piping would connect to the pool heater, the jacuzzi, the drains, the pool cleaner, and all of the suction to keep the pool water clean at all times.

Samantha eventually overcame her fear of the pool, in her last days before passing, in 2002. But she loved Gary!

All in, the pool itself cost us about $50,000. But add to that all the landscaping, tile work, and the stamped concrete that made up our pool patio. When all of that was considered, our pool project cost us well over $100,000.

Fortunately, that year, Gary and his brother, Robbie, made frequent trips to Atlantic City. Gary, as it turned out, was adept as a blackjack player. Fairly often, Gary's gambling host, Sonny, called to invite Gary and Robbie down for the weekend, with an opportunity to win $10,000. In addition, Gary and Robbie would be put up as Sonny's guests for the weekend, plus they'd receive a free camcorder. Robbie, who had been in the Air Force, obtained his private pilot's license, and on a few of these "AC" occasions, he and Gary would fly down for the weekend, or sometimes just the night. Robbie was very serious about his flying capability and made sure to be fully "with it" while flying. Fortunately, while Gary was sober during these occasions, their typical meal down in AC would be getting "comped" at the Noodle Bar. On several occasions, Gary came back from AC happy to report that he'd won as much as $20,000 (in one night!). He went on that year, in total, to win nearly $90,000! I made sure to put that cash to good use: finishing our pool project with a cabana. In comparison, poor Robbie was not so lucky at the tables. Ultimately, he came back with the story of his winnings as "the $10,000 camcorder" trip. (Sorry, Robbie.)

For the cabana, we were referred to a great contractor named Hank Emr, from Allendale. As it turned out, Hank was by far the best, and neatest, contractor with whom we ever worked. In May 2000, Hank framed out our new cabana and gave us an idea for what he had planned—the style, the color, the windows, the doors, and his thoughts for what would be inside. A refrigerator was number one. We needed the extra space to keep things cold in the summertime, and it would be useful for additional storage in the off-season. We'd need an air-conditioning unit, and a TV, to watch the all-important games during the summer. We'd need counter space and storage drawers, for all of the additional cookery and plates and trays to store during both party season and the off-season. Every day, Hank made his "Palm Pilot": a piece of 1 by 8, cut about 8 inches long, upon which he would write his list of things to do the next day on his cabana project. He did an amazing job!

Our poolside cabana, built to perfection for us

In 2001, instead of waiting until our Christmas party, I undertook the challenge of planning our first pool party gala. This was a big dream of mine: to finally put to use the pool, cabana, and yard, and entertain our friends and family at the same time. We didn't have a specific budget, but I took it to be unlimited. I turned into Martha Stewart for the party-planning process. The yard, pool, and landscaping around the pool were in place. After the pool, we set about laying sod in the back and front yards. When it came to the actual party, I had a vision of what it would look like. There'd be cocktail tables, interspersed around the pool. Each would have its own tablecloth, a vase with flowers and some candles. In the days before the party, I had to go to buy medium-sized vases, one for every table, for a total of sixteen. We had a larger oblong table on the top level of our deck, and that would come in handy. We also set up a tent on the right side of the cabana, where more tables and a dance floor could be set up. There was also room for a DJ, and I envisioned floating centerpieces to be placed in different areas of the pool, with flowers and candles on each. I had to go and buy Styrofoam pieces, at Michael's in Ramsey Square, and also get some solid rope/string to attach the centerpieces on each side of each area of the pool, so as to hold the centerpieces stationary. The day before the party, I went to the Ramsey Nursery and purchased enough flowers, of all bright colors, to mix in bunches in the vases. Once purchased, I headed home to commence the flower cutting, and mixing them into colorful bunches for each table centerpiece. Each vase was arranged perfectly. On the morning of the party, everything was falling into place. I was gratified that this "gala" was coming to fruition. While it had been extremely hot in the days preceding our party, the weather was perfect for our party. The date, August 11, 2001, was my dad's seventy-first birthday, and exactly thirty days before September 11, 2001. Who knew?

Late afternoon/early evening, our guests started to arrive. First, the people from Salomon Brothers arrived: Keith Petersen and his (very pregnant) wife, Ethan and Michelle Heisler, Carlotta Chan, and Dave Lane.

My family members arrived: my brother-in-law, Robbie, along with his girlfriend at the time, and my brothers John and Robert, who came early for finishing touches. The neighbors started coming in droves: Laina and Danny Funsch, Jeff and Beth Rosenberg, Catherine and Bill Krame, Mark and Margaret Gregorek, Harold and Lorraine Clarke, Donna and Lenny Castriani, Dave and Cathy Nelson, Kathy and Ron Laurent, Joyce and Donald Becker, Danny and Kathy Loughran, Rhonda and Mark Safarian, Liz and Mike Madden, Teri and Michael Giamborta, and Kimberly Blue and Bill Cooke. My personal trainer, Shep Haight, arrived, along with a few others from the gym. My goddaughter Lorianne and her then-boyfriend, Frank Marchiano, showed up, as well. I was thrilled that they came! Four years later, they were married, and they now have three beautiful boys!

Lorianne Diana and Aunt Deb at the pool party gala
August 11, 2001

In total, the list grew to "ninety of our closest friends," as Gary commented on our great party. The bill was $10,000, which would be a wedding reception to many, but ours was just a good use of our hard-earned cash, showing it off for all our friends to see.

A typical pool party at 17 Seminary Drive

SPECIAL FRIENDS I MADE WHILE AT 17 SEMINARY

Rio Vista was a beautiful section of Mahwah, New Jersey. One could say that throughout the neighborhood, one home was more beautiful than the next. The lawns and landscaping on each were elaborate. It had a "beautiful" feel throughout this section, built on the grounds of a former seminary (Immaculate Conception Seminary)—the one attended by our pastor at Church of the Presentation, in Upper Saddle River. Our home, on Seminary Drive, which ran through the entire 465 acres, was nice-sized but nowhere near as large as many others. For a long time, I remained wowed that we really lived here! There were events planned by the Rio Vista Mahwah Homeowners Association designed to get the people who lived there together to socialize. The main event for several years was the "progressive dinner." This event was a hit from its inception. During the event, each resident would spend time at one home for appetizers, one for the main course, and one for dessert. This way, each attendee was afforded the opportunity to see each of these "beautiful" homes, with their sculpted lawns and beautiful landscaping, their pools, and their beautiful exteriors and interiors. Of course, there was generous amounts of alcohol at each venue. The first year we attended was 1997, the year after our first Christmas party. That meant we knew most of the people in attendance. In that year, the cocktail hour, with hors d'oeuvres, was at Mike and Liz Madden's home, on Seton Lane.

A WEEKEND FORAY TO NEWPORT, RHODE ISLAND

In 2000, we were invited on a trip to Newport, Rhode Island, with a group of about a dozen other couples. The hosts were Dave Nelson and his wife, Kathy. Along for the weekend were me and Gary, Margaret and Mark Gregorek, Harold and Lorraine Clarke, Sandy and Bill Compagnone, Margaret and Lou Valenti, Carl and Sue Augusto, Pamela and Dan Castro, Gloria and Bob McHale, Jerry and Marian Ferrone, and Kathy and Rich Beylon. The first part of the weekend was the mansion tours. Of all of these summer "cottages," the Breakers, owned by the Vanderbilt family, was most elegant—and enormous!

Vanderbilt mansion: The Dining Room

Vanderbilt mansion: The Breakers

Source: https://www.newportmansions.org/explore/the-breakers

The next afternoon, we got a tour of Dave and Kathy's beautiful home in Newport. The house was built into a rock cliff, and boasted some amazing features, like a full stone shower. The next night, we attended the Governor's Ball at Salve Regina University, at which Dave Nelson was on the Board of Directors. The governor at the time was Republican Lincoln Almond, who served from 1995 to 2003. That was a very nice occasion. We all got the opportunity to meet the governor and mingle with the other guests. It was made especially fun with our time with Harold and Lorraine Clarke and Margaret Gregorek. Harold was, and is, hysterical!

Finally, on Sunday, our visit ended with a brunch at The Inn at Castle Hill.

A perfect ending to a perfect weekend.

The Inn at Castle Hill, Newport, Rhode Island

Chapter Fourteen D

The Traumatic End to Gary's Life, June 2006

In January 2006, I went off on another business trip to visit Vanoil, in Edmonton, Alberta, Canada. I was working for Starlight Capital at that time. It was during that trip that I'd been texted by Ron to alert me that Gary was aware that Ron and I had been having an affair. Gary had also made Ron's wife aware of the affair. I sat in stunned silence in my hotel room, not knowing what to do. I texted Ron, and he made me aware that his wife had confronted him and that his biggest concern (justifiably so) was that his wife might take his children away from him, and that would be too much to bear. I flew home the next day, along with Murray, and I cried most of the cross-country flight home. Upon arriving home, Gary was furious but more hurt than anything else. He'd bought me a vase of flowers, acknowledging that he had done things in the past that had driven me away. When questioned if I was in love with Ron, I said yes. Gary forbade me to ever see Ron again and said, "Stay away from him. I never want to see you with him again." I agreed, but I knew in my heart that I was unwilling to end things with Ron. That was my decision. In turn, it was Gary's decision to pick up a drink again, after ten years of complete sobriety (although he had stopped going to AA meetings, not availing himself of support and a spiritual solution he might find there). On several instances, I called Gary on my suspicion that he was drinking and he assured me, "I'll get things under control." He did start to attend meetings again, but he also continued his drinking. This continued for several weeks. This was mid-June, and our twenty-fifth anniversary was coming up, on June 28.

We'd been fighting but were planning on going away to celebrate our anniversary in Aruba (a favorite of ours). But one Sunday morning, June 24, 2006, he woke up and was headed to the bathroom off our bedroom. I saw Gary walk in and then he came out, turned around, and then walked backward into the bathroom, and I watched in horror as he grabbed the bathroom doorjamb and then fell backward, slamming the back of his head into the ceramic tub! His head bent forward, and I saw blood on the white tile. I screamed and ran over to him and he yelled, "Leave me alone, I have to go pee." He got on his hands and knees and then stood up, going into the bathroom, where he fell forward and hit his forehead on the rim of the toilet. Horrors, now he hit both front and back of his head. *What could be going on in his brain?* I said I was calling 911, so I did, and an ambulance was on the way.

First, the police came, and he was refusing to go with them. When he finally got into the ambulance, he then refused any treatment (and I since found the form that he signed). In the midst of the prior few weeks, one of the doctors at Valley Hospital, Dr. Bruce Mindich, had told Gary he needed open-heart surgery again, to replace the artificial heart valve with a tissue valve—so no more blood thinners—or he wouldn't have a good probability of living much longer with the way things were going.

Gary was furious and said he didn't want his "chest sawed open again" and if anyone tried to argue with him, he'd challenge them with, "You go ahead and have your chest sawed open, tell me how it feels, and then I'll listen to ya." My brother Robert tried, got his response, and knew the outcome wasn't going to be good. I have beat myself up over this—blaming myself that I'd killed Gary, through his broken heart—feeling horribly guilty for my transgressions, for hurting a really wonderful man (despite his own transgressions and flaws), but never did I pour alcohol down his throat. Alcohol was the only way he knew how to relieve his emotional pain, if only for a little while. Instead, he drank, and he ended up dead. Three days after his falls, after two days in a coma, his brain swollen and him being declared brain dead, Gary died on June 27, 2006, at two in the afternoon. Within minutes of calling the time of his death, a surgeon called. They were waiting in the OR to harvest Gary's organs (the only positive outcome of Gary's death). In the years that followed, I connected with the two people who had received his kidneys, both on the wait list for five years, almost giving up hope, and finally, they got word that their life was about to change for the better. One of them, a woman, told me that she had developed a craving for "Mike and Ikes," Gary's favorite candies, and for pizza, one of Gary's favorite foods. I watched as they covered his body with a sheet and rolled him into the elevator. This was it. I would not see Gary alive, walking and talking, ever again.

GARY S. GROSSER

Grosser, Gary S., of Mahwah, NJ (formerly of North Babylon, NY), suddenly, on June 27, 2006 in his 51st year. Beloved husband of Deborah Grosser (née Feltman). Devoted son of Robert H. and Eleanor Grosser and son-in-law of John P. and Grace Feltman. Cherished brother of Lynn Galbraith (Chris), Robert M. Grosser (Mary), and Susan Cochrane. Also survived by many loving nieces, nephews, and friends. Cremation was private. Memorial visitation, Thursday, 2–5 and 7–9 p.m. at the Overton Funeral Home, Inc., 172 Main St., Islip, NY. Religious service, 7:30 p.m. at the funeral home. (Published in *Newsday* on June 29, 2006.)

DEB'S DEBACLE: GARY'S SERVICES AND FUNERAL

I barely made it through the next few days. My brother John and his wife, Kelly, brought me to their apartment in Glen Cove. I ended up looking for alcohol and took a bottle of Ketel One gin to have with me during the wake (not smelling like alcohol, I hoped!).

A friend helped me by getting me some Librium so I wouldn't go through alcohol withdrawal (the most dangerous type of withdrawal symptoms among withdrawal types; i.e., heroin, opioids, benzodiazepines). Drinking on Librium would be a dangerous thing, combining liquid alcohol and the Librium in pill form. I only took a few swigs of that Ketel One gin, but that was too much to avoid smelling like alcohol.

Many of Gary's colleagues from AT&T showed up, in a bus! Gary's immediate boss, Ken Hickey, and his wife, Monique, showed up to pay their respects. Chuck DiNapoli, one of Gary's bigger bosses, also came to his wake. Meanwhile, I made it through the wake, barely hanging on. My friend, Louise, and Lin (my new AA sponsor, at that time) came to the wake, and I was able to make one statement, at the end of the wake, about "holding on to those we love because we don't know how long they'll be in our lives." I didn't make a complete fool of myself, but I wasn't the stoic, grieving widow I would have wanted to be.

I completely lost it when we took a charter fishing boat ride out to spread Gary's ashes over the Great South Bay. Gary, his brother Robbie, and his dad knew the charter fishing guys for years. I got into an argument with Gary's mom, me saying that "[Gary] didn't have to die, if he had the surgery to fix his valve the right way." And I said other stuff I shouldn't have, so when we got into the dock, Gary's mom became visibly upset, as we were pulling back into the marina. Gary's cousin Greg kept saying: "Get her off the boat, she's a drunk." My brother John was there to meet me, along with Kelly, and they would take me back to Mahwah. So, I got into the back seat of the car with John and Kelly and they drove me back to Mahwah, New Jersey. They poured me into my front door (after me yelling obscenities at Kelly). (Yes, this qualifies as embarrassingly ugly.) And it was shortly after that, that I went to rehab at Crossroads Centre, in Antigua, this time for a full month.

A Major Crossroads in the Road of My Life

Crossroads looked beautiful on its website, and in person. Many in AA would say Crossroads was too cushy, and I needed to be broken, then built up, but I was already broken. My husband of twenty-five years was dead, and I started to drink heavily again (during which I got another DUI), so I think I hit bottom pretty hard. While on the plane to Antigua, I sat next to two teachers who were going there on vacation. They asked what I wanted to drink, and I replied a double Absolut vodka, with tomato juice and horseradish. I figured this would be my last drink ever, and we continued to have a nice flight. In AA, it's said that "only an alcoholic would drink over the problems that alcohol caused in the first place."

When I arrived at the Antigua airport, my Crossroads escort met me to facilitate my move through customs. He brought along a cab driver, who took me to baggage claim, and got me to my cab (actually, it was a van) to Crossroads. But not before I spied a liquor store kiosk, where I purchased a small bottle of vodka and a bottle of Gatorade. For the next ninety minutes, I proceeded to mix a few Gatorade and vodkas, "relaxing" myself for what lay ahead.

While at Crossroads, I learned that it was not uncommon for an alcoholic or addict to have their "last hurrah," and they were known to have pulled up to the entrance with a mirror filled with cocaine, or, like me, drinking their "last" drink.

Crossroads was in a lush part of the island, on Willoughby Bay, in St. John's parish. It was founded by legendary guitarist and recovering addict Eric

Clapton and Richard Conte, CEO of Priory Hospitals Group in London. It was funded in part through Eric Clapton, the Priory Hospitals Group, and the government of Antigua. It opened its doors in 1998. The thirty-six-bed residential treatment center was also costly. The cost of a twenty-nine-day stay at the center was $27,000, private pay only. They'd accept insurance but the fee had to be paid up front. If your insurance reimbursed the cost, some of the fee could be recouped.

Thus, a few weeks after Gary's death, I had to come up with the $27,000. My friends Joyce Becker and Karen Boaz were both helpful in getting me accepted as a resident at Crossroads. They made the calls to Crossroads and got all the info about the program, the fees, what I'd need to pack, everything. They even arranged for my driver, Dan Arnautu, to pick me up to drive me to Newark airport. The morning of my departure, Joyce arrived early and helped me to blow dry my hair, as I was nervous and a little shaky to do it well enough myself. Thank you, Joyce. I'll never forget all of your help.

From the Crossroads website: "Founded in 1998 by iconic musician and recovering addict Eric Clapton, Crossroads Centre Antigua is located on the island of St. John's Antigua in the West Indies, just north of the equator in the Caribbean. A beautiful location to begin recovery, Antigua enjoys year-round sunny weather and is known for its white sand beaches and crystal clear blue water."

The Crossroads treatment philosophy is that recovery needs to treat all aspects of the person in recovery—mind, body, and spirit. The program was based on a 12-Step recovery program; thus, a resident would wake, have breakfast, do some light exercise, then head back into the facility to attend an AA or NA meeting. In the afternoons, there could be an organized exercise program, such as yoga or stretching. There was also the opportunity to use the center's pool. There could be organized exercise by the pool, or in the pool, which could include water volleyball and using foam pool noodles for exercises.

One of my favorite activities was to go for a nice, hard run. Here I was, on a beautiful island I'd never been to before, but it was still rehab. I needed to de-stress, and running always helped me. Around dinnertime, I would leave my bedroom and the building, and just start running the perimeter of the grounds. Over and over, I'd go, in part checking out the scenery of the grounds, but also feeling as if I might escape, anywhere. But no. I returned to my building, and my room, and headed off to dinner. The meals were always healthy, and tasty, and filled the void in my stomach, post my run. On the first night there, one of the new residents had taken off and there was a search going on to look for him. He was maybe nineteen years old, a young guy, and he went swimming in the bay, I guess, in an attempt to leave the center, but he was found shortly and brought back to the grounds. As it turned out, the guy had been convinced to go to Crossroads but was told by his family that he didn't have to stay. Reality can be tough, upon the realization that you were brought to rehab, under false pretenses.

We'll Always Have Paris: December 26 to 31, 2006

After the shock and horror of Gary's death, followed by a month at Crossroads for a third try at rehab for alcohol, I came back home to a five-bedroom house, with a master bedroom closet filled with Gary's clothes. Where to begin? To start the process of removing Gary's clothes from his closet, I began to pick out some things that I thought would probably fit my brothers: some nice leather jackets and coats, some of his sweaters and sweatshirts, some button-down work shirts, some ties, and even his tuxedo (he never got to wear that as much as he could have). I remember taking a full carload of his clothes to nearby Salvation Army bins, near the A&P in Mahwah, and I cried out loud (in loud sobs) when I placed them in the bin, "I'm sorry, Gary! I miss you! I love you! Are you okay, in heaven?" I was shaking, crying, but it felt like a cleansing, and I think Gary answered me back. He was okay. He was in heaven, with his father and some of his friends he grew up with who had passed. After the closet cleansing, it was a start, but I could not bear to be around during the dreaded "happy holidays."

My friend Kimberly Blue, with whom I worked at Salomon Brothers, mentioned that she was going to be in Paris right around Christmas, so I found that as an awesome way to be "away" at the precise time I knew I could not bear to be around. So, December 26, 2006, the day after Christmas, I flew off to Paris, agreeing to meet up with Kimberly at the Charles de Gaulle Airport in Paris. We had exchanged flight details, and we met as planned at the airport. She had arranged for a ride to our hotel.

On the first night in Paris, we went out to dinner early. Our reservation was for 8 p.m., and the place was empty. We were seated promptly and proceeded to order right away. Kimberly ordered a veal dish, and I stuck with my favorite, the Dover sole. After dinner, Kimberly said she was too tired and was going to go straight to bed. As this was my first time in Paris, I said I wanted to take a cab to see some sights in the city! After all, this was Paris!

We were not far from the Plaza Athénée, and from there, I found a cab and began my adventure. My cab driver's name was Jean (what a surprise).

He took a route along the Seine, and Jean interjected with stories throughout our ride. At the time, the United States was about to carry out sentencing for Saddam Hussein, which was to put him to death by hanging. Without missing a beat, Jean declared, "They should use the guillotine, it's much nicer!" (Something only a Parisian cab driver could say.) On December 30, 2006, sentencing was carried out. Our next stop was the Louvre Museum, in the center of Paris, and Jean offered that the Louvre

Museum was once the house of the kings of France. As we drove around the enormous structure, I asked, "Does the king need a house this big?"

Jean declared, with a thick French accent, "Of course, he is the King!"

Finally, I asked to see the tunnel in which Princess Diana was killed.

Chapter Fourteen E

The Conveniences and Things We Enjoyed While Living in Bergen County

Totally Tan, Lush Day Spa, Restaurants, and the Mecca of Shopping Malls

While living in Mahwah, Gary and I were in close proximity to many places we liked, to shop, to dine, and to utilize their services. Mahwah could be likened to a hub, with neighboring towns as the spokes we frequented. While Mahwah had some shopping, neighboring Ramsey was where we spent much more time. We'd go food shopping at Shop Rite, in Ramsey Square, which was bordered by Route 17 and Franklin Turnpike. There were a huge number of other stores that we also frequented.

On Main Street, in Ramsey, we frequented Totally Tan, owned originally by Joel Occhuito, and later by his son, Johnny. Gary and Johnny had a particularly close relationship, always finding humor in each other's stories and antics. Gary and I liked to have tans in the winter, and year-round, if possible. For me, tanning became an alternate treatment for my psoriasis.

Gary just enjoyed looking healthy and tan, always. While I've opted to have UV light therapy since my accident, tanning was an enjoyable therapy for me. Of course, in more recent years, the dangers of UV rays to my skin have made tanning or sun exposure less appealing, thus I've opted to no longer tan, although I did like the look of being tan.

ANDREA LYNN COLE

In Ramsey, I also found Lush Day Spa, to take care of my hair care needs. It was at Lush that I came to know Andrea Cole, a hairstylist. Over my lifetime, I've always been somewhat at war with my hair. Growing up, I went from having no hair, to curly hair, to longer but frizzy hair, always fighting against the impact of humidity and wishing I had "Jan Brady hair" instead (long, straight, and silky blond). I'd gone through the phases of using lye-based straighteners (only to suffer hair breakage and fried ends). When Keratin came onto the marketplace, I thought I'd found the answer to my prayers and the solution! I loved the end result, but Keratin was costly ($300–$500 each time) and time-consuming (three to four hours or more from start to finish). Still, finding a solution to a lifelong war, it was worth it.

Then, there was color. Having been born a brunette, and for the most part liking it, I started to dabble on the lighter side. I started with blonde highlights. Then, I went to chunky highlights, then, I went to full-on blonde. And yes, I loved being a blonde and it felt like I was having more fun. When I look back, I noted that I had undergone much of a whole-body transformation, and then I just added blonde to the mix.

Me (at right), during my blonde phase with my sister-cousin, Gigi Burrows, at Avra in New York City in 2010

Andrea has been a loyal friend and hairstylist for me over the last three decades. She's cut, colored, highlighted, styled, treated my hair, and she has been very accommodating over the years. If she wasn't in the salon, I'd go to her home. Sometimes I'd bring Kayla, my golden retriever, with me. Andrea's children adored Kayla, and it was a treat for them. Andrea's had her own share of tough times over the years. She was married and then got divorced, and there were some nasty custody issues. Andrea has always been a devout mom; she loves Hannah, Luke, and Sarah. I learned just recently that she moved to Raleigh, North Carolina, and she had another baby girl, named Charlie. She got remarried to a new husband, Joe Croniger. After all of the upheaval and hardships she endured, Andrea is a survivor. I couldn't be happier that she finally found the happiness that she needed and deserved the whole time. Now, that's a happy ending!

Andrea Lynn Cole, my hairstylist and my loyal friend

In 2000, I underwent breast augmentation surgery. I also joined New York Sports Club in Ramsey. I hired Shep Haight as my personal trainer. That launched me into weight-based training, plyometrics, and high intensity interval training. I also maintained my running, I attended spin class, and used the elliptical trainers. I was going to get ripped, shredded, cut. For the most part, I succeeded. Because I earned a hefty income while on Wall Street, I could easily afford all this transformative activity. I found myself developing a shopping habit. I remember being able to walk into virtually any store, no matter what the price point of the merchandise, and pretty much buy whatever I wanted. At Nordstrom in the Garden State Plaza Mall, in Paramus, I had a personal shopper in the fragrance and cosmetics section. If I liked a certain fragrance, I could arrange to have it purchased and sent to my home.

I went through a Gucci sunglasses phase, buying the pair I liked, right there on the spot, despite the $400 price tag. I found stores that I liked, such as Cache and Bebe. There were beautiful dresses, suits, and pants (including leather). If there was a dress or a top that I liked, I'd buy the dress, and the top, in multiple colors. Spending $500 or even $1,000 in a day, while I was able to afford it, did not seem problematic to me.

Yes, in hindsight, I can now see that I had an addictive personality and things were filling up the emptiness I felt inside. I was placing way too much importance on money and things versus doing more to better myself and to help others.

Gary and I used to enjoy going out for group dinners. For these, we often went out to some of the favorite local restaurants. There was Aldo's in Wyckoff, Savini's in Allendale, Houston's at the Riverside Square Mall in Hackensack, Dimora in Norwood, New Jersey, and Seasons in Washington Township, New Jersey. There was a slight leaning toward Italian cuisine, and we also enjoyed American fare for steak and seafood, although seafood was offered at the Italian places too. We'd go to celebrate birthdays, anniversaries, or virtually any occasion worth celebrating. Most all of the venues were upscale and would easily be comparable to places in New York City, although Aldo's had a homier feel, with Aldo usually visiting each guest's table to be assured that service and all were going well for his guests.

Generally in attendance were Gary and me, the Quinns, the Loughrans, the Laurents, the Beckers, and sometimes the Littlehales. If there were birthday celebrations, family members also attended (Gary's family, my family members, and others who were requested to attend). One year, Tom Quinn's and Gary's birthdays were close in dates and their combined ages would exceed one hundred. I ordered a half sheet cake and I got a candle for "100." At the restaurant, I heard people saying: "Ooh, someone's turning a hundred," as Gary and Tom's cake passed the other diners and the waiters were singing: "Happy Birthday to you" . . . It was classically funny to us all.

It was during our time in Mahwah that Gary and I became close with Danny and Kathy Loughran. Danny was one of the traders with whom I worked at DLJ, and he was married to Kathy. They'd known each other since they were fourteen years old and then married several years later. We had many fun times with them. In our time at Malcolm Road, Danny and Kathy lived in Upper Saddle River, New Jersey. On a couple of occasions, they had a huge party at their home, which, for the occasion, they dubbed their home

The Double LL Ranch (given their last name). It was a great party, with good food, lots of festivities, and much fun for all.

Several years later, Gary and I were invited to their casita out in Scottsdale, Arizona. We liked to play golf together, and Scottsdale had some amazing courses. During these years, Danny and Kathy also had their two daughters, Jacqueline (Jackie) and Mary Rose. The girls are now twenty-five (Jackie) and twenty-three (Mary Rose). Jackie looks strikingly like Danny, while Mary Rose looks more like Kathy. Jackie attended University of Vermont, and Mary Rose attended the University of Dayton, in Ohio. They are both well-rounded, beautiful girls. I'm very happy to know them all as a family!

Danny, me (holding Mary Rose), and Gary in our family room, circa 1999

Danny and Kathy inspired me to get involved in fundraising for Operation Smile. It's an amazing organization that performs surgery on children with cleft palates and cleft lips. It was founded in 1982 by a cranio-facial surgeon, Dr. William McGee, and his wife, Kathy, a nurse and clinical social worker. In 1999, I was working at Salomon Brothers, which became fertile ground for raising money for a good cause. The strategy of asking for support from the trading desk worked well. As I went down the line to each trader, they needed only to hear what the prior trader donated to take into consideration for their donation. In total, I was able to raise $10,000 just from the Salomon Brothers trading desk. Operation Smile was happy with my success for them.

It was through Danny and Kathy that Gary and I got to know Teri Tosi and Mike Giamborta. Teri and Mike were both attorneys. Teri became instrumental in settling a case in Gary's favor related to Coumadin. Teri was always the attractive and successful attorney, who loved her family and friends. I found this picture of Teri, between Jackie and Mary Rose Loughran, in 2015.

Jackie, Teri Tosi, and Mary Rose

Again, all this self-discovery came about because of a near-death accident. My living circumstances and surroundings are not what I pictured for myself, at sixty-one years old. And while I don't plan on staying where I am forever, I can enjoy this self-realization that the shallow, fleeting things I once valued so highly are just that: shallow and fleeting. Instead, the richness of a deep and lasting friendship or relationship have become much more desirous for me. I will remain grateful for the clarity this entire experience has provided me. I have a deep and sustained clarity that causes me to value things and people in my life differently now! This is all because of my near-death experience.

POST-MORTEM: LIFE WITHOUT GARY

After Gary's death, I was on my own, in my big house, specially built for the two of us or a family. Shortly after his death, I'd begun to reconcile the fact that I was alone. My brother-in-law, Robbie, who was watching Taylor, our second golden retriever, while I was at Crossroads, decided that Gary "wanted him to have her." Distraught at first, I ultimately decided that Taylor would be better off in a family environment, and Robbie, his wife, Mary, and her two girls would give Taylor a happy home. It was not worth a fight with the family that was still reeling from Gary's death. Thus, I thought it best that I seek another golden to keep me company. I was driving home from my home group meeting in Kinnelon, and I passed a sign: Golden Retriever Puppies For Sale! I wrote down the number on the sign and called the new breeder. Upon calling, I learned that there were three boys and two girls in the litter, born August 12, 2006. I made an appointment to meet the new pups the following weekend, September 9, 2006. I called my friend Laura May Piccolo to accompany me on this expedition. Just the anticipation of having a new puppy to keep me company filled me with excitement. The breeder was way up on Route 23 North. It was a residential neighborhood, in a house. Laura and I went in and asked to see the puppies. There is nothing cuter than baby golden retriever puppies!

This litter did not disappoint! Not long after being there, Laura spotted the one I would eventually take home! She was a beauty, and my heart melted the moment I laid eyes on her. Laura quickly said, "It's this one!" I agreed, as the puppy gave me her tiny paw and was eagerly standing over the rim of their enclosure.

"How much to hold her?" I asked the breeder.

"One hundred dollars."

So I handed over $100. They shaved a tiny bit of hair on her paw so we could identify her upon return. I was already excited to be getting my new forever friend! The breeder took my deposit and informed me that the earliest I could pick her up was Saturday, October 6. The puppies would be eight weeks old by then.

On Saturday, October 6, I would head back north. Prior to that, I picked up Lin, my sponsor in AA. She'd come for reinforcement and to hold my new puppy on the way home. I'd been considering names and had thought of the Eric Clapton song "Layla," which was nice but not a good dog name. I decided "Kayla" would be it! "Come, Kayla! Come here, girl." Yes, that was the one!

On October 6, 2006, I picked up Lin in Ringwood, and then we were off to pick up Kayla. Lin held her in her arms for the ride home, and we made a pit stop on the way back to show Lin's husband, Jay. Finally, I brought Kayla home to 17 Seminary. I'd procured a crate to train her to sleep, needing to wake her up throughout the night and take her into the yard to relieve herself. It worked like a charm. Kayla was a good girl quickly! I also bought a dinner bowl for Kayla. For Kayla's entire life, either me or my dad (post my accident) cooked for her every day. I'd make a mixture of ground chicken, with carrots and some mixed dry food for crunch. She seemed to love it and cleared her bowl and cleaned every morsel of food in that dish. When I first brought her home, the bowl was way bigger than she was for the first few months. Kayla was a delight to have around. We went for walks and then long hikes, as often as possible. When I'd get in the car, I was quick to put her in the back seat as she *loved* going to the Ramapo Reservation on Ramapo Valley Road. She would start jumping about when she'd hear the car start! Of course, I'd have to take my baby Kayla!

Sweet baby Kayla at eight weeks old

While on my own, I was still being included in neighborhood social functions. There was a lovely young woman, Emily Clarke, eldest daughter of Harold and Lorraine Clarke, the ones with whom Gary and I had attended the trip to the Newport, Rhode Island, in 2000. It was 2008, and Emily was graduating from Mahwah Senior High School. There would be a party and I was invited. The party was held in the Georgian Court backyard of Emily's home. Emily was always extremely poised, compassionate, and kind. We bonded easily. I knew that Emily would turn out to do great things, and even in hindsight, she really did. After high school, she went to Rutgers to study nursing. She graduated there in 2015. Her first nursing job was at University Hospital, in Newark, New Jersey, from 2015 through 2018. In Newark, she worked in telemetry and in the trauma ICU. In 2019 through the present, she's been at University of California, San Francisco (UCSF) Medical Center. In San Francisco, she's been in neurosurgical ICU. Emily would have likely been my neurosurgical ICU nurse when I had my accident had she been at the same hospital. She also attended to many COVID-19 patients during the pandemic.

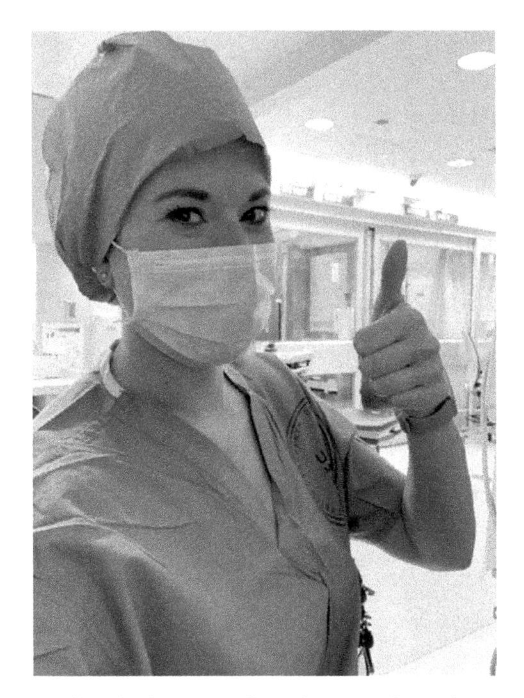

Emily Clarke, one of my favorite front-liners

Chapter Fifteen

My Triathlon Career and My Ironman at Lake Placid, 2003 to 2011

While I started with Starlight Capital in April 2003, I also began to become immersed in an unrelated, but significantly compelling, arena: the field of triathlon.

Transition to Triathlon, Twenty Years after My First Running Race in 1983

One day at the gym (I belonged to NYSC-Ramsey), I saw a friend and we were both working out on machines in the same area. Her name was Louise, and she was doing assisted pull-ups, and I was on the Roman chair doing hanging sit-ups and leg lifts. She said, "Have you ever done a triathlon?" I said, "No, but I'd like to try one." She said, "Well you look strong. You should do one. Would you like to start training?" I said, "Sure, how do we start?" She said, "I can use the pool over at Ramapo College since I'm an alumni and it's an Olympic-size pool, so let me know when you can go." I said, "Great. How about tomorrow or Monday?" It was Saturday. She said,

"Cool, how about 7 p.m. tomorrow?" I said, "Sundays are okay?" She said, "Sure, we just have to turn out the lights in the locker room and make sure the showers are turned off entirely." I said, "Sounds good to me. I'll meet you in the parking lot out back."

And so it began . . . weeks and months of swimming, spinning (in our basement or at the gym) as a biking proxy until I got a bike, and running on the treadmill for miles and miles. I went over to Ridgewood Cycle and found a Fuji for $1,500, "a decent bike for a decent price." When I first tried to ride it, Louise was so cute. Since the pedals were "clip in/lock on," she followed me around the parking lot (like a mom whose kid just took off his training wheels) to make sure I didn't do the all-too-common tip over when one had to stop a bit suddenly but forgot they were "locked in," becoming one with the bike. I also learned that Ridgewood Cycle did weekly bike rides on Saturday mornings at seven—"wheels up latest at 7:30" it would say on the Excel triathlon team training board. So now, I was learning airline pilot terminology. I also learned that triathletes paid a ton for their bikes, sometimes spending upwards of $6,000 to $10,000, and that was without wheels. Racing wheels (Zipps) could run another $1,000 to $1,500. Fifteen hundred dollars is twice what I paid for my first car (and that came with an engine in it). It was a 1972 Toyota Celica. I bought it from my uncle John Bockino (now a retired college professor at Suffolk Community College, in Selden, New York). It already had eighty thousand miles on it from going back and forth from college, in Boston, and it had dirt all over the back seat, like he carried trees back from the nursery or something. Oh, and the Celica was a stick shift, and I had to teach myself, although Carol Latva and I did get a few lessons while working at Dr. Jaffe's office and working with Lori DiTata and Lynda Gould, who both had Triumph TR6s, which were also manual transmissions. I got the hang of it after a couple of days, and I ultimately loved driving a stick, preferring it to automatic, especially when I later came to own or lease a BMW 5 Series (one of the fruits of a tough job in a lucrative field).

Oh, but the Celica's color, mustard yellow, had to go. I'd just learned about Maaco and I got it painted a nice blue color. That, and four new tires: "Now you're talking."

My first triathlon was a sprint distance at Harriman State Park on June 7, 2003. We had only done pool swimming, no open water swims yet, but we learned through David Baker (whom we called "Gladiator," at his request) that we could swim at Indian Trails Club, in Franklin Lakes, from the dock, out to a buoy and then back to the dock, and that would be a half-mile swim. And we were already signed up for a second tri, the Franklin Lakes Triathlon, on Saturday June 14, 2003, just one week after. Then we needed wetsuits. Louise reminded me that we could get a big discount at Ridgewood Cycle, so we did. We guesstimated what size we'd wear, and we went for long sleeves since it was still chilly in May. The wetsuits arrived, and we were happy. But we had yet to try the wetsuits on and when we did, we realized how fast we'd get hot, and how little we could really move in them (neoprene linings and rubber outsides is not a comfortable combination). More like wearing a boa constrictor for fun? No way could we drive with the wetsuits on. Our first open water swim at Indian Trails was Memorial weekend, May 24, 2003. It was the first time I met Cathy Konner, a friend of Bob Slagle's. The water at Indian Trails was in the low sixties, still a breath-taking, face-numbing temperature, but by the first loop, we were ready to go again.

MY TRIATHLON CAREER AND MY IRONMAN AT LAKE PLACID

My triathlon career included dozens of sprint distance tris; several Olympic-distance tris; one half Ironman (or 70.3 miles) in St. Croix, which was awesome but brutal since it had one really steep incline hill, called "the Beast"; and one full distance Ironman (140.7 miles) in Lake Placid (former host to the 1980 Winter Olympics), which I did in 2005. The whole experience was surreal and I loved every minute. I describe the Ironman like "valet parking during transitions." You swim 2.4 miles and then two "wetsuit strippers" would get you out of the wetsuit, and then one of them would help you get dressed for the second leg, the 112-mile bike ride, including your helmet and biking shoes. Then they would get you to your bike and you'd get teed up to start your ride. Finally, after you were done with the ride, someone would help you get undressed from the ride and ready for the last leg, the 26.2-mile run, just for fun. Along the way, we also had to eat and drink and so we previously prepared "special needs bags." We'd put in all the food or other needs for the day to fuel our bodies. The bags would be filled with extra Gatorades, bananas, Clif bars, and maybe a PB&J sandwich (my special needs bags also included several tampons, because, as luck would have it, I got my period on my Ironman day).

There were certain points along the route when you could "call out" for one of your bags, and they seemed to magically appear at the next stopping point. Seasoned pros told me to "eat when you're not hungry and drink when you're not thirsty." So, I progressed from sprint distance and Olympic in 2003 to the St. Croix half in 2004 and the full Ironman in 2005. Now, I wasn't an elite triathlete, but I was a competent age grouper and I did compete nonetheless. It was a wonderful period in my life and, in light of my accident, all my training and racing saved my life. My doctors, who performed multiple surgeries on me to save my life after my accident, concur with that view.

Spinning, Followed by Bagels on Saturday Mornings

Gary and I were fortunate to have a big house with a furnished basement. It was painted gray, with beige Berber carpeting and a nice beige leather circular sofa with a queen-sized pullout and a recliner on one end. And, we had a big sixty-inch TV to watch while spinning. With all TVs being flat screen these days, it was tough to almost give it away when I was moving (which didn't happen until 2009).

We were fortunate to have the room in our basement to fit up to sixteen bikes, with trainers. Most had the triangular, rear-wheel-mounted trainers, but Doug and Evan Piche brought roller trainers. They had rectangular frames and rubber rollers, and they would ride their bikes on the rollers, and they had to maintain balance. It was more realistic. Unfortunately for Doug Piche, he fell once and hit his head on one of the carpeted basement stairs and got a nice gash in his scalp. (Poor Doug, he's no longer with us, RIP.)

But most of the time, we were without incident, and we watched the Tour de France videos and then once we just watched a movie. The nicest bathroom in the house was in the basement. When we remodeled it, we built a steam shower, with beautiful blue and white Italian tile. We offered anyone who wanted to, to take a nice steam shower, after spinning but before bagels. One Saturday, Rob Isabelle availed himself of the steam shower, and in the midst, he ran out of the bathroom to get something, and like a serious triathlete, he still had on his heart monitor! We had many laughs, including the day I set up a snack table next to Brendan's bike, with candles and a bowl of pretzels. I mean, you can't make up these stories. This was just us.

ST. CROIX HALF IRONMAN

One day while spinning, we decided as a group that we would sign up for the St. Croix Half Ironman, obviously on the island of St. Croix. The group we'd been spinning with, Rob Isabelle, Brendan Lenihan, Dave Baker, Doug Piche, Evan Piche, Bob Slagle, Gary, me, Kirsten Kincade, Louise Moggio, Allison Llerandi, and Karen Finnerty, were pretty regular attendees.

Sponsor hotel for The St. Croix Half Ironman: The Buccaneer in St. Croix

That group also the attended for the St. Croix Half Ironman in 2004. We were all gearing up for that race and talking about "the Beast," a huge, steep hill during the bike course. We talked about getting to the top of the hill and spitting in a hole at the top, having conquered the Beast, instead of it conquering us.

A destination race is more complex, as it required us to disassemble our bikes to be shipped in boxes for the plane and have them reassembled at the destination. We also had to make lodging arrangements for our stay; it was likely to be a four-day, three-night stay, and of course, we needed airline arrangements. The sponsor hotel for the race was The Buccaneer in St. Croix, often featured as a prize trip on Kelly Ripa's Travel Trivia segment on her show, *Live with Kelly and Ryan*. So, about half the group stayed there, while the other half found a condo for rent and stayed there. We had a great time, race included. At one point during my fifty-six-mile bike ride, I passed a group of spectators and heard one woman say, about me: "She still has her lipstick on!"

I yelled back: "CoverGirl Outlast." I actually did write to Procter & Gamble and recounted the story to their sales staff. Not only did I not hear back from them, but I got no free samples or anything. Oh well, I still had a half marathon to run. So, I finished the bike and now on to the run. Somewhere during the run, I saw a guy walking, and I said, "Come on, let's go, let's finish strong." We ended up running the whole half marathon together (and it was extremely hot), even though I'd never met him. That was one of the cool aspects of triathlon racing: you had co-competitors rooting you on, or vice versa. We weren't out with ill will, hoping the other guy tripped or fell; just the opposite, it was a good, competitive spirit in these races.

THE TRIATHLON CAMP SETUP

Part of training for a triathlon was the "setup." Unlike the description of the Ironman as "valet parking during transitions," sprint and Olympic distance was more like "be your own Sherpa." It just meant you had to be organized. So, when you "set up" for transitions, you had to bring everything you might need that day, and "set up" camp. Going in the order of the events: (1) You had to bring your wetsuit; if you had any lube or sunscreen to put on that day, bring it. (2) You needed your swim goggles. (3) You needed your bathing cap (usually provided with your race number). Before putting on your wetsuit, you need to get "body marked." Which means that one of the "body marker volunteers" needed to write your race number on your arm and/or leg with a Magic Marker or Sharpie pen. For the bike leg, you need to find your spot on your designated bike rack to put your bike. You need to make sure you had an adequate number of Gatorades and GUs, both electrolyte replacement aids, and a little bit of sugar to put some kick in your running step, pedal, or swim stroke. All of the items you'll need have to be laid out on a towel or something where you can organize stuff like your biking shoes, running sneakers, flip flops, or the like, for when you are going to, or coming out of, the water. Depending on the race, bringing extra bottled water to wash off sand or other debris on your feet is very helpful, if you have it (it also means your feet will be dry and smooth when you put on socks and biking shoes). For the running leg of the race, I always had a brush to de-tangle my hair, a baseball cap (to cover over the mess, which I always thought I looked like while racing), and of course, sunglasses and maybe a quick swab of Chapstick "ultra-hydration." All these little things can make a race successful, or at least comfortable. Or you could at least try and look good.

THE IRONMAN AT LAKE PLACID, JULY 24, 2005

The Llerandi kids at Lake Placid, 2004: Spencer, Ashlyn, and Grayson

After training for a year, just for the Ironman, we were finally at the place where it would all happen: Lake Placid. We arrived on Thursday, July 21, 2005, and we'd be up there till Monday, July 25. Lake Placid was a perfect venue for the Ironman. The structure of the course, multiple places for spectating: it was the perfect place. Lake Placid was the host site for the 1980 Winter Olympics. There are still many remnants of the Olympics. The entire town was prepared for the weekend that lay ahead, having been the host town for many years. There were parts of the running course where large crowds of spectators would be present as most of the runners went by. Nestled in the forty-six High Peaks in the Adirondacks, Lake Placid offers majestic views. On the ride up to Lake Placid, and having spent one day to train for the bike course, we knew what we would confront on the course. It did not contain rapid, steep climbs, but rather, long, slow, grinding climbs, overlooking some beautiful terrain. Surrounded by mountains like White Face, we knew it would be a challenge. When we were up at Lake Placid for my Ironman, my family was a great cheering team. They were there, at the start, watched the swim, and saw me go off for the bike. The 112-mile biking distance is covered in two fifty-six-mile loops, and at the completion of each loop, I passed my family along the way.

When I was about to complete the second bike loop, I came upon my dad, who had convinced race officials that he was a large shareholder in Ford Motor Company (Ford being the race title sponsor), and therefore should be allowed to see his daughter in the race! It was a welcome sight to see the man whose approval I always sought, and he was always there to offer words of encouragement (which I would surely need as I started the hardest part of the race: the 26.2-mile marathon run).

The transition from swim to bike is relatively easy. The swim completed, and now dressed and equipped for the bike, off I went. The transition from bike to run is not so easy. Wanting to go off with a quick step in my pace, for me, it felt more like someone had sliced my hamstrings in the back of my legs. I knew right away that this was going to be a long, hard run. On the positive side, I also knew that, having gotten through this much of the race, I was going to finish my first-ever Ironman! That feeling was going to have to carry me for 26.2 miles.

After running and walking the last half of the marathon (the third leg of my Ironman in Lake Placid), it made me happy that I had a good adrenaline rush, while I ran (not walked) the oval at the high school in Lake Placid to the finish line. (It was almost like a runner's high, which I've experienced many times.) At the moment I'd been waiting for—crossing the finish line—I was able to put my arms up in a "V" for "Victory." After that, I saw my dad and my mom, who both hugged and kissed me, and some of my friends, who were up at Lake Placid to spectate. I was able to run across the finish line with Ashlyn Llerandi, my friend Alyson's daughter. Alyson is a very accomplished runner and triathlete, with a sub 1:30 half marathon time and I think the half is her sweet spot in racing. Her daughter Ashlyn was an accomplished pole vaulter, earning herself a "full ride" in her fourth year at Villanova. I also ran with Nicole Kincade, my friend Kirsten's daughter. Nicole Kincade was in high school in 2005, but subsequently went to Princeton, in New Jersey, for college, and had a stellar career in volleyball. Unlike me, Kirsten Kincade is an elite triathlete, who has done the World Championship Ironman in Kona, Hawaii, many times, including 2007. She was running it for the benefit of the Matthew Larson Foundation (see Ironmatt.org). Matt was diagnosed in 2002 with choroid plexus carcinoma, a rare but very deadly brain tumor cancer. Matt left this world in April 2007 and is surely in heaven.[2]

2. Fifteen years after my Ironman in Lake Placid, Ashlyn Llerandi just married Joe D'Andrea, on August 8, 2020, and Nicole Kincade just got engaged to her boyfriend, Mike.

Ashlyn & Joe; married on August 8, 2020;
first child, Joseph Michael, welcomed in April 2021!

After the race and being so warmly greeted by my family and friends, it was time to bring this ol' horse home. I was able to maintain a deliberate pace to walk the distance from the finish line to where my bike had been stowed on the bike rack, with my number, and then back to the hotel and car (to put my bike on the bike rack for the ride home). Finally, when I got to my room, and bed, all of the adrenaline that carried me across that finish line began to drain from my body, and soreness and stiffness began to replace the elation. I was tired! Realizing that, I struggled but maintained a deliberate pace back to the car, and then to the hotel and our room. There was a pillow with my name on it, for sure!

It wasn't until the next morning that my stiffness really started to set in (it's called DOMS: delayed onset muscle soreness). But I was able to get my things together, load them in the car, and Gary, my parents, and I set on our way home. Gary had been great and supportive of me the whole time! Just as he'd been at St. Croix the year prior. Who knew that one year later, he'd be dead?

In the years following my Ironman at Lake Placid, I continued to race in triathlons, although at the sprint distance and Olympic distance level. I continued to do the Franklin Lakes/Wyckoff YMCA triathlon (in 2010, at fifty-one), and the West Point Triathlon (including 2011, at fifty-two, the year of my accident). I also did the annual Mahwah 10K and Ridgewood 10K, on Memorial Day weekend.

Me, pre-race, at the Porta-lav

First leg, emerging from the swim

Second leg, longest part of a triathlon: the bike

Third leg, the hardest part: the run

The reward part of a tri: the finish

Chapter Sixteen

Post-Accident Living Arrangements

Kessler Rehab Institute, West Orange, New Jersey

After my accident in 2011, my first cognizant moment was reading my patient bracelet at Kessler Rehab, stating that I was admitted October 7, 2011. So, yes, there was a memory lapse, but I think that was a good thing. Remembering that I'd done cartwheels down the steep, wooden steps and smashed my face on every step would not be something I want to remember. The nine-year recovery period (so far) that ensued is somehow worth remembering. All the care, concern, patience, tolerance, and love that I've received has opened my eyes to so many things. First, all the people who cared for me in the process of restarting my life have inspired me to "give back" to those who gave to me, and to "pay it forward" through this book, inspiring them to know that a normal life is possible once again.

While at Kessler, I was assigned to two senior physical therapists: Shannon Ferguson (now Motisi) and Dave Monteleone.

Kessler is a renowned rehabilitation facility; for instance, professional football players went to Kessler. Actor Christopher Reeve went to Kessler after his tragic fall from a horse. All I can attest to is that at Kessler Institute for Rehabilitation, from October 7, 2011, to April 12, 2012, my therapists had me running on my last day of treatment. Admittedly, I did not run fast, and my two therapists each took a hand, but it showed me that my body and brain knew the mechanics of how to run again! It proves to me that I just need the proper training, and I can run again. The only flaw with my present rehab facility is that Gurwin is a geriatric rehab facility, geared to a much older population (average age: eighty-six). But Gurwin's skilled nursing care and wonderful staff (whom I've grown to know and love) make up for the flaw, for now.

Shannon Ferguson, now married to Dave Motisi; Shannon was my physical therapist while I was at Kessler. She had Dave as her boyfriend then, but marriage and the kids (Brook and Drew) came five years after!

Also, while at Kessler, I went through a phase when I became a human vomitorium. A byproduct of my TBI, I had several episodes when I became dizzy or light-headed, resulting in nausea, followed by an uncontrollable need to vomit up whatever was in my stomach. Fortunately, one of the therapists there, Rich Klauber, assisted me in the clean-up process. There were episodes in the back of the ambulette, when I couldn't get near the door or open a window, before the vomit started flowing. Not a pretty thought, but true. Thankfully, that was short-lived.

My Brother and Sister-in-Law's house, Huntington, New York

After my initial surgeries and rehab at Kessler, I lived with my brother John and his wife, Kelly, at their house in Huntington, New York, from where I attended another rehab called Transitions, a North Shore/LIJ (now Northwell Health) affiliate program. Kelly had arranged that I would have an aide. She found Yolanda Miller, a devout, Jesus-loving, Bible-reading woman from Jamaica. Yolanda wanted a job that would allow for her ability to read her Bible, every day. Working with me fit the bill!

Living Independently Again, Garden City, New York

In the fall of 2012, I moved into a one-bedroom apartment in the Avalon Gardens apartment complex in Garden City, New York. It was a beautiful complex, each unit having brand-new features such as granite countertops and stainless-steel appliances. The complex had just been built. We were originally scheduled to move in, May 2012, but several buildings in the complex were destroyed by fire. We moved in during September 2012. Yolanda and I got to work setting up our bedrooms, putting clothes away, and checking out the new place, including the fitness center and the pool. During the late summer/early fall, we availed ourselves of the fitness center almost every day.

I continued to attend Transitions, and I liked going there because of the ongoing PT and OT that it offered.

Yolanda and I went about getting groceries, cooking our meals, and getting acclimated to living independently again. Periodically, either John or Kelly would stop by to see how things were going. It was during this time that I took my survival of my near-death accident for granted, experimenting with just a small amount of alcohol again. My ability to procure any alcohol was difficult. I devised a way to get the small four-pack that I thought could be hidden easily.

At the time, we were calling for taxis to take us to the local Stop & Shop. The cab driver who picked us up was named Sam. Sam was also from Jamaica, thus he and Yolanda would get along well. He also worked with a partner at All-Island Taxi whose name was Chappy. Our fare for getting to and from the Stop & Shop was about $10 each way. Both Sam and Chappy surmised that as two American women, we might have more than adequate funds to pay a generous tip. On more than one occasion, Chappy agreed to pick up a four-pack of the wine of my choice, and I'd pay him $10, in addition to the fare we'd pay to go back and forth to Stop & Shop. While Yolanda and I went off to Stop & Shop, Chappy would go off to the liquor store and procure my four-pack. It was easy enough to shove a four-pack into the bag with groceries, and upon arrival home, I was quick to grab the bag with my "hidden" goods. Once inside, I'd get the bag with the goods to my bedroom and shove the four-pack into one of my dresser drawers or the closet. It sounds like I was so clever, but in the meantime, I was playing with fire, and at the same time denying to myself that there was anything wrong with what I was doing. It wasn't long before my "stash" had been discovered by Kelly. She was horrified, hurt, angry, and felt betrayed. How could I do such a thing, after all that had happened to me? How could I take that for granted?! I couldn't tell Kelly enough how sorry I was. Understandably, she was not ready to speak with me about it. After all that Kelly and John did for me to help me, and here I was, at the brink of screwing up my relationship with them. It wasn't until I'd been sober for almost six years that I was able to discuss the topic with them, and they were receptive to listening to me. These were the kinds of situations that proved to them that it was premature for me to live on my own again. Money was the other deciding factor.

In December 2013, I was facing eviction. In late December, I ended up in NUMC, in East Meadow, New York. Apparently, I had a grand mal seizure. My aide at the time, Thelma, called 911 and an ambulance and got me to the ER at NUMC. As it turned out, I hadn't taken my anti-seizure medication (common for brain injuries), Keppra, and that's what triggered my seizure.

OAK HOLLOW NURSING AND REHABILITATION CENTER, JANUARY 2014 TO FEBRUARY 2016

On January 13, 2014, I was discharged from NUMC, and I moved into Oak Hollow Nursing Center, in Middle Island, New York. Oak Hollow Nursing Center also offered physical, occupational, and speech therapy. Thankfully, at each place I was assessed and did not need much or any speech therapy, but I did avail myself of the physical and occupational therapy. At Oak Hollow, I had the pleasure of meeting Julie Schmid, a career RN for over forty-five years. Her daughter, Kimberly, worked there also. The resident base was varied in terms of age group, as was its staff. I enjoyed my time there, which lasted two years. One area that I found to be slightly deficient was its physical therapy department. Oak Hollow was acquired about the time I left there to go to Gurwin. Ultimately, under its new name Surge, the facility has implemented many changes, upgrading many of its services. But Julie Schmid will always be one of the most caring, compassionate nurses I encountered during my nine-plus-year journey of recovery.

During my stay at Oak Hollow, I had my first exposure to those who were Jehovah's Witnesses. The woman who came once a week was Doris Nemeth. Her husband was named Frank, and they had three boys. The whole family were Jehovah's Witnesses. I'd remembered Jehovah's Witnesses as people who stopped by our house growing up. They'd ring the bell and drop off literature, which I came to learn was called Watchtower. They'd stop and chat about Jehovah God, and they were usually very nice. But after their visits, it was never discussed in our home again. Doris proceeded to come every week and initiate discussions about God, and Jesus, and His ultimate ransom sacrifice by dying on the Cross at Calvary. Her line of discussion was compelling, and mainly I liked that there was some intellectual and spiritual stimulation. I liked Doris and Frank very much. After my stay at Oak Hollow, Doris made arrangements with other JWs to come and meet with me at Gurwin.

After my experience at Kessler, I was growing anxious to get back to the idea of me "running" again. At one point, one of the physical therapists at Oak Hollow suggested that we take a look at Gurwin and said that their physical and occupational therapy was "top notch."

Chapter Seventeen

Gurwin Jewish Nursing & Rehabilitation Center

My Home for Five Years

On February 26, 2016, I moved into Gurwin Jewish Nursing & Rehabilitation Center, in Commack, New York, where I am living now. My sister Donna was helpful in me getting into Gurwin, as she had already been a performer there, singing at their evening cabaret. The Gurwin story is a special one and answers the question, who gets into the nursing home business in the first place?

FOUNDING PRESIDENT OF GURWIN

"Joseph Gurwin was our founding President and benefactor, a kind and generous man whose dedication to philanthropy brought lasting joy and enhanced the quality of life for countless people throughout the United States, and throughout the world.

Mr. Gurwin came to New York from Lithuania when he was 16 years old, with only $100 in his pocket and the intention to send for his parents when he was financially able. Before he could, they perished in the Holocaust. Because he didn't have the opportunity to care for his own parents, he and his late wife, Rosalind, embraced the chance to name the Gurwin Center, and the opportunity to help care for the parents of others.

A familiar face at the Center, Mr. Gurwin took great pride in the services Gurwin provides, always mandating that we strive to be "the best of the best." He regularly attended resident events, and was committed to enhancing the quality of life for each resident. Mr. Gurwin considered it one of his greatest achievements that his dream of caring for those who cared for us became a reality.

While Mr. Gurwin is no longer with us, his generosity will live on, not only here at Gurwin, but also throughout the world where his many projects enrich the lives of the people they serve."

Source: Wikipedia, https://en.wikipedia.org/wiki/Joseph_Gurwin).

Chapter Seventeen A

Gurwin Jewish Nursing & Rehabilitation Center

Nursing: The Main Component

Skilled nursing care, both acute and sub-acute, are the main ingredients in staffing a nursing center, and the staff at Gurwin are very seasoned. They've had decades of nursing experience. The director of nursing at Gurwin is Lynette Rutherford. She has been a nurse for more than two decades. Reporting to her are the nursing care coordinators (NCCs). Kim Thomas, Meryl Lenner, Lizy Thomas, Elaine Searson, Brian Codrington, Chrissy Roach, and Sobi Biju are several of the NCCs, but there are several others who cover each unit on each shift. They cover many units, sometimes responsible for much of or the whole facility, if necessary. The NCCs visit each unit for which they are responsible, checking on the current activities on a given unit. In turn, the nurse manager on each unit, for each shift, is responsible for the delegation of assignments for the certified nursing assistants (CNAs) on each unit.

GURWIN STAFF

I can't say enough good about the staff at Gurwin, but I'll give it a shot. Overall, the staff are very competent, with skilled nursing care high on their priority list. There is staff at Gurwin, twenty-four hours a day, in three shifts: 7 a.m.–3 p.m. morning shift, 3 p.m.–11 p.m. evening shift, and the 11 p.m.–7 a.m. night shift, as people typically breathe twenty-four hours a day, last I checked.

MORNING SHIFT

This is the most active shift in the twenty-four hours staffed at Gurwin. The staff on this shift appear more alert and arrive ready to go. The "all staff report, please, all staff report" call is heard on the PA a bit earlier on this shift, as all staff are apprised of what's happened in the prior shift and what's anticipated in the current shift. The details need to be thorough and accurate. Taking "report" is serious business; thus, staff must be alert and attentive to the details shared.

On all the shifts, there is a designated NCC. There is also a nurse manager (or charge nurse) on each unit. She's the one who's in charge of delegating the CNA assignments. Depending on how many CNAs report for the shift, it will determine the resident count that each is assigned. There are twelve units at Gurwin, with roughly thirty-eight residents per unit. The more CNAs that show up, the lower the resident count, the more manageable the shift. For every task that a CNA must perform, everything must be documented. Gurwin uses the Optimus system, which allows for input on every area of a CNA's tasks. There are entries for ambulation (walking), meals (percentage eaten), bowel movements (S, M, L), dressing, and additional food items, fruit, ice cream, glass of water. Documenting can consume as much as an hour total (12 percent) of an eight-hour shift. Things that can add unnecessary time to their shift include incident reports. These can involve resident falls or other mishaps. These, too, must be documented and can be time-consuming, during an already busy shift.

I've come to fully appreciate all that the CNAs here have to do. Many of them are married and have children. While several of them are not married, they have one or more children and still come in to perform their duty. In the era of COVID-19, I've come to marvel and admire what all of these courageous, ambitious, and selfless people are capable of doing each day. And they still have their personal lives. They struggle to pay their bills and deal with their school-age children's school activities and education, all the while wishing they could catch a break and maybe find someone to help them with their enormous workload. Unfortunately, that often doesn't mean a man (although many might like one). They are confident in themselves, they've set goals, they care for the residents on their assignment, they love their children, and sometimes, they like to have a good time!

Below, I write a little about each nurse, their role in the nursing hierarchy, and my interaction with them. Later, I do the same for all of the CNAs I have interacted with during my stay at Gurwin.

Donna Shannon: Until early 2020, Donna was the 4 East unit nurse manager on the morning shift. Donna had been a nurse for what she describes as "since the Mesozoic Era." In 2020, Donna retired, at the age of seventy-four. She was great at what she did every day, and her cool, calm, mature demeanor will be sorely missed. Donna has a daughter named Debbie, who has triplet boys who were born on my birthday, May 6. These are all linkages from Gurwin to me.

Roseanne Fienga: Current nurse manager on 4 East on the morning shift. Taking Donna Shannon's role, Roseanne Fienga had already been a charge nurse on 4 East, but now she is in that role permanently. Roseanne is a great nurse; she's funny, no-nonsense, good at what she does every day. When I used to have my head bandaged daily, the resulting look was like what she called a *Cupalina*, or a dome, in Italian. We got many laughs out of that one. If Roseanne were on the show *Laverne & Shirley*, she'd be Laverne!

Rowena Ormita: 4 East unit charge nurse from 3 p.m. to 11 p.m. Rowena is originally from the Philippines. She is a very competent and caring nurse who also does her job quite well. She's been a nurse at Gurwin for seventeen years, but her career as an RN goes back twenty-five years. I knew Rowena mostly from my two years on 4 East.

Lizy Thomas: Lizy is an NCC for many units, sometimes the entire facility, at Gurwin, on whatever shift she works. She is definitely not one to mess with. She can be intimidating, which is why many CNAs fear her. I used to be intimidated by her, too. But when I started to refer to her as Priyanka (as in Priyanka Chopra, the dark-haired, red-lipped attractive star of *Quantico* who is married to Nick Jonas), she seemed startled that I was being so kind to her. Fact is, I like her very much. I respect her role as NCC, and I know the responsibility that comes with her job. Understanding that, we get along with our mutual love of the Lord, and mutual respect.

Kim Thomas, a Gurwin veteran

Kim Thomas: Kim is an NCC at Gurwin. She started at Gurwin in 2001, and she's been here all twenty years. She started as a CNA, then went back to school twice, to receive her Licensed Practical Nurse (LPN), and then her RN. During this same time period, Kim had three children. They are twenty-two, nineteen, and five years old. Her oldest is a boy, Kion. Her nineteen-year-old is a girl, Kijanai (who also works at Gurwin), and her youngest, a girl, is five, and her name is Kya. Kim is also a grandmother! She has an adorable granddaughter named Kali. I guess they've adopted the Kardashian system of names—every one is spelled with a K. Kim is the "cool" NCC. Certainly no-nonsense, on a professional basis, but it's always nice to have her on the unit.

Brian Codrington: Brian is an NCC at Gurwin. The first time I met Brian, I was down on the second floor, walking down the middle hallway. At the next turn, I made a left, and then another left, taking the shortcut to the elevators. Brian asked me where I was headed, and I replied, "To the family room Brown Bag Room, to use the microwave." He asked if I was permitted to walk on my own (I was), and he just told me his name. I had no idea who he was, or what he did at Gurwin. Much later, I found Brian to be a helpful person when I was in search of chewing gum. Kindly, Brian would stop by and drop off a half pack of gum, and always referred me to Kim Thomas as another likely source (thank you, Kim). Brian has been in nursing since 1994. He's been at Gurwin for eleven years and has been an NCC for the last several of those years at Gurwin.

Brian Codrington, NCC at Gurwin

Marcia Hercules: Marcia is the unit nurse manager from 3 p.m. to 11 p.m. on 4 West. Marcia, pronounced Mar-see-uh, has been a nurse for fifteen years. She is extremely sweet, caring, and kind to me. I think we get along well. She does her job very well. That means she also adheres to the rules, at all times. The Health Insurance Portability and Accountability Act of 1996, or HIPAA laws, relate to patient privacy rules and dictate that a nurse should not give out any sensitive information about another patient's treatment plan, medications, or current condition. We had a slight bit of friction one night on this matter. I had been asking about my roommate Florence Yudenfriend's medication and whether or not she had taken something that would make her sleepy. Even when I told her that Florence's children tell me everything that goes on with Florence, she said, "That's fine but you'll have to ask them about her medication list." Marcia stood by the rules, and I respect and admire her for that. And I love her just the same.

Loune Alex Cantave: Loune is the unit nurse manager on the evening shift. Loune has been at Gurwin for fifteen years. A bright light, always helpful, kind, and considerate, she's also very efficient.

Chrissy Roach: Chrissy is an NCC at Gurwin. When Chrissy answers the phone in the nursing office, she says, "Hello, nursing, this is Chrissy." When you ask her last name, she says: "Roach, like the bug." I guess she's gotten used to responding in that manner. Head them off at the pass, answer it for them! I like that!

Anna Buchta: Anna is the 3 East nurse manager on the evening shift. Anna is a very efficient, get-the-job-done-now kind of nurse. She's of Swedish and Polish descent. She's pretty and has an athletic build. Although the evening shift appears that it might be a bit more relaxing, it is anything but that. Think the day shift in reverse.

The activity starts with taking report and setting the assignments for each CNA. After that, everything is geared to dinnertime. Pre-COVID-19 lockdown, all residents went to the dining room on each unit. Many residents have their own "assigned" seating. Basically, it's where they choose to sit, and do so, every night. Generally, where they sit at dinner applies to lunchtime, as well. Getting the dinner process going is a pretty hectic activity. CNAs line up to set up trays for each resident. The trays are generally set up with silverware—knife, fork, teaspoon, and soup spoon—along with a dinner napkin. Each CNA is usually familiar with their assigned residents' drink preferences. Thus, they'll add a large cup with ice or ice water, and a coffee or tea preference, before the tray is delivered to the resident's table or room (if they eat in-room).

After dinner, residents can attend "evening cabaret," or stay on-unit and watch TV. Some may have a shower night. These activities usually wrap up between 8:30 and 9 p.m., after which the bedtime process begins. Each resident gets a gown and a towel, and either the assigned CNA or the resident will get them ready for bed. Some residents go to bed quite early, like 8 p.m., and many more usually between 9 and 10 p.m., and other late-night folks (like me) stay up till 11 p.m. or midnight. For me, I have used most evenings to work on my manuscript. Slowly but surely, it's getting done! Finally.

Kayla Miga: East for the morning shift. Kayla is a young pretty RN on 3 East. She's been in nursing since 2014, starting as an LPN, and ultimately going back to school to achieve her RN. She brings a lot of youthful energy to the unit and can hold her own under pressure. I've also discovered (through observation) that Kayla is a lover of body art. Here is Kayla's picture upon her graduation, having received her Registered Nursing degree. Congratulations, Kayla!

Newly engaged RN, Kayla Miga, having received her RN

Deidre Gaither: Diedre has been a nurse for twenty-two years. Most of that time, twenty-one years, have been at Gurwin. She's very capable and seems easy to work with. Depending on the shift or the unit, I've seen her take the role of nurse manager. Deidre, or "Dee," has a husband and three children, ages thirty-two, twenty-six, and eighteen. She has two boys and a girl; the girl is their middle child.

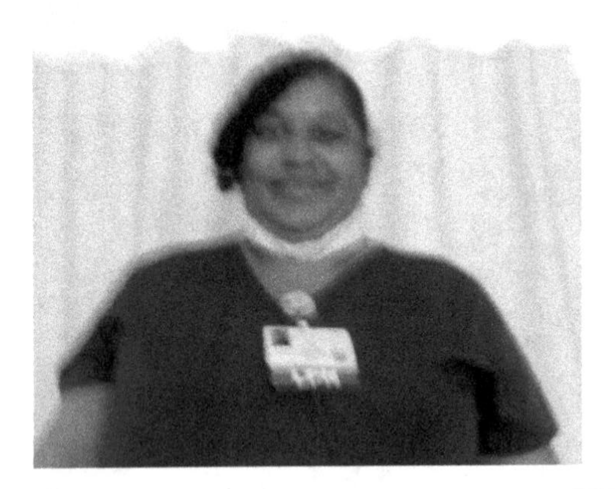

Deidre Gaither: Twenty-two-year veteran LPN

Brianna Taormina: Brianna is a nurse on the day shift. When I first met Brianna, she was on 4 East. She was youthful, energetic, and lively. She originally had blondish colored hair, but then she went dark, or brunette. After she changed her hair color, I took to referring to her as "Brownanna," to which she responds. She still has all of the youthful, energetic qualities that I always liked about her, and she's moving to be a nurse on 3 East, where I live now.

Brianna Taormina

Katie Seikel: I first met Katie as a nurse on 3 East. She is a sweetheart. She now works on 3 North in the Schachne Pavilion. Katie has been at Gurwin for twenty-one years. She started in 1999 and started as a CNA. In 2012, she returned to school and is now an LPN. I also came to learn that she is the mother of another Gurwin employee, John Peter Rajotte, who worked both in the gift shop at Gurwin and was also a supervisor in the Volunteer Department, training all new volunteers and showing them the ropes. John Peter and his wife, Amanda, are a beautiful couple. In August 2019, John Peter and Amanda had their first baby, a girl, and they named her Logan Riley. Her arrival on August 10 brought much joy to not only the happy couple but to Katie as well. One morning, Katie mentioned that she would be visiting her new granddaughter in the afternoon, after she got off from work. I asked her to send me a picture when she got to the hospital. This was one of my favorite pictures. I told Katie, "You clean up nice."

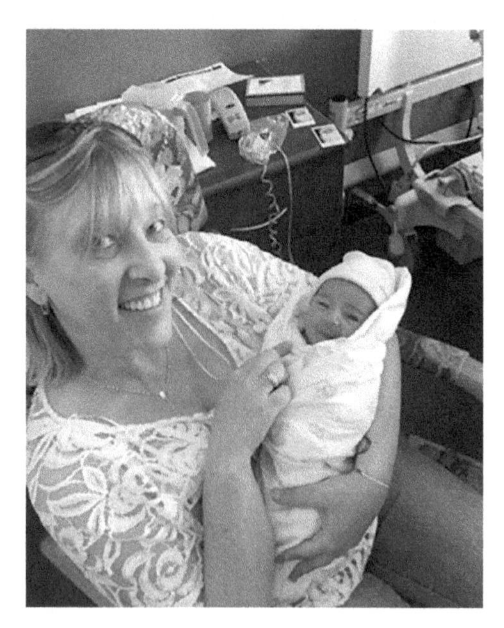

Katie Seikel and her newborn granddaughter, Logan

Martha Ababio: Martha is a nurse on the evening shift. Martha is a tall, very pretty RN at Gurwin. She's been in nursing since 2007, starting as a CNA at Gurwin. She kept going to school and ultimately achieved her RN status in 2015. After achieving her RN, she also went to work for the VA, in Northport, while working per diem at Gurwin. It's just one more example of dedication, hard work, and how it helps people to realize their goals.

SPECIALIZED NURSING: WOUND CARE AT GURWIN

There is a specialized group at Gurwin that focuses on wound care. The supervisor in that group is Johanna Graham. She's been in nursing for more than twenty years.

Wound care deals with all types of wounds caused by surgery, as well as compression wounds (bedsores), and wounds as a complication caused by diabetes. As those who've ever had them know, the pain from wounds can be excruciating. Such was the case for my recent former roommate, Estelle Goodman. Her screaming that "something is stabbing my back" was the result of a bedsore that Estelle had prior to her passage just a few days after. She was a month shy of turning ninety-six. I miss her sweet laugh.

CNA (CERTIFIED NURSING ASSISTANT)

Certified nursing assistants are the entry-level positions in nursing. Arguably, they have the toughest job. They get more than their fair share of the "dirty work." They get to do all that is *not* required of a nurse, whether an LPN or an RN. Upon arrival for their shift, the nurse manager "takes report." She reviews what happened on the prior shift, whether there were any issues, or incidents that required an incident report, and whether the issue has been resolved. Next, the nurse will assign the CNAs their resident assignments.

The allocation of residents to CNAs will be determined by the number of CNAs who show up for the shift. If they're short CNAs, they end up being "overloaded" with too many residents with which they are assigned. It doesn't make the CNAs too happy, for sure.

I've gotten to know most all of the CNAs who've been assigned to me. Since my arrival, that's been four units (4 West, 4 East, 4 North, 3 East) and seven rooms (477, 466, 452, 436, 425, 369, and 366). I've always been impressed about the jobs they have and their personal lives (which must be managed). Many of them have children, some very young. Some are continuing their education to move up in pay grade. Somehow, they make it work, both while at Gurwin, and the job they'll return to upon arriving home. I have tremendous respect and admiration for all of these women and men, both young and more mature. They come in, do their job, encounter some difficult situations, yet they always manage to remain pleasant and polite and helpful to all whom they are assigned! God bless you, CNAs! You are my peer group, my friends (whether or not you agree), because I genuinely care about all of you!

There are numerous CNAs with which I've become close (whether they know it, or agree with it, or not). To even those with which we've had a thorny patch or two, I still find ways to appreciate the tough job they have to do, yet they do it every day.

Katrina Robinson Hairston: My self-proclaimed BFF (who looks like Kerry Washington, from *Scandal*). Katrina has gone above and beyond in assisting me. Most notable was when she came to work at 3:30 a.m. to accompany me to then–North Shore University Hospital (now Northwell Health), as I had to be there at 5 a.m. to be prepped for a 7 a.m. surgery. She waited with me up until I was wheeled in to the OR for a surgery that would last fourteen hours—an Ironman-length surgery. The surgery ultimately was extended into the next day due to a complication, but it was resolved. (My throat had gotten swollen around my intubation tube; I required two large doses of steroids to resolve it.) Total surgery time, as measured from intubation to extubation, was thirty-two hours! Sadly, Katrina Robinson Hairston passed away in 2019 from a bleeding ulcer. After Katrina left Gurwin, her health insurance lapsed and she was unable to see a doctor, which possibly could have prevented her death. Rest in peace, my beautiful friend! You will be very missed!

My self-proclaimed BFF: Katrina Robinson Hairston; you will be missed!

Cassandra Joseph Moise: I've known Cassandra since my two-plus years on 4 East. She's been a CNA for seven years. She's very competent, capable, and kind, and I like her very much. I hadn't seen her for a while as I made my moves to 4 North, and now back on 3 East, and just recently, in October 2020, I learned that she'll be moving to 3 East! In January 2020, she had a baby girl and named her Avery. It is her and her husband's first child. They are very happy to be parents! Cassandra always had a beautiful figure and she's now working on losing all of her "baby weight." She already looks great. She'll be back to Sultry Cassandra in no time.

Cassandra Joseph Moise, before she was Avery's mom

Karin Joseph: Karin is a nurse on the morning shift. She has thirty years of experience at Gurwin. Karin was my day shift nurse while I was on 4 West. She was always very efficient and never wanted any nonsense. In the end, she always had a kind heart and was eager to please.

Margaret Dasque: Margaret has had an eighteen-year tenure at Gurwin. Margaret is another very compassionate nurse who works the morning shift throughout the week. She's dedicated, is helpful to new nursing staff to show them the ropes, and she's a great example of how to comport oneself as a nurse. I jokingly call Margaret the "food-pusher," as she's always inquiring of the residents if they would like another piece of bread, or fruit, or cake. Sadly (for us residents who loved her), Margaret moved to Adult Day Care. It was a move she liked; however, in the pandemic, Adult Day Care has been shut down until it's safe to re-open (i.e., until there's a vaccine).

Zushia: Zushia, pronounced Zeh-shuh, is a CNA and works the 3 p.m. to 11 p.m. shift on 4 East. She's relatively new to Gurwin and only been a CNA since 2016. One of her goals is to complete the requirements for her LPN. She's only twenty years old but is poised, seeming older. Her name is Polish and means "Sophia." She's excited to be included in my book.

Islande Pelony: Islande, pronounced Iz-len, has gone on a couple of medical visits with me lately, and she was helpful and attentive. She has big, beautiful, brown eyes, and I compliment her on her eyes often. She was the one who told me of Katrina's passage.

Chilene Bijou: Chilene, pronounced Chi-Len, works the morning shift. When I started this book, and it came to talking about Chilene Bijou, she was a day shift CNA. Currently, she switched to doing double shifts three days a week. No matter the shift, without question, Chilene has been one of my favorite aides at Gurwin. She typically arrives early, she's very efficient, and when I was wearing them, she knew how to braid my hair very well. Wearing a braid, or braids, was a new thing for me, but while I had them, I used to seek out aides who know how to braid hair (this was in 2017, as my hair started to grow post my new scalp installation). She has a ten-year-old daughter named Sabrina, whom I'm anxious to meet. Chilene tells me that if Sabrina doesn't see her mom going to work, and make eye contact, that Sabrina will cry and call her mom the second she gets to Gurwin, bemoaning the fact that she didn't get to see her! I really look forward to meeting this little girl! Chilene has switched to doing doubles almost every weekend she works. Those are grueling days. She's also going to school for respiratory therapy. I admire all these very hardworking women!

Chilene Bijou and newborn Sabrina

Scherley Simon: Scherley is a CNA on the evening shift. Without question, Scherley was one of my favorite aides on the evening shift while I was on 4 East at Gurwin. She's beautiful, very sweet, and extremely competent. Her nickname among her family is "Luscious Lips." She has gone above and beyond, helping me get cleaned up after a bathroom accident at the very end of her shift, and she did so without complaints about me to others on the evening shift. It's bad enough that I have to wear adult diapers (now pull-ups), but my pride had to be checked at the door at Gurwin. I've also said, "There's nothing brief about a brief" here at Gurwin. All of them require a bit of adjusting in the crotch area to make the brief a bit more comfortable than briefs are originally designed. Scherley has a son, Jasiya, who's now twenty years old. Scherley lives with her boyfriend, Mike, whom I call "Magic Mike." Scherley says he lives up to the name. (I can only dream of such things until my freedom occurs.)

Scherley "Luscious Lips" Simon

Granville Ferguson: Granville is a CNA on 4 East for the evening shift. Ferguson, or "Fergie" (as most call him), is a six-foot-two-inch Jamaican guy. I find him to be attractive, yet there's no nonsense between residents and employees (too bad). He is a good CNA, very efficient, and usually, the male CNAs work with male residents. Fergie is married and has two children, a boy and a girl, both teenagers. At one point, it was Deb who made some suggestive remarks, but it was made clear that Fergie is a "loyal, married man" and doesn't go there anymore. To me, being a loyal, married man makes a man even more attractive. In December 2018, Fergie had, as part of his shift one night, to attend to a resident who had died. His name was Philip Cangemi. Philip had two daughters: Deanna and Kathy. Philip died from natural causes, at ninety-eight years old. Earlier in his life, Philip had been a tailor, as his profession, in the 1940s. After Philip passed, Fergie was charged with escorting his body down to the morgue at Gurwin. I recently had occasion to speak with Deanna, and she told me that the weekend prior, August 8, Philip would have been one hundred years old (he was born August 8, 1920).

Fergie and his boy

Jodian Jarrett: Jodian is a CNA on the evening shift. Jodi has been a CNA for ten years. She's worked on 2 South, 4 East, and now 3 East, where I currently reside. Jodi is very efficient, very pleasant, and I'm always happy when she works my assignment. She's not married, but she does have a son, Aiden, who's four years old.

Jodian Jarrett, a definite favorite for me

Iris Larios: Iris is a CNA on the day shift, on 3 East. Iris Larios is a very sweet and efficient CNA. She has two children, whose names I love. She has a daughter, Serenity, who's eleven, and a son, Christian, who's eight years old. She's engaged to be married to Brandon Drummond. Again, I marvel at these young, mature women who show up for their duty every day while also caring for young children and a personal life. God bless Iris. I hope she and Brandon are very happy together and that they have a wonderful new family life together.

Iris Larios, great at being a CNA and a mom

Karline Ferguson: Initially, Karline and I didn't have an easy go of coming to an understanding of each other. She was quick to scold me if ever I was doing something non-kosher. From observation, however, I came to realize that Karline did care what people thought of her, and she used her abrupt responses as a protective mechanism. The day I found out she had a son, Reese, changed everything for me. All of a sudden, her abrupt, scolding responses could be viewed as a protective mom who would also go to any lengths to protect her child. In this instant, her "child" could be me. She was just looking out for my best interests, and based on prior experience with other residents, she'd seen people get hurt doing what I was attempting to do. It really does come down to "walking in her shoes" to understand from where she was really coming.

Farah Pintro: Always pleasant and kind, Farah is a very good CNA. She's been at Gurwin for fourteen years. She also has two children: a boy, twenty-seven, and a girl, fifteen. She is always helpful when she can be, even when other staff needs her help. One might call her "a good egg." It's always a pleasure when Farah is on our unit.

Sweet and friendly Farah Pintro

Julianny Martinez: Julianny is a CNA on the night shift. Working the overnight shift seems to work for several aides, such as Julianny (pronounced like the former mayor of NYC). She has four children: Chelsi (eleven), Skylar (eight), Hailey (five), and Carter (two). For most of the shift, her kids are asleep. Tonight, this ambitious gal is working a double, from 3 p.m. to 11 p.m. and 11 p.m. to 7 a.m.—sixteen hours of nonstop graveyard shift fun. I find that double is about the worst you can have, but many seem to like it; it's quieter, and most of the residents are asleep for most of both shifts.

Julianny Martinez, mom of four prefers the overnight shift

Misbah Khalid: Misbah is a CNA on the night shift. I met Misbah first as a ride-along for one of my medical appointments. More recently, she's been a CNA on the night shift on 3 East. Misbah has a five-year-old daughter named Sara. Misbah very pretty, nice, and always responsive to my generally simple needs during the overnight shift. She's been a CNA for about three years. Her longer-term plan is to attend medical school. This girl is definitely going places! I am very impressed!

Misbah Khalid and daughter, Sara

Eliana Lujan: Eliana is a phlebotomist. By far, she is the most gentle vampire I have ever had the pleasure of being stuck with a needle by. No pain. No muss, no fuss; she is the best. It's over before I know it! I wish there were more like her! She's always pleasant to see around the facility.

THE CLINIC AT GURWIN

Along with doctors that attend to each unit, there are doctors that come into Gurwin in many areas of specialty. Doctors from gastroenterology visit Gurwin once a month. There's usually a long list of people lined up to get into to see him or her. Dermatologists also come in once a month. As I was a patient in this area, I first visited with the doctor at Gurwin, who referred me to a dermatologist at Stony Brook Dermatology, which set in motion a series of three visits per week at Stony Brook Dermatology to receive short-wave UVB therapy to treat my psoriasis. To accomplish this, it required transport three times per week and regularly scheduled UVB light therapy. Ultimately, it was very effective and was superior in one main respect over immunosuppressant drugs, which are now used fairly often. Immunosuppressant drugs were not good for me to use, as I was still undergoing surgeries. Also, more recently, in the era of COVID-19, immunosuppressants are *not* to be used by immuno-ompromised patients. "Manning" the clinic is Annmarie Trimigliozzi Bianchini. She's been with Gurwin for fifteen years. Also acting as transporters for the clinic are Marlene O'Connor and, for a time, Leone Harvey (until she returned to school in 2019).

Annmarie Trimigliozzi Bianchini

Marlene O'Connor

My favorite ride-along, Leone Harvey

CHAPTER SEVENTEEN B

GURWIN JEWISH NURSING & REHABILITATION CENTER: LIFE WITH THE EMERGENCY BRAKE ON, FOR NOW

I arrived at Gurwin on February 26, 2016, and presently, on August 16, 2020, I'm just a month away from my four-and-a-half-year anniversary at Gurwin, and nine years since my near-death accident, on August 31, 2011. Time has gone by quickly, but I made the choice to be productive in an environment that I hope to leave within a year, while appreciating the valuable currency of time that I would never have had if I never had my accident. I've chosen to recognize this time as that which will allow me to finally complete my long-hoped-for book project.

Along with all the other therapy I receive at Gurwin, I also receive psychotherapy. I've had a variety of therapists spend various amounts of time with me, but lately (for at least the last three years) I've been seen by Dr. Christine Marra, a highly qualified PhD in psychology. Dr. Marra has been speaking to me about my life, both pre- and post-accident. We've discussed my Wall Street years, my marriage, my guilt over my transgressions, Gary's death, my history with alcohol, my feelings about living at a nursing home, as well as all my surgeries, and what plans I have for the future. Today, she summed it up nicely: it was as if I were "living my life with the emergency brake on"!

Emergency brakes: we need them in an emergency, but left on, the rubber on the tires burn and the car doesn't operate properly, if at all. But it is a good analogy to describe my life right now. That's why taking life one day at a time is the best way for me to operate. I need to maintain my patience, and remain hopeful, as I won't accept that I'll never be able to live independently again. In order for me to do that, I need to explore all of my options, and very importantly, figure out my earnings limitations in the context of Medicaid income limits. Getting Medicaid was a lengthy and involved process. My attorney, Arnold Reiter, and his paralegal, Joan Tie, spent much time and energy with the myriad of paperwork necessary. My dad and my mom also had to go to bat for me to qualify. After hearing all that they had to say, I was authorized to receive Medicaid. The once financially successful Wall Street analyst was reduced to being subsidized by federal Medicaid insurance benefits, and for Social Security Disability (SSD) benefits. Having once enjoyed making tens of thousands of dollars per month, my full monthly income now—my SSD ($1,700), a pension from Gary's employment with AT&T ($1,000), and a small pension for me from my ten years at Lehman Brothers ($700)—is approximately $3,500 per month (25 percent of my monthly cost at Gurwin). The remainder (75 percent, or $11,500) of my monthly living costs at Gurwin ($15,000) is subsidized by Medicaid.

Along with working with Dr. Marra, I've also been evaluated by neuro-psychologist Dr. Myling Sumanti. She evaluated my current cognitive state from a neurosurgeon's perspective.

> "Neuropsychology is a branch of psychology and neurology that aims to understand how the structure and function of the brain relate

> to specific psychological processes. It is scientific in its approach and shares an information processing view of the mind with cognitive psychology and cognitive science," according to https://www.sciencedaily.com/terms/neuropsychology.htm.

Dr. Sumanti gave me a full battery of tests to determine my level of cognition, following my traumatic brain injury. These were like no other test I had ever taken. They seem to be designed to test the brain's ability to detect and then realize the type of information being sought. For instance, there were a series of words—color names written in different colored ink, but the words didn't match the ink colors. For instance, you would read the word "red" but the colored ink was blue. She would ask me to say the color, not the word. Using the example I just gave, I'd say "blue," even though the word said "red." It might sound simple but in the midst of the test, it could become a bit maddening. Add to that, part of the test, at certain points, I'd have to start counting in reverse, by seven. After reading several colors, she'd say, "Start from ninety-seven." And I'd have to answer: ninety, eight-three, seventy-six, sixty-nine, sixty-two. Again, it *sounds* simple.

And as the tests would continue, they got harder and took quite some time. I'd be asked to draw a picture from memory of a picture in a book. Suffice it to say that these were not easy tests. Once completed, Dr. Sumanti would evaluate my responses and return her analysis of my performance of these tests. To me, these tests seemed analogous to walking, chewing gum, and throwing a tennis ball in the air, all at the same time. But I liked them! I find the field of neuropsychology fascinating, and Dr. Sumanti is a true scientist. Thank you, Dr. Sumanti!

During the evaluation of my performance, Dr. Marra sat in for the review of the findings. Generally, Dr. Sumanti acknowledged that my tests were intentionally hard, in order to evaluate the level of recovery, in the physical brain, as it pertained to the psychological process. Her findings were that many of my cognitive scores were high, but that in certain areas I demonstrated rash or poor judgment. For example, I went looking to see if Dr. Sumanti was on Facebook, and upon finding her, I sent a friend request. That was a poor decision, in her evaluation, as (1) she could not accept my friend request due to the doctor-patient relationship that would make it inappropriate, and (2) it's just not something she would do, as her personal preference. She suggested that I ought to have a backstop, or person I should check with prior to acting on impulse. She suggested that Dr. Marra would be a good point person.

Chiropractic Care by Dr. David Shapiro

A vital area of care for me has been the Chiropractic care by Dr. David Shapiro. He visits with me and treats me for my ongoing neck and back pain that usually results from my many hours at the computer. Dr. Shapiro has been extremely helpful with his expert hands and a useful tool called the 'Activator'. It hits upon many of the pressure points in my neck and back that relieves the pain greatly and leaves me feeling much more relaxed and pain-free as I head back to my computer.

Chapter Seventeen C

Gurwin Nursing and Rehabilitation Center Facility

Where I've Stayed at Various Points

Since arriving at Gurwin in February 2016, I've resided on many units. I started at Gurwin on 4 West, in the Weinberg Building (a newer building added after opening in 1988). After my sixteenth surgery, in August 2016, I was moved to 4 East, where I remained for two and a half years, in two different rooms (466 and 452). In the latter part of 2018, I was moved to 4 North, in the Schachne Pavilion (the original building). I was there for about six months, during which both of my parents passed away. While on 4 North, I was in two different rooms (436 and 425). After the death of my father, I was offered a room back in the Weinberg Building, which I eagerly accepted. The rooms in the Weinberg Building offer significantly more living and storage space. I compare the two as living at the Ritz Carlton (Weinberg) versus the Holiday Inn Express (Schachne). The Schachne Pavilion was the original part of Gurwin, when it began as a 300-bed nursing facility. It had been a Commack middle school, and the Rainbow Room (used for recreational events and evening cabaret) had been the school's gymnasium, replete with a basketball court. The Weinberg was built later and housed 160 additional beds.

4 West: My First Stop at Gurwin

When I first arrived at Gurwin in February 2016, I was fifty-six years old. My new room there was room 477. There, I learned the routine of being at Gurwin: mealtimes were held in the dining room for 4 West, just one door down from my room. Mealtimes in the dining room were generally just lunch and dinner. Breakfast was usually in my room. The three meals were the main activity each day, although physical and occupational therapy usually preceded or were just after lunch (unless specified by the PT personnel). Recreational therapy hosted activities for residents, and they occurred in the afternoon (around 2 or 2:30 p.m.) and generally lasted between one hour and one and a half hours, depending on the activity or entertainment.

On 4 West, for the 3 p.m. to 11 p.m. evening shift, the CNA who usually took charge was a guy named Sherman Gonzalez. He was the one who orchestrated the flow of dinner. When CNAs came into the dining room to pick up trays and deliver them to residents, Sherman was the one who maintained a constant flow of trays moving and dinners being served. If additional food items or supplies were necessary, he was the one to call downstairs to Nutritional Services, and a runner was usually dispatched to provide the necessary food or materials.

4 EAST: RESPIRATORY THERAPY, OR THE VENT UNIT

When Gurwin added a vent unit, designated as a floor with ventilator-only rooms, Gurwin's population became more skewed to a younger age. The Vent Unit, on 4 East, which was started by Robert Heidelberger in 1999, mandated an area requiring specialized, respiratory therapy—trained personnel. Most all of the RT staff have been at Gurwin for many years, having acquired initial training at other facilities. Jean, Elaine, Biju Jose, Wayne Fray (aka Kaiser), Paulette, and Nidia are among the qualified respiratory personnel at Gurwin. As Robert Heidelberger retired in 2019, Delta Young is now the head of the respiratory unit on 4 East. I wonder how much these team members could have been helpful during the coronavirus pandemic. Hopefully, they'll never have to know.

Robert Heidelberger, founder of the Vent Unit at Gurwin

4 EAST: MY NEXT STOP, FOR OVER TWO YEARS

I was on 4 West from February to mid-August 2016. On August 15, I had my thirty-two-hour surgery. After my stay at North Shore University Hospital (now Northwell Health), I returned to Gurwin, where I learned that my old room, 477, was no longer available, and I'd been moved to 4 East, to Room 466A. I was the only occupant until Kelly Dolan moved in to join me. After six months or more, Kelly was moved to Room 452A. That was a help for her, as her neck positioning did not easily allow for her to see the TV. Bed A was perfect to meet Kelly's need. Shortly thereafter, Bascilia Jayes moved into 466B. Bascilia was a very sweet woman with a lovely family, who came to visit and tend to her daily. She had a son, Arturo Cancinos, and daughters, Sandra and Silvia. There was also a brother, Jorge. They visited often and spent much time while visiting. Arturo tenderly cared for his mom, saying, "All her life, she did for me, now, it's my time to do for her." In late 2017, I was offered to move to room 452. Turns out, I'd be back with Kelly! In late 2018, I was asked to move into a new room, in the Schachne building, 4 North. Danielle Marblestone, my social worker, sold it to me: "Well, you'll be closer to the front of the building, for when you're going to move out of here." Sold.

While I was on 4 East, I began to have numerous outgoing medical visits. First, these included post-op visits with my surgeon, Dr. Armen Kasabian. Ultimately, I was going to see him or his physician's assistant almost weekly for more than a year. I also commenced a course of UV therapy treatments at Stony Brook Dermatology, also for about a year, three times per week. For transport, the unit receptionist on 4 East, Gloria Alvarez, would arrange for the pick-up and return for these visits.

Gloria Alvarez and her children

THE AMBULETTE EXPERIENCE

Gurwin uses an ambulette service called Care & Comfort, or C&C. Care & Comfort has a fleet of vans and buses equipped to transport varying amounts of wheelchairs and people.

Each van or bus is equipped with a lift. It's either a side-loader or a rear-loader. The lift is designed to lift the wheelchair, with its occupant and the driver, who will maneuver the wheelchair once in the van. It sounds simple but I've become somewhat fascinated by the equipment design that seamlessly moves the wheelchair/occupant into the van, without having to manually get the chair up in the air, and the person with it. When the lift is on the ground, we are wheeled onto the ramp and once there, the rear plate lifts up, creating a backstop, and the driver then presses a button and activates the lift. As the motorized lift rises up, eventually it becomes level with the floor of the van, and then the alternate side backplate slides down and then slides into the grooves of the waiting plate, allowing the wheelchair to be wheeled into the van, and then positioned to be secured into the van floor. Once in the van, there are two main things that need to happen: (1) the wheelchair needs to be secured into the floor, and (2) the patient needs to be secured into the chair through the use of seat belts around the patient's waist.

Care & Comfort could be very frustrating at times. I had occasions where I, along with my ride-along CNA, had to wait for three hours; one time the doctor's office closed and we were left to wait in the lobby or outside. It was that time and another occasion when I suggested that the company change its name to "Careless and Discomfort." That was definitely the exception versus the rule (thankfully), and most times the rides were on time, and the drivers were pleasant, and we could have a decent conversation or listen to music. I got to know most of the drivers by name as I had so many appointments. Everyone at the company knew Dallas, as he'd been there for so long. There was Ernesto (one of my favorites). He is a very sweet Latino man from Ecuador. He used to like to play his salsa and merengue music. There was also Bill, Michael, Tito (like Puente), Chris, and so many others. Generally, they were all friendly and each had to defer to the dispatcher to determine if they could wait for the duration of the visit versus having to call and wait the mandatory "hour" for another ride to pick us up.

Death Is a Part of Life

As a nursing home with a large portion of the population being eighty-six (median) or older, death is a normal part of the coming and going here. Since my arrival in 2016, I've borne witness to the passage of many residents here. On 4 East, there was Philip Cangemi, who passed in December 2018 at age ninety-eight. Then, in February 2020, right before the coronavirus pandemic hit, Irving Fuchs died at ninety-eight, just four months before his ninety-ninth birthday. Of all people here, at Gurwin, Irving got out before the world stopped. He would have hated the quarantine and virtual lockdown—curtailing all ability to move about Gurwin, its facilities, and halting all activities in which Irving liked to participate. He loved to play Bingo, blackjack, and three-card poker, winning at most everything he played. All to win a scratch-off lottery ticket, which most often did not yield anything. But it was the playing that Irving most enjoyed—raising his hand thirty-two times for the number of Bingo games he'd won. Irving also enjoyed Gurwin's outings to restaurants. He loved Bertucci's in Hauppauge. He ordered virtually the same meal every time: chicken parmesan (non-kosher, by the way), served with pasta and warm rolls with butter. Some coffee or tea, and an ice cream, and Irving would be in heaven. One of the recreational therapists, Don Mulvey, was terribly sad upon learning that Irving was gone. Irving longed for Sunday to come, so the card games could resume. I even posted about Irving's passage on Facebook:

Irving Fuchs in 1940

IRVING FUCHS

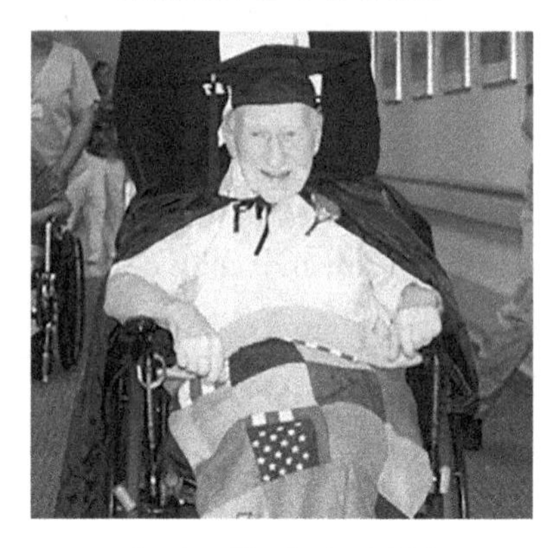

Irving Fuchs in 2018

On February 4, 2020, the world has lost a special man. Irving Fuchs was ninety-eight and a half. Irving was a great man. A storied, WWII Veteran, who flew in the US Air Force, and went on numerous bombing missions over India and Burma. After returning home at the end of the war, Irving married his wife, Mary, and had three children: his sons, Stanley, and Richard, and daughter Karen. He has ten grandchildren and eleven great-grandchildren. Irving became a letter carrier for the US Postal Service, to support his family. He did that job, faithfully for more than forty years. As a co-resident, at Gurwin, all I can tell you is that Irving Fuchs will be sorely missed by so many here. While at Gurwin, Irving was the Valedictorian for the Adult Ed Program, two years, while at Gurwin. Up until his last days, Irving was sharp, a very kind man, funny, and always had a comeback for a comment. He was also a mean 3-card poker player. He will be sorely missed by the Therapeutic Recreation Dept, at Gurwin, especially Don Mulvey. Rest in Peace, Irving Fuchs. You deserve it. We know you are with our Lord. God bless and sincere condolences to the entire Fuchs family.

Rosemarie Scinicariello was part of my 4 East experience. She shared a dining table with Irving Fuchs and Philip Cangemi for more than two years until they passed. Rosemarie is vice president of the resident council at Gurwin. She originally came from Bay Ridge, Brooklyn, same as my hometown in Brooklyn. As she's Italian, she became very friendly with Susan Fantazia, wife of Philip Fantazia, whom I wrote about in an earlier chapter. The most interesting time in Rosemarie's life began in the early 1960s when she went to Paris in her junior year at college, at Mount St. Vincent's, in the Riverdale section of the Bronx. She studied French and Italian. She studied in Paris for nine months and Florence for four months. She graduated in 1965. She met Nick Scinicariello and they married in 1970. They adopted two children, a girl, Danielle, in 1984 and David, in 1986. Sadly, David passed, in 2010, at just twenty-three, from cancer. Rosemarie went to further her education in the mid-1990s and attended Fordham University, and NYU, ultimately achieving her master's in French education.

Rosemarie Scinicariello, in the left forefront in photo, holding her diploma, in 1965

4 NORTH: A COMPLETELY DIFFERENT BUILDING AND EXPERIENCE

On 4 North, I moved into Room 436. The nurse manager on 4 North was Cynthia Cunningham. My roommate there would be Bernice Cruhlac. Bernice was sweet enough, it seemed, but there was a little issue with her voice. On one hand, she spoke in very high-pitched falsetto, and alternately, she spoke with a very low bass tone. When I met her granddaughter, she explained that Bernice had been perfectly functional ten years prior, but then her husband died, and she had a nervous breakdown. Ever since then, she stopped doing things for herself; she no longer dressed in the beautiful clothing she once had, and she could no longer go out of the house and do for herself. Bernice must have been terrified of the dentist. She had a frequent refrain of "I've got no teeth!" or "They're taking me away."

Nurse manager on 4 North, Cynthia Cunningham

When I write about things like a resident's mental state, personality, or behavioral issues, and their resulting effect, I do it only as an example of what life in a nursing facility can be like. In the phases of human development, human beings go through the infant stage, the toddler phase, young child phase, pre-adolescence, puberty, teenage years, young adulthood, and finally adulthood. That lasts for multiple decades. Ultimately, even absent dementia, or Alzheimer's disease, older adults can start to regress. There are days when the unit sounds more like a playpen or nursery than an adult home. When some of them become hungry, tired, or are in pain, they behave much like a child or infant: crying incessantly, screaming (as if in pain), calling out for *help*! Instead of being the adorable infant, looking at everything in the world as new, no, rather, they are a seventy-, eighty-, or even ninety-year-old man or woman, needing his or her diaper changed, a shower, a pillow, a blanket, or something to keep them warm, or something to eat or drink. In the nursing facility environment, patients can range in age from twenty to over one hundred years old, with the median age in the mid-eighties. There are those who have had specific brain or neurological disabilities (such as TBI, like me) or longer-term, progressive conditions such as multiple sclerosis or ALS. There are also those who have chronic brain conditions such as cerebral palsy or autism, for which there has been no cure.

The CNA's ability to work with people who have cognitive difficulties in expressing themselves due to their unique brain disorders is the principal reason I have such high regard for the job that the nurses and the CNAs do at Gurwin every day.

Lucy Cavaco: Lucy is an RN on 4 North. While on 4 North, I met Lucia (or Lucy) Cavaco, a long-tenured, compassionate, registered nurse. Lucy's very capable and caring for others. Lucy's married to another worker, Kevin Cavaco, from housekeeping. Together, they have a son. They seem very happy together. Lucy has endured her own health crisis, even prior to COVID-19. Her prognosis is excellent, having gone through treatment for her Stage II breast cancer, enduring chemotherapy, radiation, and surgery. Her selflessness in coming to work to help others every day is a huge statement to Lucy's character and that of many of the dedicated nurses at Gurwin. I remain awestruck at these amazing, selfless human beings and their dedication to helping others. God bless them all.

Lucy Cavaco at left and friends

BACK TO THE WEINBERG BUILDING: 3 EAST

After my father's death, I was moved to 3 East, back in the Weinberg Building. This unit had a whole new group of personnel, much of it seasoned. The nurse manager of 3 East for the day shift is Vida Antwi. Her call to "take report" is slightly different than Donna Shannon on 4 East. Vida: "All staff, please report to the nurses' station, for report." Vida runs a tight ship. She can be intimidating to some, but we seem to have hit it off since the beginning of my stay here. She is very responsive to my questions and need for details. We've evolved to me calling Vida "Vidalicious" and her calling me "Debalicious" (we've both come from the era of Destiny's Child and "Bootylicious"). At mealtimes, she summons the staff: "All staff report to the dining room. Breakfast trays are here, breakfast trays are here.

Please make sure all hallways are clear. Make sure all hallways are clear." Vida is married and has three children: two boys and a girl. All of her children have gone to college, or graduate school, at some of the most prestigious schools: Wharton (University of Pennsylvania), Yale, and (SUNY) Stony Brook.

My first room on 3 East was 369. My roommate was Evelyn Becker. She was born in the same year as my dad: 1930. She turned ninety on June 24, 2020. She has two children, a son, Jim, and a daughter, Evelyn. After about six months, I was moved to Room 366, where I live presently. I had four different roommates in Room 366: Laura Adams, who passed away the first weekend I was there; Rosemarie Rainone, who passed away in November 2019; and up until July 11, my roommate was Florence Yudenfriend, who just turned ninety on May 31, 2020. Florence has a lovely family. She had three daughters, Randy, Judy, and Vicki, and a son, Richard. I call the Yudenfriends my "family" proxy, as up until the coronavirus crisis, one or another Yudenfriend came regularly to visit Florence, or as her daughter Judy calls her, "Flossie." They are a very tall family—all of them. Even Florence, who just turned ninety, has very long legs. The girls, and their children, are all about five foot eleven. Florence (Gertsky) was married to Lester Yudenfriend. They married on July 4, 1948, and were married for sixty-nine years, up until Lester's death in August 2017. Florence was eighteen when she married, and Lester was twenty-two. Each of their four children have been prolific in "going forth and multiply," as Florence has fourteen grandchildren and two great-grandchildren (Sofia and Liam). All of them adore "Flossie."

Their first daughter, Randy, married Jordan Glaser, and together, they had five children: Allison (she's a doctor, specializing in infectious diseases; she works with her father, Dr. Jordan Glaser, at Staten Island Hospital); Lauren; Zoe, engaged to be married; Jake; and Jonathon. Sadly, in April 2016, Randy passed away at sixty-one from ovarian cancer.

Their second daughter, Vicki, is married to Aaron Werman. Together, they have two boys: Max and Gabe.

Their third daughter is Judy, who married Mitch Goldberg, and together, they also have five children: Rebecca, married to Miki, who together have two of Florence's great-grandchildren, Sophia and Liam; Emily, who married Howard in June 2021; Daniel; Justin; and Carly (Justin and Carly are twins).

Their fourth child, and only son, is Richard (aka Sonny Boy). Richard is married to Sigal Shaye, and together they have two boys: Jonni, married to Michelle, on Friday, May 22, 2020, and younger son Zachary.

Sadly, on July 11, 2020, Florence Yudenfriend passed away, peacefully, with her daughter Judy present with her. It was as Judy hoped: Florence did not suffer, she died peacefully, in the presence of family. Just forty-one days prior, on May 31, Florence turned ninety. While I was the first to sing "Happy Birthday" to Florence, her whole family came to celebrate her birthday. They couldn't see her in person, however. In the era of COVID-19, Florence was able to celebrate "with" her family from a window at the end of the hallway from our room. Florence was in her Geri chair recliner, and each of her family members were able to approach the window, and were visible to Florence, and they waved and yelled up to Florence at the window. They held up large signs, saying "Happy Birthday Florence" or "Happy Birthday, Mom" or "Grandma, we love you!" Judy, Vicki, Richard, Allie, Zachary, Gabe, Zoe, Mitch, Aaron, and Sigal all showed up, waving and hollering "We love you, Florence!" It was a birthday celebration unlike any other she had experienced in the past. But it did make her happy. And that was the family's objective, and hope. Mission accomplished, Yudenfriends! Good job!

On July 4, 2020, Florence and husband Lester would have celebrated their seventy-second wedding anniversary. She passed exactly one week later. In my belief system, Florence and Lester will be celebrating their next wedding anniversary together!

Florence and Lester Yudenfriend on their wedding day, July 4, 1948—simply stunning

My sincerest condolences are sent to the Yudenfriend family. I will miss you all. God bless and rest in peace, Florence. You can re-join your husband, Lester, and daughter Randy. You are now together again, and with our Lord.

My fourth roommate in Room 366 was Estelle Goodman. I was hoping that Gurwin admissions would move her into my room after she returned from her hospital stay. A few weeks prior, she suffered a fall and broke her right hip. She went to Huntington Hospital and had surgery there. She then had a minor setback with an infection. Upon her return, she was moved into 366, with me. Prior to her accident, Estelle was remarkably "with it." And we became fast friends. I'd begun to call her "my ninety-five-year-old BFF." We would attend evening cabaret almost every weeknight, and I was her helper, as I transported her, in her wheelchair, both to and from evening cabaret. Her room, 350, was immediately to the right, back on 3 East. Estelle had the cutest infectious laugh, which most all who'd met her always found it charming. The Estelle Goodman who moved into 366, however, had been through so much and was not like her old self. She was very tired and low energy, which given her recent injury was understandable. The worst part was that she wasn't eating, which is so important for healing, especially having had a broken hip. Estelle was probably one hundred pounds or less, and for her not to eat made it even worse. Shortly thereafter, she developed a bedsore, and she was in agony. She always would complain that "something in the mattress is stabbing me!" But it was the bedsore, which could result in excruciating pain. It pained me to hear her screaming in pain. Ultimately, her family ordered hospice care, which brought her some relief, with the doctor prescribing morphine and the nurse administering it to her. As it was with Florence, when she passed just a month ago, I knew it wouldn't be too long before cute little Estelle Molly Kakoshka Goodman would be gone also. Therapeutic recreation (TR) came by almost daily to connect Estelle with her family. Even till the end, Estelle was concerned for her family: her daughter, Gail; her son-in-law, Stephen Goldfarb; and her grandchildren. As things were getting worse, TR brought the iPad up with headphones, so that Estelle could at least hear her family speaking to her via FaceTime. Her daughter, Gail, said that Estelle should "Go see Daddy for your anniversary." Estelle passed away on August 6, 2020. On August 10, Estelle and Morris (her husband who predeceased her, in 1994) would have been married for seventy-five years! I don't find occurrences like this are by chance. It is not uncommon when the date of death is timed in accordance with an important life event. Now, Estelle is with Morris, her three older brothers, and younger sister (who all predeceased her). My faith allows me to believe that. It is so comforting to no longer have a fear of death because of that. When my day and hour are done, the Lord will call me home. Until then, I plan to do good things and make the world a little better for me being around.

Estelle, in the 1940s, about the time she met and married Morris Goodman. Another movie star!

THE CENTENARIANS

Since my arrival on 3 East, I've learned that there are at least three people who are at, or older than, age one hundred. Previously, I'd come in contact with a few centenarians, but now they are my neighbors: Mae Guldin, Maria Perez, and Shirley Cooper are all one hundred or more years old.

Mae S. Guldin lives two doors down from me, in Room 364. On January 12, 2020, Mae turned one hundred years old. I went to her room that morning and sang:

Happy birthday to you,
Happy birthday to you,
Happy birthday, dear Mae
Happy birthday to you

I continued:

May you live a hundred years (oh, you already did that)
May you drink a hundred beers
Don't get plastered you little bad girl
Happy birthday to you!

I stopped by for a brief interview a few months later, to learn more about Mae's life. Turns out, Mae was a very successful businesswoman, in an era when women did not own businesses!

In the 1960s, Mae owned Atlas Temp Inc., at 194 7th Avenue. Note that Mae was forty. Atlas did staffing for typists, stenographers, and court reporters. In 1979, she opened Morceaux Choisis, Ltd., in the Manhattan Arts & Antiques Building, on Second Avenue and 56th Street. Note that Mae was nearly sixty when she started this new business. She sold art, antiques, jewelry, rugs, and some clothing. During the 1960s and 1970s, it was uncommon for a woman to be a business owner. Ultimately, she retired in 2004, at eighty-four! I guess that having hope for my entrance back into the work world is not so far-fetched!

When Mae turned one hundred, I asked, "Mae, how did you manage to live until one hundred?" Without missing a beat, she replied, "I had one really good man, and of course, lots of good sex!" Sounds like Mae is becoming a role model, of sorts, for me!

Leo and Mae Guldin, circa 1943

Leo and Mae married in 1943. They had two sons, Matthew and Gregory. Mae will always tell you that she was "a one-man woman." Leo passed more than thirty years ago and she never married again, despite being a successful business owner and sought after by many men. Her husband, Leo, was "it" for her. Until they meet again . . .

The other centenarians on 3 East are Shirley Cooper and Maria Perez (101), who are a bit older than Mae. Maria Perez passed in October 2020. She was born in December 1919.

Out of curiosity, I looked up what someone in their sixties is called. The answer: sexagenarian. Well, some things in my life will need to change for that to happen!

Upon entering the facility, one can tell that Mr. Gurwin put much thought into the layout and design and ingredients of what went on here. Gurwin would be a place where residents would find all of their needs, and some of their wants, as if it were their own home. There would be good food three times a day.

OTHER ATTRIBUTES ABOUT GURWIN JEWISH NURSING & REHABILITATION CENTER

Dining at Gurwin: Dining at Gurwin would occur in each unit's dining room, to allow for some socialization among the residents. Gurwin was a place where one could dine with dignity. While meals were served on trays, the plates and silverware were just as they'd be at home. In the COVID-19 world, special sanitary precautions are warranted, and our food is served in individual plastic bags, rather than trays. I mused that Mr. Gurwin, God rest his soul, would not be happy about our pandemic dining arrangements. Thankfully, dining has returned to the normal format, albeit, we still must adhere to limited attendance in the dining room, with one person per table. Personally, I haven't taken issue with my in-room dining arrangement.

In non-pandemic times, there would be daily and evening activities to help maintain some intellectual stimulation, and perhaps even set some goals for the future. As it turns out, Joseph Gurwin became a resident at Gurwin during the years before he passed in 2009.

Evening cabaret/therapeutic recreation: The big activity in the evening, after dinner, is evening cabaret, which is hosted outside entertainment from 7:15 to 8:15 p.m. Many acts are prescheduled for the various musical tastes of the residents. Groups include Just Friends, Roberta Fabiano, and several others. My personal favorite is Donna Lee, as she's my sister! I'm the oldest of five, and Donna is second in our family lineup. She was always talented: she's self-taught on the piano, and also plays the viola, alto saxophone, the organ, and I think even a little guitar. While growing up, I always felt a little perplexed that after dinnertime, at home, Donna got to play the piano, but Deb always had to wash the dishes. (At the time, I felt a bit like the Cinderella story.) But when Donna comes to perform, I'm always proud that the audience at Gurwin will be treated to a performance of so much talent. Donna is a talented performer, and she always puts on a great show. She is capable of singing just about any performer's work, over multiple decades.

As a result, she tends to get a larger-than-normal audience in the Simon Rainbow Room, which is named for a large donor family (the Simons) and for the rainbow of colored squares adorning its walls. Performers adhere to a tight one-hour schedule, and residents often times participate in any sing-alongs as required. It's a nice way to wind up the evening, as 8:15 p.m. is bedtime for many residents.

The therapeutic recreation team includes Nicole Hopper (supervisor), Patti Dowsett, Donald Mulvey, Johanna Catulo, Chelsea, Maria D'Amelia, and a few others. They have been working on each of the units during our COVID-19 lockdown. Each one does a great job of keeping the residents occupied: playing Bingo, three-card poker, blackjack, word games, board games, and sometimes hosting hot chocolate or coffee and cake or pastries, all in the name of keeping everyone somewhat happy and occupied. They deserve much recognition for their efforts during the lockdown and prior to that time. Therapeutic recreation also runs the adult education program.

Adult education at Gurwin: Since the beginning in 1988, Gurwin has offered an adult education program through the therapeutic recreation department. It's offered courses in a wide variety of topics, and each year, for the last thirty years, they've had graduating classes. In 2019, I participated in this program, and while not graded on a numeric basis, there are candidates elected to valedictorian and salutatorian. In 2019, I was elected as valedictorian. As it turned out, the speech I'd prepared in advance had to be delivered. Who knew that it would occur on the same day as my nineteenth surgery, this one to correct contractures on three fingers on my left hand? Fortunately, my surgery time, and my same-day surgery status, allowed for me to make it back in time to deliver my speech. "From gurney to Gurwin," I started my speech, and it was very well-received. The reception afterwards and my brother Robert's attendance at the event was quite welcome, as I hadn't eaten since eleven the night before! My speech appears in the appendix, at the end of this book.

Gurwin Jewish, a kosher facility: Since the name of the facility, Gurwin, is Jewish, it's no surprise that the kitchen adheres to kosher rules. All meals are prepared in a kosher kitchen, and the preparation is overseen by Rabbi David Shain. He has been at Gurwin for sixteen years. He'd performed the oversight function elsewhere for a couple of years after he became a rabbi, in 2001. He then joined Gurwin to perform the same function. Around the same time, Rabbi Shain married his wife, Devorah, who ultimately bore him five children: four girls and one boy, Samuel (the middle child), who comes with Rabbi Shain during Jewish services, every other week. His children's names (and ages) are Sara (sixteen), Chanie (fourteen), Samuel (twelve), Tzivia (ten), and Rivkah (eight).

Rabbi David Shain, of open mind and open heart

Rabbi Shain has shown himself to be of open mind and open heart. On September 30, 2018, I was baptized as a born-again Christian at Gurwin Jewish Nursing & Rehabilitation Center. Rabbi Shain attended, as a witness to the process.

As Rabbi Shain attended my baptism, I respond in kind and attend weekly services at Gurwin, on Saturday mornings. I've also participated in holiday Seders during Passover and Rosh Hashanah. Since Christianity is founded on its Judeo-Christian roots, I believe the two religions are integrally linked. Also, let us not forget that Jesus Christ was the most famous Jew that ever walked the planet. Notwithstanding language translation difficulties between the Judeo and the Christian, I believe it would be unfortunate to not find the similarities between the two. Amir Tsarfati and Jonathan Cahn, two Messianic Jews, have provided much in the way of bridging the gaps that have historically existed between the two. I openly discuss my view points with the Rabbis at Gurwin.

A more recent addition at Gurwin is Rabbi Uri Lesser. He arrived in the middle of 2019. I haven't gotten to know him as well as Rabbi Shain, but he is very pleasant and kind whenever he stops by during this elongated period of lockdown due to COVID-19. As it will be the case, "this too shall pass."

HOUSEKEEPING AT GURWIN: A LITTLE BIT ABOUT THE PERSONNEL

Tom Heinisch and Owen Martin are the director and assistant director, respectively, of housekeeping at Gurwin. Both have been around since almost the beginning of Gurwin (about thirty-two years). There are head housekeepers at Gurwin, also, who do the training of the other housekeepers. There are 460 beds at Gurwin, split between two buildings: the Schachne Pavilion (the original building, with 300 beds), and the Weinberg Building, with an additional 160 beds. That means that there are 260 rooms that need to be cleaned every day. Four hundred sixty toilets to be cleaned, sinks to be washed, mirrors that need to be Windexed. There are also 260 floors that need to be swept, mopped, and floors that need to be waxed and buffed. Those are the bigger items. Each room has a few trash cans that need to be emptied, and furniture with surfaces that all need to be cleaned. Most days, the rooms require a cleaning but on certain days, the rooms are turned into "Terminal" rooms. That usually is best accomplished if each resident vacates the room for a period of time (determined by each housekeeper's capability).

I am impressed that most of the housekeepers have children and husbands or wives, for which they work their jobs at Gurwin to provide for. This, in addition to putting in an eight-hour shift at Gurwin, which I don't believe is an easy job for them to do. Below, I mention several of these very hardworking, polite, and caring people who make Gurwin shine every day!

Blanca Ayundante: Blanca Ayundante (pronounced Ah-yoon-dahn-tay) is in housekeeping, a very important function at Gurwin, as Gurwin is cleaned constantly. It is always being cleaned, buffed, shined, and never smells, like many others. I know, through my sister, who sings at dozens of facilities across Long Island. She assures me that Gurwin is tops in the "clean-smelling" department, and for that I am grateful. Blanca is always pleasant and courteous. I just like saying her last name, "Ah-yoon-dahn-tay." She has three boys: Renzo, George, and Luis, aged seventeen, fifteen, and twelve. She is very proud of them and says they treat her well, as they adore her. She deserves being adored. I recently saw a picture of her son Renzo receiving an award from Suffolk County Executive Steve Bellone. Blanca was beaming with pride, and understandably so! Renzo had been working at Gurwin before he started with the US Marines. We thank Renzo for his service to the country.

Blanca Ayundante, mom of three boys, and a great housekeeper at Gurwin

Daysi Ramirez de Hidalgo: Same letters, different spelling than Daisy. For a few months, she was a fill-in for Blanca Ayundante in housekeeping. She has two boys and one girl: Esdras, twenty-three; Daniel, twenty-one; and Jenny, nineteen. She's also a very pleasant, capable, thorough housekeeper.

Jeronimo Ortega: Jeronimo has been in housekeeping at Gurwin for twenty years and works on the evening shift. On the evening shift, he participates in much of the common area cleaning. He's always cleaning tables and mopping floors, and always has a good attitude. That is most important. On the days when it seems kind of blah, people like Geronimo always have a kind word, always anxious to help with even the simplest things. There's not a day at Gurwin when I don't meet someone anxious to lend a hand.

3 East Housekeepers: Always Pleasant, Considerate, and They Do a Great Job

Since I've been living on 3 East, there is a whole different group of housekeepers; it's worth spending a moment to acknowledge their daily efforts to keep Gurwin "shining." These include Sandra Garcia, Susan Gilroy, Sheila Singh, and Brandon Miller.

Brandon Miller: Brandon is a very friendly and courteous young man. He works in housekeeping at Gurwin, mostly on the morning shift. The day shift housekeepers have the task of cleaning each room daily. That means sweeping and mopping the floors in each resident's room, emptying trash, cleaning the bathrooms including toilet, sink, shelves, and all of the furniture in each room: dressers, tables, and nightstands. And let's not forget the windows, mirrors, and TV screens.

Brandon Miller, kind and capable, with a nice smile

Sandra Garcia: Sandra works morning shift on 3 East. Sandra has been at Gurwin for four years. She is very capable and does a great job. She's married and has two sons. Pre-COVID-19, I'm sure the day shift, from 7 a.m. to 3 p.m., fits well with the boys' school schedule. She can be home with them shortly after they arrive home.

Sandra Garcia, another hard worker, always with a smile

Sheila Singh: Sheila's been a housekeeper at Gurwin for fifteen years. Like many others, she's married and has children. Sheila's job and its compensation are an important part of her family's household income. Sheila likes being at Gurwin and always does a very good job. She sometimes bemoans that it's a tough job. "Day after day, the same thing, but it needs to be done." And so, she does it. Thank you, Sheila; you're an important reason of why I'm here at Gurwin and not somewhere else.

Susan Gilroy: I've gotten to know Susan more recently, on 3 East. She, too, is a very competent and thorough housekeeper at Gurwin. Susan's wish-list includes her plan to visit Gilroy, California. In Northern California, in Santa Clara County, Gilroy is known as the Garlic Capital of the World. Gilroy also boasts a number of boutique wineries with "tasting" rooms. If she hasn't been there already, I'm sure Rachael Ray, "lover of all things garlic," will ultimately visit Gilroy!

Louis Morrison: A tall drink of water, Louis is a very nice man who also works in housekeeping on the evening shift, from 3 to 11 p.m. On this shift, much of the overall facility clean-up gets done: sweeping and mopping the dining rooms on each of the four units in the Weinberg Building, and the eight units in the Schachne Pavilion. They also have to clean and wax every hallway and common floor area on each unit. They are also responsible for the lobby, the kitchen, the clinic, and the Rainbow Room.

Kevin Cavaco: Kevin has been at Gurwin for fifteen years. He's a very capable and kind guy in housekeeping. He's actually married to Lucia Cavaco, a nurse on 4 North. Together, Kevin and Lucy have a son, Matthew.

Mike DuPont: Mike always yells at me when I pass through the "shortcut" on the second floor. Like everyone at Gurwin, deep down, he's a nice guy! When I've used the cut-through to head to the elevators, Mike usually scolds me as I make the short trip. Again, Gurwin is always anxious when it comes to cut-throughs, as there are loading docks and other places where if you don't know what's coming through, you might get hurt. Fortunately, I'm very alert at all times, and I make the trip quickly.

Charles Dewar (like the Scotch) and Simon Haye: Charles and Simon both work the evening shift, where much of the common area work gets done. All the unit hallways, dining rooms, and TV areas need floors to be swept, mopped, and waxed. In terms of floor-waxing they utilize these Zamboni-type machines that they ride throughout each area requiring cleaning. The Zamboni, or ice resurfacer, was invented in 1949 by engineer Frank Zamboni.

Mike Henry: Mike has been a housekeeper on the morning shift at Gurwin for sixteen years. He has a wife and three children: two boys and a girl. Mike, like many others in housekeeping, is doing a most important job, especially in the midst of the pandemic. I pray for you all, and God bless you!

SHORTCUTS THROUGH THE "BOWELS OF THE BUILDING"

Since being at Gurwin, I eventually came to know the entire "bowels of the building." I remember when I first arrived, and I had to go for physical or occupational therapy, someone usually came to transport me to my appointment. I remember long hallways, with eventual right turns, and more turns, and it seemed like a blur to me. Eventually, however, I came to learn the entire labyrinth of hallways, where each hallway leads, and how to get back from where I came. Gurwin's elevators have front and rear doors. If you go out of the rear of the elevator, that leads to the second-floor hallways that lead to the cafeteria and Nutritional Services office. It can also lead back to the hallway from which I can get to the clinic gym, or lobby gym, and the front desk. Pre-COVID-19, when I'd go to church with my friend Heather Roff, we took an even further shortcut, through 2 North, straight down to the front lobby. Those were the good ol' days!

ENGINEERING AND MAINTENANCE

With 260 rooms, it's inevitable that a toilet's going to clog, the A/C won't work, a light fixture or TV needs repair, or a TV or bed remote needs replacement. For those things, we call engineering and maintenance. Given the system at Gurwin, it's best to tell the nurse or CNA so they can make the call, as orders get sent through to their iPads, and it can be completed much more quickly.

In this department, there are a few people that I usually try and call myself. There's Bill Diakakis, who's been at Gurwin for about fifteen years. It turns out that Bill and I have a connection through one of my jobs, about thirty-five years ago, at the Bonwit Inn. He is the son-in-law of one of the owners, Charlie Tsunis (who unfortunately passed, in 2001, nineteen years ago).

Bill and Anastasia Diakakis

Recently, there's been the appointment of a new manager in engineering. His name is Luigi Iannucci. He's a young guy (mid-thirties) but he's been very responsive to issues we've had with hot water. There was a brand-new water heater installed in 2020, but periodically there's been no hot water, which is essential in a healthcare facility. On the numerous occasions I've had to call because the water has been freezing cold, he's seen to it that the situation gets rectified quickly. On shower days, that's most important!

NUTRITIONAL SERVICES DEPARTMENT

Juan Ortiz: Juan was one of the initial hires at Gurwin, when it first opened in 1988. Juan learned that Gurwin was hiring from his sister. Juan had grown up in the Fordham section of the Bronx. He was looking to live and work out of the hustle and bustle of the Bronx's city environment.

Juan is the head of production and procurement manager for all things nutritional at Gurwin. He's had to deal with many vendors for both the key ingredients for the main dishes, as well as the accompanying sauces, broths, dressings, and toppings. He must do this all within keeping of Gurwin's kosher menu. He also must do this in keeping with his budget.

Located on the second floor, Nutritional Services is a lifeline for me at Gurwin. Every day, several times a day sometimes, I call down to learn of menu items to possibly order an alternate from the menu, and to order my coffee. Typically, I do this for breakfast, lunch, and dinner. Thanks to the team, I usually get my "special delivery" coffee right on schedule! Thank you, Kenroy Grant, Johnel Jarrett, Debra Benson, Julia Ay, Ashley, Amy, Kristina Maier, and, sometimes, Sandy Richter for being the gracious and patient servers that you are. Without your help, I'd go caffeine-starved!

Juan Ortiz, production manager

Eddie Vanderhorst: Eddie has been at Gurwin for sixteen years. He's been a runner in the Nutritional Services department. Throughout the day, he delivers the coffee urns to each unit for lunch and dinner. He also makes individual deliveries, many times for me, and I truly am grateful for that! Thank you, Eddie V!

Eddie Vanderhorst, the runner for Nutritional Services Department

Debra Vollaro Benson, Nutritional Services manager

Johnel Jarrett, Nutritional Services Department

Several months ago, I commended Kenroy Grant for his extra-special service during the time the facility was replacing the coffee machine in the cafeteria. For the few weeks it was out of commission, he took it upon himself, from my frequent requests, to make extra pots of coffee, and thus Debbie could get what she wanted! Gurwin rewarded him with a Customer

Service Star, for going above and beyond the call of duty. He was presented with his award in the cafeteria, and I was asked to present it to him. Thank you, Kenroy Grant!

Kenroy Grant, Nutritional Services manager

Julia Ay, Nutritional Services manager

Kristina Maier, Nutritional Services Department

FOOD PREPARATION AT GURWIN

In February 2020, Gurwin made a change in its food service vendor. Previously, they'd been using Morrison Food Services, but in February they changed it to Unidine (Unidine is a subsidiary of Morrison). Gurwin's administration, along with Nutritional Services, sought to bring on a company with a broader food offering and a superior product offering, including food presentation. Eating good-quality food is important to Gurwin's 460 residents. There have long been debates about menu selection and food preparation, and always there remains the hope of getting food just like "at home." Because of the diversity in tastes among the residents, there will never be 100 percent satisfaction for 460 people at one time. But I know the chef and all of the servers work hard to put meals that are enjoyable and nutritious in front of us three times a day!

Chef James W. Junk: very accommodating

The most recent head chef at Gurwin is named James Junk. He's had decades of culinary experience, often cooking for presidents of the United States, like George H. W. Bush, his wife, Barbara and the likes of General Norman Schwarzkopf and even Governor Jerry Brown of California. Chef James has been very accommodating for me and I appreciate that. During the lockdown, and subsequent quarantine on my unit, food really has been the only bright spot in my daily routine. On Wednesdays and Fridays, Chef James normally makes pizza for the cafeteria. Separately, he's made pizza for me, which is a great treat and it breaks up the routine of the menu. Thank you, Chef James!

THE SERVERS

As food is the main attraction three times per day, much effort goes into the menu-planning, the preparation, and the delivery and serving of the food. Collectively, these roles all come under the heading of Nutritional Services. Since the beginning of my stay at Gurwin, I've come to appreciate their role in the everyday functioning of this nursing facility.

Orick Bird: Always pleasant and cheerful, originally from Jamaica, Orick is a delight. He's a hard worker, too. Many a time, he works double shifts, from 6 a.m. to 2 p.m., then 2 p.m. to 8 p.m., at which point, he's really done and very tired. Orick's been at Gurwin for nearly twenty years. I think it reflects on the facility that it has many long-tenured employees. It must be a good place to work. Gurwin has received this distinction, several times.

Orick Bird, recently retired: good for him, sad for us

Andrew Gabriel: "Hello, my friend!" Always pleasant and helpful, Andrew Gabriel, or angel Gabriel, as he likes to be called, has been at Gurwin for a number of years. He and Orick Bird, when working on the same unit as servers, are quite funny, teasing and joking and arguing with each other like an old married couple. But they always get the job done! Andrew Gabriel is a long-timer at Gurwin, with thirty-two years of tenure under his belt.

Noella: Noella (pronounced No-well-ya) works on the day shift. Noella is becoming one of my favorites, as she brings me coffee from the cafeteria each morning at breakfast. She's very sweet and tries to accommodate, within limits. There is no rule-breaking with her. Residents are not permitted behind the counter during serving time, as there is fear that residents could get hurt, as the steam tables can be hot and dangerous. Gurwin is all about residents' safety and its liability if something goes wrong.

Kenny Mavnan: Kevin works from 12 a.m. to 8 p.m. He can be both a lunch and evening server. He's generally very nice; he sometimes gets a little irritated, but he does his job just fine! He tries to be accommodating whenever possible.

Ace Johnson: Ace is a nice young man who works largely in the cafeteria at Gurwin. He also does many of the dining room set-ups in the various units at the facility. In talking with Ace, I get the sense that, yes, he likes his job at Gurwin, but my sense is that he'd rather be working on laying down new tracks in a studio producing hip-hop or rap. He confirms that he'd like that kind of life but for now, Gurwin is his paycheck; it pays his bills and maybe one day his alternate dream will come true.

A CHRISTIAN BAPTISM AT GURWIN JEWISH

As part of restoring my relationship with God, I did two things: (1) I repented for my sins, transgressions, and iniquities; (2) I got baptized. After nine months of studying the Bible with my sisters-in-Christ, it was time to fully commit myself to Jesus Christ. Having been baptized as a Catholic at three months old, I was now being baptized as an adult who had made a conscious decision to commit my life to Jesus, as my Lord and Savior. It was decided, along with the help of my sisters-in-Christ, that I do this some time in September 2018, as that was the availability of the pastor of Calvary, Chapel of Hope, Pastor Claude Stauffer. The date decided upon was Sunday, September 30, 2018. Interestingly, it was my late husband Gary's birthday. Here I was, being "born again" on the same date as my late husband's birthday. If only he could have been there. As I was unable to go to a beach or a pool for a full-submersion baptism, we did the best we could. We opted for the large bathtub in the shower room on 4 East. This ceremony had to be approved by administration at Gurwin. My friend Donna Pennacchio coordinated with my social worker, Danielle Marblestone, and discussed our need with our administrator, Joanne Parisi. Within a few days, all the pieces were falling into place. Pastor Claude would oversee and perform the baptism.

On September 30, 2018, Debbie Grosser was baptized as a born-again Christian at Gurwin Jewish Nursing & Rehabilitation Center. Rabbi Shain attended, as a witness to the process, and I believe he genuinely enjoyed the worship music and the sight of me being doused by several basins of water. Pastors Jeff, Dominick, and Albert came and played "worship music." As a courtesy, we offered Rabbi Shain some good kosher food from Bagel Boss—egg salad on a sesame bagel; he accepted and he was very gracious and grateful. All in all, it was a very special day for me. In addition to my sisters-in-Christ, Donna Pennacchio, Kerry Rohe, and Janis Mayors, and their family members, the staff at Gurwin was very kind and presented me with "Congratulations on your Baptism" cards. I was very touched by their kindness. We had a baptismal lunch to follow, enjoying pizza from LaScala and a cannoli cake! It was indeed a special day for me and for us all!

My first outing to attend church services did not happen until Easter 2019. My father's memorial had been the week prior, on April 13, 2019, as he passed on March 30, just 164 days after my mom. I attended Smithtown Gospel Tabernacle (SGT, for short) with my sister-in-Christ Donna Pennacchio; her husband, Anthony; and their twin girls, Megan and Caroline. My first regular church outings started a few months after that. I started to attend Faith Evangelical Free Church in Dix Hills. At first, my brother Robert took me, all through the summer of 2019. Then, Robert got a new job and then it was my friend Heather Roff who began to pick me up, and from there, she'd take me to church, we'd attend services, we'd "fellowship" downstairs, and then she'd return me back to Gurwin. All in all, it gave me about four hours of freedom from the nursing facility environment. Hallelujah. Within a short time, it became obvious that traveling with my wheelchair in tow was cumbersome. My walking ability had improved enough so that holding onto an arm would be sufficient for me to walk up to the church and wait for Heather to open the door and let me in. I could now navigate in and out of church, sans wheelchair! This was a big deal for me and for those who came to pick me up for church!

FAITH CHURCH: PART *LITTLE HOUSE ON THE PRAIRIE* AND PART *THE PARTRIDGE FAMILY*

Faith Evangelical Free Church, Dix Hills, New York

Faith Church has become my church family. It's a humble church, but perfect for me, and the Faith Church family that developed from it. The pastor, Cliff Tomlinson; his wife, Vickie; Chris Roff; and Sal Caliendo all participate in the worship music, as do we congregants. Pastor plays the guitar and Vickie plays piano. Chris Roff plays the drums. That gives the church the Partridge Family feel.

Services are always uplifting with the pastor's message, the principal part of the service. I've enjoyed being able to share the message through follow-up emails, which are accompanied by worship songs from the services.

Fellowship always follows services, and that means convening downstairs for coffee, bagels, donuts, and other refreshments. It's a small congregation, adding to the overall church family feel. Faith Church had been my parents' church while they were still here. Pastor speaks of my father fairly often—about his story-telling ability and the strong contribution my parents made as congregants of Faith Church. One of my mom's former coworkers, from Sterns, Angela Romano, speaks of my mom often. "She never had a harsh word to say about anyone in all the years I'd known her," she says. It just added to my prevailing view of my mom from the Beatitudes: "The meek shall inherit the earth." Angela is my friend Heather Roff's mom. Chris Roff is her husband, and their son, Noah, also attends when he can. Ralf Nemec, Karen Kirschberger, her husband Bill, and their children, Bill, Andrew, Kirsten, Rebecca, Jonathan, and Jaclyn, along with Carol Hill, Angel Cordero, and sometimes Joe Costantino, are among the regular attendees to services at Faith.

Social Workers at Gurwin: An Essential Role

I've been on four different units while at Gurwin. On each, I was assigned to a different social worker. The head of social work at Gurwin is Dorian Froelich. She's been at Gurwin for more than twenty years. She has seen Gurwin's growth and its changes throughout those twenty years. The social worker to whom I was assigned for the longest period was Danielle Marblestone (4 East), social work supervisor at Gurwin. Generally, she oversees the various social workers for the twelve units here. Social workers at a nursing facility can play a vital role, as they serve as intermediaries between residents and their families, residents and staff, and sometimes residents with other residents. With the global pandemic, they've played an important function while we've been on lockdown. It is the social worker that can go to Finance on our behalf and receive money (if it's in our accounts). They advise us when we have Treatment Plan Care Team meetings, and those occur in each unit's conference room. They can send faxes, if we request that to be done. As my physical and walking capability have improved, I've been permitted to perform these tasks, which I did regularly during pre-COVID-19 days.

Danielle was the interface between administration (Joanne Parisi), me, and Donna Pennacchio regarding my request to be baptized at Gurwin Jewish, which was important to me and my sisters-in-Christ. Danielle is kind, pretty, and I adore her as my social worker.

When I was moved to 4 North, my social worker was Marilyn Confessiore. I liked her very much, although I was not on 4 North for long. When I moved back to the Weinberg Building, to 3 East, I was assigned to Joan Seidell, but she retired in late 2019 or early 2020, after which Jonathan Morrison became my new social worker. In the COVID-19 world here at Gurwin, I've had to engage Jonathan many times to retrieve money from Finance. Most times, he is very helpful. He's a young guy, only twenty-seven, but he's got four units to which he's assigned (3W, 3E, 4W, ACU, or acute care unit). That can pull him in many different directions on a given day. On a few occasions, Jonathan was very helpful in dropping off a FedEx package at a local drop-box. Thank you, Jonathan! Danielle tells me that she'll always be my social worker, as a back-up, if Jonathan is not available. If ever I need someone as a further back-up, I can always go back to Dorian Froelich. My most recent social worker on 3 East is Jeraldine Fedoriw. Mainly, she has been helpful in being the Finance Department interface for me.

As I'm capable of performing most all of the tasks of the social workers (retrieving money from Finance, sending a fax, or mailing something), there are times when being in a nursing facility environment feels constricting. Putting a positive spin on it, being here, I can achieve, or have things done for me, whenever I need it. Still, I look forward to being out on my own and living independently once again. That day will arrive, when I'm fully ready to do so.

Chapter Eighteen

Gurwin Jewish Nursing & Rehabilitation Center Administration

The Example for Excellence Starts at the Top

As an analyst on Wall Street for thirty years, having interviewed management teams at all levels, I decided to employ that approach to the place I've lived for nearly five years. I inquired of each of the Gurwin officers if they would spend some time with me so I could learn more about their backgrounds and motivations for being in the nursing and rehabilitation center arena. First, I was grateful that each was willing to spend a bit of time with one of their residents, and while that may be a bit unusual, I found each one to be very approachable, kind, and reasonable in their understanding of what I was attempting to accomplish through these brief interviews. In all, I found all three to be family people, with the key ingredients necessary to be part of a nursing facility environment: compassion, an implicit belief that people are mostly good, and importantly, a solid understanding of the profound changes that occur in humans as they progress into advanced ages. All three began with a basic desire to find ways to help and work with people. One person in particular sought to work with what he called "America's greatest generation to whom we owe so much." As a result, I took this opportunity to give a little "air time" to the people who hold important roles that make Gurwin into the top-tier healthcare facility that it remains today.

I'll introduce you to three extraordinary human beings: Stuart Almer, CEO of Gurwin Jewish Healthcare System; Shua Sauer, its COO; and Joanne Parisi, VP and administrator. I'll present their profiles in the order that I met them for my interview.

Joanne Parisi, VP and Administrator

Joanne Parisi, a formidable yet open-minded administrator at Gurwin

In the context of the Debbie Grosser story, Joanne Parisi could have played Sister Ruth Francis, my Catholic grade-school principal. In keeping with that story, my initial perception of Joanne was that she was no one to mess with. She could be intimidating to anyone who crossed the line with her. But like Sister Ruth, Joanne has turned out to be very reasonable, straightforward, caring, kind, and flexible. As I found being an analyst on Wall Street, getting to each person's human level, one would be surprised at what they found. So it was with Joanne. When I went for our interview, Joanne was very kind and made me a nice cup of regular coffee. And there were cookies, too! Our discussion graduated into our interview. Here are my main findings:

I asked about her upbringing. She was born Joanne Visochi (I thought she was saying Versace).

She grew up in Park Slope, Brooklyn, till age ten, then moved to Lindenhurst, on Long Island. She was born in the 1950s, and here's an interesting connection: we were both born in Methodist Hospital, in Park Slope, Brooklyn, New York.

She's been married to her husband, Neil, for forty-nine years (married in 1971).

She has two daughters, fifteen years apart. Her youngest held her wedding in June 2019, and honeymoon in Italy for ten days.

Joanne went to Suffolk Community College to obtain her two-year degree, followed by SUNY Stony Brook, where she graduated with a BA in English and secondary education. She then went to Queens College, MLS (Master Liscense Social Worker).

For her first job out of college, she worked at Brunswick Hospital as a clerk in the ER department. She learned a tremendous amount in that role. Her goal was to teach but she always wound up in record-keeping and information systems. She kept moving toward hospital administration. She helped build a library at Brunswick Hospital.

Joanne came to Gurwin in 2006, as chief information officer. Her initial position had been as project director for Gurwin's transition to electronic medical records (Optimus). In 2012, she became assistant administrator. In January 2016, she was promoted to associate administrator, and finally, in 2018, Herb Friedman retired, Stuart Almer was appointed as president/CEO, and Joanne was promoted to VP/administrator of Gurwin. She worked hard, and she climbed the ladder. I believe Joanne finds her position very gratifying, as she deals with the needs of all 460 residents and their families. It has been very challenging during these days of COVID-19. I'm certain that they'll deal with all of the attendant issues with safety first as a key component in any decision that is made in these uncertain times. We're all just waiting for the light at the end of this long, dark tunnel. As the COVID-19 vaccine rollout has begun, that light has finally appeared! This means a full reopening of Gurwin visitation has begun. This warrants a true Hallelujah!

STUART ALMER, PRESIDENT AND CEO AT GURWIN HEALTHCARE SYSTEM

Stuart Almer, a kind and effective CEO who thinks big

It's almost as if Stuart Almer knew he'd be in the role that he currently holds. He was appointed as president and CEO of Gurwin Healthcare System in late 2017, effective January 1, 2018. His father, Irwin Almer, is also a resident at Gurwin.

Stuart has always been interested in finding ways to help people. The healthcare industry seemed like a good way to effectuate that, and he planned his career accordingly.

He attended college at SUNY Purchase and pursued a degree in sociology. He thoroughly enjoyed his educational experience while there. He graduated in 1982.

He met and married his wife, Geri, in 1989. They have two children: a son, Zachary, twenty-six, and a daughter, Nicolette, twenty-four. Zachary is currently following in his dad's footsteps in the healthcare business. Nicolette is pursuing a degree in dentistry.

Stuart makes no bones about it: he thinks big and has always had big ambitions.

After graduating college, he initially started working in the hospital arena, working at Peninsula Hospital Center, in Far Rockaway, Queens. That hospital closed in 2012.

He then broke into the nursing home segment, working at a nursing home called Parker Jewish Institute for Healthcare and Rehabilitation in New Hyde Park, on Long Island. While there, Stuart had known of Gurwin Jewish, and was friendly with the administrator at the time, Mike Scarpelli. Mike kept in touch with Stuart and advised him that the current executive vice president and administrator at Gurwin, Herb Friedman, would be retiring in 2017, and Stuart joined Gurwin, with that role in mind. In 2015, he joined Gurwin and began to oversee day-to-day operations as Gurwin's administrator and COO, while preparing for his eventual role to succeed Herb Friedman. In September 2017, Herb announced that he would be stepping down as executive vice president and CEO at Gurwin's Nursing & Rehabilitation Center, while transitioning to be president and CEO of the newly created Gurwin Healthcare System.

SHUA SAUER, COO

Shua Sauer, a reliable COO,
a solid advocate for me and biking

Shua was elevated to his current role in 2018. Previously, Shua had known and worked with Stuart Almer, Gurwin's current president and CEO, in his role at Parker Jewish Institute for Nursing and Rehabilitation. Shua has always been geared for a nursing home environment, having graduated with a Master's degree in nursing home administration from Hofstra University, in Hempstead, New York. Shua was drawn to Gurwin, not only for its long-standing good reputation but also the demographic of the resident base: Shua is passionate about serving what he calls "America's greatest generation to whom we owe so much." Shua is married and has six children, ranging in age from twenty-five down to "bar mitzvah age" (about thirteen).

I've been very grateful to Shua for having honored his promise to move the recumbent bike to my unit while Gurwin remains under quarantine orders. His responsiveness and flexibility in delivering on his promise has literally changed my life at Gurwin for as long as our quarantine continues.

Shua also believes, as I do, in giving back, and he currently teaches in the master's program for nursing home administration at Hostra University. Thank you, Shua Sauer!

Chapter Nineteen

Ancillary Services at Gurwin: No Need to Air Our Dirty Laundry—It's Done for Us

Tony Waul: Laundry at Gurwin

Along with everything else that is provided at Gurwin, our laundry service just adds to the list. Certain employees at the facility have been here since the beginning. One is Tony Waul, head of laundry services at Gurwin. Tony can be seen at all hours. If one happens to wake up at 5 a.m., Tony can be seen at the end of the bed, removing soiled laundry from the bins in our room. He's there on Tuesdays and Fridays, when clothes are returned to their rightful owners. Oh, and every piece of clothing needs to be labeled at Gurwin. For instance, if someone gets a gift of clothing from family members, they first have to be dropped off at the front desk (in the lobby) and labeled—every sock, every undergarment needs to be labeled, lest they get lost in the mystery of laundry.

Tony makes the rounds as each resident's laundry gets dropped off at their rooms. God bless you, Tony Waul.

In my bid to get busy living, one task I've taken up is to do my own laundry, each night, in my bathroom sink. Much like Will Smith in *The Pursuit of Happyness* (which I love), I wash the five regular outfits that I wear throughout the week. I've graduated to a wardrobe consisting of various print leggings, or "jeggings," and T-shirts or a long-sleeved, quarter-zip top, all purchased at Walmart or Amazon. This is a far cry from my days spent shopping at Nieman Marcus or Nordstrom, but hey, I live at Gurwin Jewish Nursing & Rehabilitation Center, and it works for me!

Methods of Survival I've Devised at Gurwin

In a kosher nursing facility environment, I've come up with a few "inventions" that make my off meal time dining experience more enjoyable for me. I've made a few discoveries that have become part of my daily and nightly rituals. As I'm also trying to lose or maintain my weight, I've come up with a few ideas.

For dessert options, I've come up with Quaker caramel rice cakes (purchased at Walmart, through Amazon, or at grocery stores), with a thin layer of peanut butter and a few slices of banana. Tonight, I actually made a variation by spreading my rice pudding onto my rice cake and it was actually quite tasty.

I discovered that since skim milk contains no fat, it can be mixed with almost any juice (which would normally curdle whole milk). Thus my favorite is cranberry juice cocktail, skim milk, ice, and a packet of Truvia. It actually tastes very good, and it's filling at the end of the evening.

If you use orange juice, it tastes like a Creamsicle. Cranberry juice tastes more like strawberry milk, and grape juice can be used also.

LORI COELLO: HEAD OF VOLUNTEER SERVICES AT GURWIN

It turns out that Lori Coello was in my senior graduating class at North Babylon High School! My brother John brought a box of my belongings that had been stored at his house, and my Class of 1977 yearbook was among them! Lori did not like her picture from the yearbook (although I think she looks fine), but we all tend to see ourselves in the worst light. Lori and I also have something else in common. We both love to watch *General Hospital* every day at 3 p.m. While Lori works at that time, she DVRs it every day. Periodically we get caught up in the drama.

Lori Coello, supervisor of Volunteer Services

John Peter Rajotte: Previous Supervisor of Volunteers at Gurwin

John Peter Rajotte and I met through his other role at Gurwin, manning the gift shop. At first, I heard people referring to him as "JP," and I asked what his JP stood for. He replied, "John Peter," which immediately prompted me to tell him of my grandfather, father, and brother, who were all named John Peter! Ever since then, he became JP to me, and I was DG to him. John is a very personable, kind, and compassionate guy. You can tell that about him. He works as a supervisor for all new volunteers at Gurwin, explaining the volunteer's duties and roles. He takes his role very seriously. In 2015, John met and married his wife, Amanda, a yoga instructor. In 2019, he and Amanda welcomed their new baby girl, Logan Riley. Turns out that JP's mom is Katie Seikel, a nurse who used to work on 4 North, then on 3 East.

John Peter Rajotte and his yoga-instructor wife, Amanda

GESTURES OF KINDNESS

This is a whole topic to be covered while at Gurwin. Since I've been here, there has been many an occasion when I needed change of a $5, $10, or $20 bill, and one day, I even needed a dime to get me to a dollar, which is what I needed to procure my Diet Coke. Yesterday, it was the Pick family, when I needed change. There were five people, two of them men, and they automatically reached into their pockets to come up with the needed change for a $10 bill. Later, in the Family Brown Bag Room, it was Jeanette who loaned me a dime to get the necessary change for my Diet Coke. I tell people that I am writing a book about my whole ordeal, including my time at Gurwin, and I will be including a section entitled "Gestures of Kindness"—seemingly small, almost meaningless gestures to most, but in my changed perspective, they mean the world to me! Almost daily, there are occurrences such as these, where small gestures of kindness change the trajectory of my day, in a better direction.

For instance, I went to the cafeteria to get my Diet Coke, and I needed someone to help me get the cap off. Sounds simple, mindless, but I needed a hand strong enough to release the cap, sometimes hard to open, sometimes wet; I just needed enough strength and friction to get to that delectable brown, carbonated liquid, which would offer sweet flavor (without sugar) and quench my thirst! I found that hand attached to a man named Miguel, in line at the register in the cafeteria. He opened my bottle cap, which took just a second, and helped pour it into my waiting cup, with ice, so that I could begin to consume my thirst-quenching beverage.

There are innumerable instances like this that happen every day at Gurwin. I'm sure those who come to my assistance don't give it a second thought, like the people who have given me five singles when I only have a $5 bill, or four quarters when I only have a $1 bill. No, they might not give it a second thought, but I do! Previously, I'd have taken it for granted. But not anymore! And that is the essence of my book: to never take it for granted and always be grateful for those who did for me when I could not. And for that, I will remain eternally grateful! Amen.

Every day, when questioned by people about the book I'm writing, which includes cameos of some interesting people I've met at Gurwin, they ask, "Who's going to be interested in our boring stories? You're trying to sell books, right?" To which I respond, "Every person here has a story, has a history worth knowing about. And people are going to be interested to read my story, but also the snippets of peoples' stories that I've included, too."

PHYSICAL THERAPY AT GURWIN

The director of physical therapy (PT) at Gurwin is Joseph D'Ambrosio. He's been with Gurwin for more than thirty years. He was hired personally by Joseph Gurwin, due to his excellent credentials and experience. Joe's assistant and rehab coordinator is Maureen Rieder. She's always very helpful and pleasant.

Director of PT at Gurwin, Joseph D'Ambrosio

SOME OF GURWIN'S PT STAFF WORTH MENTIONING

Broadly speaking, I've found most all of the PT staff at Gurwin to be very capable, and they seem to love what they do to help people. Many residents at Gurwin come for short-term rehabilitation and are sent home quickly. The physical therapy staff works with these patients to determine what their ability is in terms of walking, their balance, strength, and endurance. They perform numerous exercises to improve their strength, whether it be leg lifts using ankle weights, or heel-toe, to determine flexibility and to work all of the muscles involved in walking. Many patients have just had knee- or hip-replacement surgery, and their rehab protocols are determined accordingly.

During my time here, I've always enjoyed going to the lobby gym, on the main level.

Scott Gordon and his son

Scott Gordon: It is in the lobby gym that I originally used the recumbent bike. One of the first PT people I met there was Scott Gordon. A few times, I came upon Scott using the recumbent bike himself. His strategy was to utilize the bike for high-intensity interval training (aka HIIT). He would put the tension at very high levels for short bursts on the bike. He would work up a good sweat, elevate his heart rate, and, my favorite, burn calories. Scott is always upbeat and pleasant, and he is fun to joke around with.

Brian Cangemi: Brian is always very pleasant and usually working with several patients/residents at Gurwin on any given day. It turns out that Brian's uncle was Philip Cangemi, one of the residents at Gurwin from my time on 4 East, who passed in 2018. His uncle would have been one hundred in August 2020.

Brian Cangemi

Brad Hain: Brad is six foot three and is a very pleasant physical therapist. Actually, Brad is a much more average-height guy but he asked that he be "much taller" in my book. None of that takes away from his pleasant nature and competence as a physical therapist. Today, he and Tova, a PT assistant, came up to my room to evaluate my roommate, Francine Miller. Francine is here for short-term rehab following surgery at NYU Medical Center, in the Kimmel Center (named for late-night talk show host Jimmy Kimmel, who made a large donation after his son Billy needed some early cardiac surgical treatment shortly after his birth). After her surgery there, Francine had a short stay at St. Catherine's Hospital in Smithtown, New York. She'll require additional treatment upon her return home. Despite her lung cancer diagnosis, she's got a positive attitude and remains hopeful. She's very alert and "with it," something I haven't had in a roommate before now. I wish her well upon her departure from Gurwin.

Raymond Wolf: Ray is a long-tenured physical therapist. He is strikingly good-looking. To many (like me), he was regarded as the only good eye-candy at Gurwin, but professionally, he is very good at what he does to help people. He is married, with a family. For several months, Ray left Gurwin to work in his own PT business in Deer Park, New York. Due to the pandemic, his stand-alone business got hammered, and he since has come back to Gurwin. We're glad you're back, Ray!

Coleen D'Orio: I liked Coleen immediately when I was assigned to her as my PT. Also, I found out that she lived where I grew up, in North Babylon. She even lives along my initial jogging route when I'd just started running, back in 1978. I was nineteen years old. I'd start at my house and run toward Deer Park Avenue. I'd cross over, and make a right, going North on DPA, and make an immediate left onto Belmont Avenue, which when continued would lead straight to Belmont Park (not the racetrack), and I'd make another left, onto Phelps Lane, going past the Phelps Lane Pool Complex, and other neighborhoods. Finally, I'd head back toward Deer Park Avenue, I'd make a left, ultimately crossing over Deer Park Avenue onto Taylor Avenue, then back to Powell Court, and home.

Coleen Cody D'Orio (on right)

In 2016, after my scalp installation surgery, the pain was in my legs, given the graft sites in my upper inner left thigh and the vein harvest from my lower right calf.

Physical therapy resumed, and that was the tough part. This nimble, flexible runner was reduced to a painful, leg-buckling, struggling walker. But I could start from there.

My exercise, and walking, was painful for the first few weeks. It's interesting that my surgery was to build me a new scalp, but it was the large graft site from my inner left thigh and the harvest of a saphenous vein from my right calf from my knee down to my ankle that caused the soreness post the surgery. Then, I started to regain my strength, and my balance was improving. Every time I go for a walk and I am permitted to walk on my own, I am grateful. These were things I always took for granted. But not anymore. I have come to understand and appreciate these things, and I am able to view the world from a new perspective.

OCCUPATIONAL THERAPY

Anita Wong: I got to know Anita after my nineteenth surgery on my left hand. I described the surgery in detail earlier in the book.

Laura Abrams: Laura was my OT for a week while Anita was on vacation to visit her son who lives in Alaska.

Stuart Natividad: I haven't been treated by Stuart, but I love his laugh. He's a very jovial and outgoing guy. Stuart is married and hopes to have a family someday soon.

Stuart Natividad, occupational therapist with a great laugh

THE AMBULATORS AT GURWIN

There are a group of therapists who assist residents in rehab with their walking capability. Depending on the resident's capability, they will use a walker or another device to assist with their walking. In some cases, residents are able to walk on their own, which is a good thing if they are at Gurwin for short-term rehab prior to returning home. A resident's ability to walk up to one or two hundred feet may be what makes them ready to go home. Insurance coverage, under Medicare, usually will determine that a given resident is able to return home once they can walk the required number of feet. The halls at Gurwin have railings, which are sometimes used as a fall-back, or walking aide, if a resident gets tired or winded while walking. Getting residents back on their feet, and building their stamina, is a key goal of the ambulators. The ambulators have been mirrors for me to determine the level of progress I've made since I arrived nearly five years ago.

Mercedes Martinez: Mercedes has been a CNA, and now a rehab aide, at Gurwin for over twenty years. Mercedes and her team have been helpful to residents at Gurwin on virtually every unit.

Elijah: Pronounced Ah-lee-hee-yah, Elijah has been at Gurwin for twenty years. Spelled as the biblical name, Elijah, the pronunciation is much more fluid, and I find it enjoyable to say out loud.

Jacqueline (or Jackie) Jules: Jackie has been a CNA and a rehab aide for eighteen years. I came to know Jackie as a CNA while I was on 4 East. Jackie was always very capable, no-nonsense, and she gets the job done. Jackie will often work double shifts if one of her daughters is looking for a special "something." She's a tough cookie and a hard-working girl! Not one to mess with, I find her bark is always worse than her bite. Deep down, she's a very caring and selfless human being.

Maria Salinas: Another long-tenured rehab aide, Maria has been with Gurwin for fourteen years.

SHOWER DAYS: AN INTRO TO SOME CULTURAL DIFFERENCES

At Gurwin, each resident is assigned shower days. We are given two showers per week, usually spaced a few days apart. Each resident gets "cleaned up" every day, but unlike living on my own and showering daily, the shower days are set, according to room numbers. My shower days are Tuesdays and Fridays, on the day shift (7 a.m. to 3 p.m.). The showers are given in the designated shower rooms on each unit. I've had to get over any modesty or embarrassment about my body, and the CNAs are always professional and kind during the shower process. While writing this book, I toyed with the idea of portraying our showers as being like the scene in *The Shawshank*

Redemption—being hosed down with a high-pressure nozzle, and then being doused with lye, to prevent bed bugs and lice—but in reality, the process is much more like being treated like Prince Akeem (Eddie Murphy) in *Coming to America*. My hair gets washed and conditioned, and then my body gets scrubbed and washed clean. I get to shave my legs and underarms (if desired). During the body wash, I've gotten to learn the cultural differences of cleaning our private parts. As many of the CNAs are from Haiti, Jamaica, or other islands, and even Ghana, I've learned the various terms used, in other places, for the words we might use in America for "vagina," "pussy," or "hoo-ha" (there is an actual list of fifty different terms for these "private parts"). I have learned that in several of the islands, the term "poon-poon," "puni," or "punnai" might be used interchangeably. Understanding the use of these different terms allows us to communicate more comfortably and have fun, speaking the same language.

Also, as many of the CNAs are from the Islands, I've also learned that many Island men do not like to perform oral sex on their women. Recently, an aide told me that there's a "movement" afoot, called "You've got to lick it before you stick it." I think it's only fair and there are those that *do* perform it, but again, I learn something new here all the time! Thank you!

SECURITY AT GURWIN

Security is pretty tight at Gurwin. There are a few main people who've been with Gurwin for several years. The head of security is Angelo Bonura. He's been with Gurwin for fourteen years. All of the people who man the front desk are very capable, courteous, and kind. They are the initial face that visitors see upon arrival at the facility. Lisa Lynch answers the phone. She's also been with Gurwin for fourteen years. Erica Freeburg is another helpful person at reception at Gurwin. There's also Joe Chambers, who is a security guard. It turns out that he is the cousin of a friend of mine, Doug Chambers, who I knew back in the late eighties/early nineties. Doug now lives in Florida with his wife and daughter. It's interesting to me about how many linkages I have to people here, from people in various periods in my life. There are other people who cover the front desk phones that over the five years I've been here have been helpful to me, particularly during these strange times of COVID-19. Susan Sucozzi is always extremely pleasant and efficient, facilitating several things for me. The pandemic, and the facility's resulting lockdown, has severely curtailed and even prohibited residents' movement about the building. This has been especially difficult for me, as I used to move all over the building in order to do as much walking as possible. My hope is that the arrival of the vaccine will rectify all of these restrictions at 68 Hauppauge Road.

Chapter Twenty

The Feltman Children, All Grown Up

Donna Marie Feltman, today, is Donna Lee Feltman Maida. While growing up, it was discovered that Donna was very musically talented, and to this day, she has a beautiful voice. At home, we had a baby grand piano, and that's where Donna taught herself how to play. She also learned to play the alto saxophone and viola. In her young teen years, Donna was invited to audition for the show *Star Search* (the precursor to today's *American Idol*). Not wanting to pass on the opportunity, Donna, Ray Vino, and I flew out to Los Angeles. It was exciting. Donna performed Barbra Streisand's "Watch Closely Now." Ultimately, she did not win a spot but did receive an honorable mention from the judges. Over the years, Donna has been part of many different bands and orchestras. She did record a single for one of Danielle Steele's books, *To Love Again*. It was sold along with each book. It was during the time Donna was a lead female singer in the band Rapture that she met her future husband, Ronnie Maida. They married in March 1993. Five years later, they welcomed their first and only daughter, Natalie Grace Maida. She became my goddaughter and niece. She was a precious, beautiful baby, and then she went on to become a beautiful young woman. In May

2020, she graduated from my alma mater, SUNY Stony Brook, with a BA in psychology. She also garnered honors with distinction, after making the dean's list every semester. Aunt Debbie was quite proud of Natalie's many diverse accomplishments. Dean's list every semester and sorority president—all challenging to manage! I imagine she will go on to do great things! Today, Donna is a lead female singer in a ten-piece band called That 70s Band. It's become hugely popular all over Long Island and around the Tri-State area. Pre-COVID-19, there was hardly a date when she wasn't working. She was also a regular singing at Gurwin's evening cabaret. She's always a big hit here, and I'm thrilled to show off my sister "Donna Lee" (a stage name). As I finish writing this book, I look forward to the ultimate easing of restrictions, so that activities in the Rainbow Room, like evening cabaret, can reconvene!

***Donna, Ronnie, and Natalie Maida—
a musically talented family***

My brother John Peter Feltman III grew up, graduated from North Babylon Senior High School, and went on to Nassau Community College. John is in the pharmaceuticals sector. John is married to Kelly (also in the pharmaceuticals sector), and he has two sons, John Gregory and Matthew Thomas, with his first wife, Renee Caputo. Renee is now married to former high school sweetheart Dominic Caputo, and together they have a daughter,

Emily, now sixteen. Both John and Matthew have graduated from college and are currently at various stages of graduate school. John is now pursuing a career in teaching, while Matthew, who just graduated from James Madison University in Virginia, is deciding whether to pursue business or law school. Both boys are amazingly smart, they have great personalities, and I'm sure they'll succeed at whatever profession they choose. I just want them to be happy and fulfilled. Turns out that Matthew has exceeded all height expectations, at six foot five inches tall!

Brother John and Kelly at a family baptism

The Feltman grandchildren, James Philip, Nicholas Michael, Matthew Thomas, John Gregory, and Natalie Grace in 2019, after my dad's memorial

My brother Robert, the other brunette in our family, also lives on Long Island. He has been married to his wife, Eileen, for nearly twenty years. Robert has worked in a profession based on his education: computer, electrical, and mechanical engineering. He made a change several years ago into the finance sector, not unlike my dad. Due to losing his job in the wake of COVID-19, Robert is currently pursuing a job back in the insurance and finance arena after the pandemic, which has been tough for everyone. Eileen has been supportive of Robert these last few years, helping him with diet and lifestyle modifications to help his type 2 diabetes. She's been an angel to help him with that. Like me, Robert and Eileen do not have children, but I have always thought they'd be great parents.

Robert and Eileen Feltman—twenty years and counting

Last, but not least, my brother Michael Joseph currently works in home care. He's been a live-in home healthcare aide. One of Michael's most important roles was the home care assistance for my mother, Grace, while she was suffering from metastatic breast cancer, and just five months later, having to deal with the passage of my father, John Peter Feltman. Michael was present when my father, sitting in his usual chair in the den, literally said: "I know this is going to be inconvenient for all of you, but I have to go and see about your mother," after which my dad slumped over and died of an apparent heart attack, but we knew it was a broken heart. So great was their love for one another that my dad could not bear to be on this earth without his Gracie. While Michael performed CPR, as did the EMTs who arrived shortly after, my father could not be revived. He was already gone, in search of his Gracie. The void created by the loss of both of our parents has been enormous, but through our faith we are comforted that they are together forever, and that's where they belong. Michael is also a great father to his two sons: Nicholas Michael and James Philip. Both are in the early stages of attending college. Michael was married to Melanie, but they have since divorced. Most importantly, Michael and Melanie successfully co-parent Nick and James.

Michael, in one of his most important healthcare roles: caring for our dear, mother, Grace

The original five siblings:
Michael, Donna, Robert, me, and John

The Feltman Family at a 4th of July gathering at Cindy and Tom Quinn's home, one month before my near-death accident

Chapter Twenty-One

The Wall Street Years

A Long and Storied Career

I enjoyed a long and storied career on Wall Street—thirty years in all. I started with bulge bracket, investment banking firms, and ended up with a boutique broker-dealer in Houston called Starlight Investments. After graduating from Stony Brook University in May 1985, I hit the pavement, "resume in hand." I'd called a number of firms and finally got some interviews: one at Donaldson, Lufkin & Jenrette (DLJ), and another at Goldman Sachs. Goldman Sachs (a high-pedigree investment bank and brokerage firm) was for a back-office operations position, and I'd been advised against that because I could get "stuck" there with no exposure to the real "action." As it turned out, with DLJ, I believe I made the best career path decision for me. I learned fast and moved up quickly. I wouldn't change a thing about my path for either my personal or professional life, because all of the events contributed to who I am today, and my positive outlook for the future. There were certain decisions that I later came to regret, but still, they all made me who I am, and they all caused me to maintain the drive I continue to have. Many people who have gone through what I have endured would have given up long ago, but today I thrive. It didn't kill me; it made me stronger. And now I have a big job of rebuilding my life from the ground up. Wish me luck! And stay tuned.

A COURTESY INTERVIEW WITH LEHMAN BROTHERS

As it turned out, Gary's cousin Ken Ambrecht worked for Lehman Brothers as a corporate bond salesman. This was the summer of 1985. At the time, I didn't know the difference between a bond salesman and a stock broker, like my father was. I knew that I obviously had a ton to learn. Ken was a tall, very good-looking man with salt and pepper hair combed back and spectacular blue eyes. He wore suspenders (or braces as they were also called). Later on, I learned that his coworkers routinely referred to Ken as "the Senator" because of his looks and the way he dressed and carried himself.

Ken didn't have a specific job to offer or talk about when I met with him; this was more of a "networking, talking generally about the business" kind of meeting. We met at 55 Water Street. I also noted that there were a lot of boxes around, like it was moving day. He introduced me to Karinne Koury, his sales assistant and also to Nina Wainwright, his bond salesperson business partner. Nina was tall, with long legs and a short skirt. She had long blond hair, which was wavy, and she had the front ends pulled back in a barrette. I noted that she wore an insignia ring. Ken mentioned that she had graduated from Trinity College for undergrad and Wharton Business School for graduate school, and she was recently married to a guy named Doug Stone, who was also in the biz, and they were living on Fifth Avenue. We exchanged pleasantries and Ken told Nina that I would be talking to DLJ. Ken said to me that, if I took a position at DLJ, maybe we could "find ways to work together." Little did I know, but Nina would become one of my dearest friends, and I would end up working for Lehman Brothers. Lehman Brothers morphed from then–Shearson Lehman Hutton, division of American Express, and began to run independently. It later went public and started trading on the New York Stock Exchange under the ticker symbol "LEH." On September 15, 2008, in the midst of the great recession, Lehman filed for bankruptcy. It later was acquired by the UK's Barclays bank.

My Interview at DLJ with Mariel Clemensen: Beginning to Learn How Much I Didn't Know

DLJ was at 140 Broadway. It was the Marine Midland Building, with a big orange cube outside. I was going for an interview with Mariel Clemensen. They told me she was on the thirty-sixth floor, so I went up. I approached the receptionist and told her I was there to see Mariel Clemensen. She said, "Have a seat and I'll get her." I thanked her.

In a few minutes, out from around the corner, a tall, pretty woman with perfectly straight, blonde hair, parted in the middle (my lifetime hair envy), approached me and said, "Are you Deborah? Come back into my office." I followed her past a few desks and turned right after the third desk and into an office to the left of two other offices. I saw a man seated at a desk in the office on the right, and Mariel said, "That's Paul Parshley, he's writing a book about nukes under construction." (Okay, what are nukes?) She said, "And I just wrote this one," handing me a book that said *High Coupon Bond Redemptions*. Apparently, it was a big hit and invited a ton of inquiries from institutional clients who owned high coupon debt, debt that was issued to fund construction of new nuclear plants and for other capital needs. Now I could see (a teensy-weensy bit) how these things fit together.

In looking back, it is now easy to see that Mariel Clemensen had a huge impact on the market in her heyday. She saw the coupons that were coming out on new issues, knew they were extremely high, but knew they were likely to keep coming. But what about redemption features? She took it upon herself, and maybe an assistant, to accumulate copies of every single bond issued in the 1980s, in the electric utility universe. There was Central Maine Power, Arizona Public Service, Ohio Edison, Long Island Lighting (LILCO), Baltimore Gas & Electric, as well as several other utilities.

Then there was the issue of call prices, and under what circumstances. There was the M&R (Maintenance & Replacement fund), the sinking fund, and release of property clauses. All of that was in her book, which was a huge hit and garnered her much recognition from institutional investors. Every day, while working as her administrative assistant, I would receive calls from investors asking for copies of the call schedules, and the verbiage in the prospectus about the M&R, sinking funds, and release of property clauses. She was onto something, and the fixed income world knew it! She would sit at her desk, prospectus and her book in hand, and read the schedules and the prices to these investors, seemingly not tiring at all!

Mariel told me to have a seat. She sat across from me. Then, in one discreet move (okay, two), she flicked her long hair behind her shoulders, grabbed a tube of red lipstick out of her large Coach satchel bag and applied a fresh coat, then blotted her lips together and smiled at me. She was pretty. I liked her instantly, and she seemed to like me. She was packing up her satchel and her briefcase, and I inquired, "Are you going somewhere?"

She said, "Yes, Nelson and I are going to Italy for two weeks."

I said, "Nice, I'd love to go there one day. Are you taking all those large textbooks with you?"

She said, "Sure, I'll get to read them on the plane."

I asked, "How long is the flight? You have enough reading for three years."

She laughed, a hearty laugh, and said, "Well, I will skim the chapters for relevant pages and skip a lot."

I said, "Okay, but it's your vacation."

So she told me about the job I came to talk about, an administrative assistant, and she needed someone to help her "find out where all the bodies are buried," and to stay organized.

I asked, "And the bodies?"

She laughed again and said, "It will help you figure out who does what around here, and that's a very important skill." She began going through the inbox and tried to shove a stack of mail in her satchel, and it looked like she was wrapping up our meeting.

I asked, "So what are the hours?"

She said, "It depends on you. We generally start between 7 a.m. and 7:30 a.m. for our morning meeting up on forty-nine, and then we finish when we finish."

I said, "Okay, fair enough."

With that, the receptionist came in and said, "Mariel, your car is here."

Then Mariel said, "Thanks, I enjoyed our meeting. I hope you're here when I get back."

Wow! So I think I got the job! I forgot to ask specifically about the money. So I said, "Just one more thing, do you have a specific salary in mind?"

She replied, "How does eighteen thousand sound, with a first-year bonus of three thousand dollars?"

Barely able to contain myself, I said, "Sounds great! I'll be here when you get back. Have an amazing time in Italy!"

Mariel Clemensen, circa 1980s, my first boss on Wall Street

And so, my career begins in two weeks! Wow! I can't believe it! I'm so excited and happy! She was really nice and she seemed cool, like we were on the same level. But I know she'll be my boss. Yes! I'm so excited.

I left 140 Broadway and began my trek home. I looked for the number 2 train—found it—across the street from the back of the building; I got into the station just as the number 2 train arrived. The doors opened, and I got on. Onward to 34th Street/Penn Station, and then the LIRR. I was shaking with excitement! Wait till I tell Mom and Dad! They'll be thrilled too! I got to Penn Station and then looked for the sign for the LIRR. It was a long way down the hall and then I saw a big hallway with a number of monitors in a row, listing all the trains that would be headed to Long Island. I saw one for Babylon: the next train would be at 6:10 p.m. and would arrive in Babylon at 7:22 p.m. I looked around and saw a bar cart on the platform and said, "What the heck? I gotta celebrate." So I went over and bought a single-serve bottle of chardonnay. The vendor gave me the bottle in a paper bag and a cup with ice in it. I gave him a $5 bill and he gave me $3 change. So this was the way adults cap off their day. I felt so grown up and liberated!

The train ride home was uneventful, and we arrived on time. Then, I had to call someone to pick me up. The phone rang and I got my mom. She said hello. I said hi, and that I was at the train station in Babylon, and could someone pick me up. She said, "How did the interview go?"

I said, "Well, I have good news."

"I'll send your father down. Give him about fifteen minutes. That's great!" She sounded very hopeful and happy for me.

STARTING MY JOB AT DLJ: THE FIRST DAY

I started at DLJ on September 18, 1985. When I arrived at the offices of Mariel Clemensen and Paul Parshley, there was a paper sign on Paul's office door to "Congratulate Paul, on the arrival of his new baby boy, Michael Louis Parshley," so that was happy news for Paul, and his wife, Cathy.

Paul and Cathy Parshley, circa 1990s;
Paul was my other first boss on Wall Street

I wasn't sure if Mariel was back from Italy yet, but I would see. I was invited to sit at the desk outside their offices, which would be my desk, and so this was my new base of operations. I had to answer calls for Mariel, Paul, and Michele Mahoney, the new research assistant. I needed to take information from the callers about what they were calling about and their contact information. I quickly realized that my job would be a central hub of information flow, and I could figure out the various parties who put together the pieces of the fixed income division. First, I had to survey the lay of the land: who sat where, who did what. I took a walk out to the trading floor, where all the action happened. It was a little daunting at first, but I was one of "them" now. I belonged there and was part of their team.

When I walked out to the trading floor, I saw that there was an L-shaped desk along two sides of the floor, and the traders had their backs to the windows, facing west and north. That was where the traders sat. Branches of desks jutted out from different points along the trading desks, where the bond salesmen sat. In between them and on the ends were desks and seats for the sales assistants. The trading floor comprised areas for each product line: corporate bonds, government bonds, mortgage bonds, and preferred stocks. There was also an area for syndicate: the place where all of the literature for new sales product was kept—prospectuses, sales memos, and everything else to help get new bonds "sold." Early on, I got the feeling that I was part of something big. And it was exciting.

It was only nine o'clock, and the place was already full and buzzing. People on phones. People shouting commands, and in between, the people trying to help them. We didn't know it then, but one of our sales assistants, Mary Pat Christie, was married to a man with political aspirations for the future, and who later became the governor of New Jersey. His name was Chris Christie. There was an overhead speaker system, which allowed for traders to "broadcast" the merchandise they had in inventory and were trying to sell. I learned that we had offices in Boston, Chicago, Dallas, and San Francisco. People who worked in those branch locations had to adhere to Wall Street hours, or East Coast time. So when we had a meeting at 7 a.m. EST, the salespeople in San Francisco, Chicago, and Boston had to be in the office, or listening by phone, at 4 a.m. PST, 6 a.m. CST, and 7 a.m. EST, respectively, allowing for the time differences. Each one of the salespeople had their assigned accounts, and so they'd be in contact with their accounts' portfolio managers, research, and syndicate if there was a new issue coming to market. The salespeople always had to bear in mind their accounts' return objectives and maturity constraints. They had to be aware of all that was happening in various sectors that their accounts invested in: utilities, banking, retail, industrial, capital goods, the financial services sector, casinos and gaming, and so on. If there were ratings changes, upgrades or downgrades, the salespeople had to be aware of those, too. And it was the job of research to be on top of all that was going on, on the ratings side, and if there were new developments on the regulatory side, or a pending court ruling related to a rate case, or a broad, industry-impacting decision. There were so many different moving parts on a given day, so all hands needed to be on deck.

Morning Line: A Daily DLJ Production

One of my first job tasks was the manufacturing of our daily publication, called "Morning Line." It had a big green logo across the top of the page, with a black telephone handset and cord stretched across the green background, with "Morning Line" inscribed in the forefront. Below it, we'd type stories about companies on a typewriter (really) or on a Wang Word Processor (there was no Microsoft Word widely available at the time). The write-ups were about companies featured in the daily papers, including our opinions about whether this news was good or bad for the particular company, or the industry, in which it participated. Was it a ratings event (likely to impact financials of the company or companies, negatively or positively)? Because these were then likely to impact the way a given company's, or its sectors' bonds and stocks traded; with good news, possible upgrade, spreads go tighter, prices of the bonds go up. Bad news, spreads go wider, prices of the bonds go down. The same would generally apply to a company's or its industry's stocks and bonds.

After a while there, I dubbed the traders, salespeople, and trading floor inhabitants at DLJ "The Hogan's Heroes of Wall Street." Many times, they stood or sat in a huddle-type formation, speaking low or in hushed whispers. They were all so different from each other; all had different personalities, some were more boisterous than others, some were more scruffy or rough around the edges than others, but generally they were a group I came to like very much.

YOU'VE GOT GUMPTION

Back to "Morning Line." It was a daily production, and not an easy one. As I mentioned, this was all in advance of Microsoft Word, when cut and paste from a newspaper website was still just a twinkle in a programmer's eye, and so scissors, scotch tape, and manual placement of articles and text were all we had. And there was no such thing as blast emails to branch offices and departments (or a website where such items could be posted). We had to manually make copies and fax copies to the branches and to departments, like investment banking and the equities trading desk. The ease of the way things are done today was something we could only dream of. One morning, in the daily "Morning Line" production, I was in the process of making the required 300 copies—and if a copier was going to jam, it always happened when you were under pressure. So, while I was in a sweat, and trying to get the copier working again, a man standing at the doorway interrupted and asked, "Can I butt in here and make a couple of copies?"

I said, "Sorry, but you're going to have to wait, I've got 'Morning Line' going here."

He said, "No problem, I'll come back later."

In just a few seconds, Michele Mahoney poked her head into the copy room, and said, "Nice workin' with ya, Deb."

Perplexed, I asked why, and she said, "Do you know who that was?"

I said, "No, who was it?"

She said, "Oh he's just senior counsel for the whole firm. His name is Michael Boyd, and I think he's a pretty nice guy, so you're probably okay."

I said, "Well, I had to finish 'Morning Line.'"

She said, "Whatever."

Later in the morning, I asked where Michael Boyd's office was, and I was told it was around the corner. So around the corner I went and peeked in, and there was Michael Boyd, eating a bagel at his desk, and I said, "Michael, I'm sorry I couldn't let you in to make a few copies."

He said, "No worries, young lady, you had much more important things to do. I can do my copies any time. You've got gumption, though, and that's a good quality to have around here."

Wow! Phew! What a relief! I said, "Well that's very gracious of you, and I think that's a wonderful quality to have around here, and not everybody does." So, I guess I still had a job and maybe scored a few points.

The next interaction, a few weeks later, came from Dick Paini, a corporate bond salesperson. He had walked by my desk a few times and said hello, and the last time he did, he leaned over my desk and said, "Do yourself a favor, lose the schoolmarm look, let your hair down. I bet you'd look good." I'd been wearing it in a bun or ponytail most days. So, I guess hairstyling advice must be in the purview of the sales guys on the trading floor.

Dick Paini became part of the high yield bond department. Kathy Duffy was the first woman in the junk bond department. (High yield and junk bonds are the same product: sub-investment-grade debt). Dick had a large pepper plant hung from the ceiling over his desk. If Dick was upset about something going on in the midst of the business day, he would reach overhead, cut down one of his peppers, and eat them, right then and there. This caused his entire face to turn bright red and you could tell his blood pressure was high. There was another custom among the traders and salespeople. If a bond trade was done for the first time, a trader or salesperson would cut the tie of the successful bond salesman and tack it to the corkboard in the trading room—a sign that he had lost his virginity in the bond sales arena. What to do if it was a woman salesperson? One day, Kathy Duffy found out. After successfully selling a large block of bonds to her customer, Dick Paini took it upon himself to show Kathy what to cut to commemorate her successful trade. Dick reached down Kathy Duffy's jacket back and reached for her bra strap! Kathy, screamed at Paini, "Get the f#ck off me, what are you, crazy?!" Yes, these were the types of things that went on across the trading floor, and we liked it!

DONALDSON, LUFKIN & JENRETTE: HISTORY

Bill Donaldson, Dan Lufkin, and Dick Jenrette founded the firm on the principle that no one else on Wall Street was doing high-quality independent corporate research. They not only centered the firm around this notion but ended up being one of the best firms doing independent corporate bond research. As research became more of a commodity throughout the 1980s and 1990s, they had since expanded into other businesses. One of them was a dominance in high yield fixed income securities. They gained this dominance in both underwriting and trading by astutely picking up most of the expertise from Drexel Burnham Lambert after its demise in the late 1980s.

A big emphasis on research continued when I was there. In 1988, our group came in first for utility research in the Greenwich Street Research Survey, made up entirely of buy-side votes among institutional clients. And we were happy to have it.

Source: https://en.wikipedia.org/wiki/Donaldson,_Lufkin_%26_Jenrette

WE WANT TO BE JESSE'S GIRLS!

It was 1986, and the New York Mets made it into the World Series, playing against the Boston Red Sox. Since the trading desk didn't want to miss any of the "action," a few of the traders, including Danny Loughran, bought us perks, buying big-screen TVs for the trading floor. After hours, we livened up the atmosphere, and we bought beers to be delivered for the games at night.

As we watched, Games 6 and 7 were the highlights of a series that the Mets won, in Game 7. Pitcher Jesse Orosco was made extra popular with the popularity of the song "Jessie's Girl." Ultimately, one of the most memorable moments was the game-winning strikeout of the Boston Red Sox's Marty Barrett in Game 7 when the Mets won the title! Jesse Orosco was so thrilled that he threw his glove high into the air and then went down on his knees, arms in the air, as his teammates poured out of the dugout!

THE MBA CLASS OF 1986

Mariel Clemensen seemed to be making headway as she was rising in her rank around DLJ. First, she became head of corporate bond research, and then head of high yield research, as DLJ was becoming better known for its large high yield bond offerings. Deals in this arena were quite lucrative. It also appeared that she was becoming the "muse" of DLJ president John Chalsty. Mariel was charged with hiring new talent to staff the research department with the necessary expertise in various industry sectors in which DLJ was seeking to manage their bond offerings.

In 1986, Mariel sought out the fresh, new talent from some of the best schools. Thus, the MBA class of 1986 was born. As I was privy to some of the paperwork involved in recruiting this new talent, I viewed their starting salaries (all significantly higher than mine at this point). First was, where to put this new class? Turns out that just a floor below thirty-six was some space, built by one of the founders, that was, in some ways, perfect to put these new folks to work for the summer of 1986. Ultimately, it came to be known as "the hamster cage," as it was generally very hot all the time, and it was filled with reams of paper—newspaper and other documents related to their new research. One of the members of the class of 1986 turned out to become one of the dearest and most loyal and helpful friends I've ever had: Tim Foxe, or Thomas Timothy Foxe (who preferred always to be called Tim, not Tom, ever). Later we took to calling each other "Dr. Foxe" and "Dr. Grosser," and that has stuck for thirty-five years! Tim came from Columbia University. He was a very smart guy, with beautiful blue, piercing eyes. He was handsome too! One might say Tim should have been born in an earlier era, as a gentleman of sorts. He loved e-type roadsters and wearing scarves while driving fast in his e-type roadster. I'd say he stepped right out of *The Great Gatsby* era!

Tim Foxe, a great friend,
right out of the Great Gastsby era

Others in that group included Matthew (Matt) Nelson (undergrad), Rick Mallon (undergrad), Nancy Diao, Steven Rattner (who had a JD MBA from NYU), and Chuck Strasser. To keep the appropriate "pecking order" intact, the MBAs took to calling Matt and Rick "the puppies." They hated that designation.

Our Departure

We accomplished much in my first three years, including our Greenwich Survey win, and me being promoted to vice president and analyst in the corporate bond research department. My compensation package was already over $50,000. I remember, one Christmastime, after my paycheck arrived with my bonus included in it, I went to go run an errand over at the World Trade Center. As I left the building at 140 Broadway and stood at the corner of Broadway and Liberty Street, facing northwest, an X27 MTA bus bound for Brooklyn stopped at the corner, diagonally across from where I was standing, and I looked up at all the building lights, including the World Trade Center, and I got the urge to throw my hat up in the air, like Mary Tyler Moore did at the end of her TV show every week, because "you're going to make it after all" was playing in my head.

After we had only been at DLJ for three years, Paul Parshley had been approached by Shearson Lehman Brothers, and apparently, he had already met with them about our entire group going over to Shearson Lehman, and further, he had nominally agreed that we would go. Paul approached each of us about salary expectations and roles for each of us. My new role would include a title upgrade to analyst and vice president in the fixed income division of Shearson Lehman Brothers (my first VP role was in the corporate bond department, and the division title was a nice uptick). I remember telling my grandmother, Nanny, that I'd been promoted to vice president, and her response to me was, "When do you get to be president?" (It was only natural for her to ask that.) My compensation was estimated at about $65,000, and I liked that, too. Paul said it wouldn't be too long before my comp got to the $100,000 range, and I really liked that. When the department heads heard we were proposing to leave, they put on a "push" for us not to leave, but all in all, it was too compelling, and we agreed to make the move.

Lehman Brothers: Our New Beginning

When we first arrived at Lehman Brothers in 1988, the official title of the company was Shearson Lehman Hutton, Division of American Express. It later became Shearson, Lehman Brothers, division of American Express, and finally Lehman Brothers, Inc.

As it turned out, we moved to Lehman on September 18, exactly three years from when I started at DLJ. A few weeks prior, at the end of August, our group went over to meet the "new kids" we'd be working with. Thus, Paul Parshley, Jim Asselstine, Peter Petas, Michele Mahoney, Patti Byrnes, and I all went over to survey the new landscape. We were also moving to the new World Financial Center, which was supposed to be beautiful.

Lehman had moved to the World Financial Center (WFC) shortly after its completion in 1985. The WFC was a beautiful complex, just north of the growing Battery Park City. Interestingly, Battery Park City was built on the landfill that came out of the dirt from digging for the foundation for the previously existing World Trade Center (WTC), which was destroyed in the September 11, 2001, terror attacks, with more than three thousand lives lost on that day. WTC 1 and 2 (the big towers), and 3, 4, and 5 (the medium-sized buildings) came down also, as well as 7 WTC (about fifty-plus stories, that came down later in the day).

The WFC housed several financial companies such as American Express, Lehman Brothers, Merrill Lynch, Nomura, and others. It also had a retail center, housing restaurants and stores, a hair salon, and other small shops that were perfect for midday retail therapy, getting my hair done, buying small gifts for someone's birthday, and so on.

Barbara Germain from Lehman became a good friend of mine. Years later, Barbara, my parents, and I discussed her thirtieth birthday, and we heard Barbara's early impression of us. On this birthday, Perry Burns, her then-boss, led the parade as our group traipsed into her office. First, the three women, all carrying their red Coach bags (Patti Byrnes, Michele Mahoney, and me), were followed by Paul Parshley, the group's new boss, and then the "twin towers," Peter Petas and Jim Asselstine (former Nuclear Regulatory Commission Commissioner, appointed by President Reagan, who would share the group-head role), both well over six feet tall. So, Barbara's reaction was less than enthusiastic or excited, more like trying to be nice, but she was secretly annoyed that this new group, previously competitors, was going to encroach on her comfortable little world—but my, my, my, things were about to change!

Barbara Germain, my longtime gal pal from Lehman

Michele Mahoney on the right and hubby Ken Richardson on the left

WE INHERITED SOME NEW HELP FOR OUR GROUP

Patti Byrnes came over from DLJ to join us at Lehman. She was very close to her family, including her grandmother. She was a devout Catholic, once nearly fainting with fear when a prank was played, threatening her with just the idea that a male stripper had come to entertain her for her birthday.

Patti Byrnes, our admin who joined us from DLJ

Jane Paschetti was one of our new secretaries, and shortly thereafter, we hired Lisa as a new administrative assistant. Some memorable stories resulted from their presence in our group. One day, Lisa brought me a phone message that said the caller was "Fred" or "Lin," but it was the same x6705 trading desk extension. The actual caller was Fred Orlan (pronounced "Orlin"), one of our industrial traders. Another time, Jane complimented my outfit, and I said it was Evan Piccone, and she said: "Oh, I love Eva Piccone." (I guess it was gender reassignment, without the surgery.) Another time, she said we have to get to the five-fifteen meeting, "It's at five-fifteen." (Thanks for that clarification, Jane.) She also asked me once where I had gotten a particular outfit, and I said Neiman Marcus, and she replied, "Oh, I love 'Newman'

Marcus, they have beautiful things." Finally, there was that classic occasion when Paul Parshley, our boss, interrupted our less-than-important conversation to say, "Hey, we can't be talking out here, we've got LILCO calls coming in, we need all hands on deck." Poor Jane had just been on the phone with her sister, who died a short time after their call.

Just before Paul and I moved to equities, we'd inherited Hazel Talley. She was an internal hire and had previously worked with some of the traders on the desk. Hazel, originally from Jamaica, had a lilting and melodic voice. It was one that Barbara Germain and I discussed as having a "drowsy" impact on us. We came to learn more recently that the drowsy effect that Hazel's voice had on us came from something called autonomous sensory meridian response, or ASMR. I had discussed this phenomenon with Barbara one day and we discovered that we shared this! I remember being in a ladies' room in the office and just the sound of makeup casings rubbing against each other could be cause for an uncontrollable urge to drowse off. On Barbara too! If a woman on the X-27 bus from Brooklyn to downtown Manhattan had to apply her makeup, I could spend forty-five minutes watching and listening to the soothing sound of her rummaging through her makeup bag in search of her lipstick or blush. It truly had a hypnotic effect on me.

Hazel Talley, who had a good coma-inducing voice

Hazel's voice had the same effect! She would often talk about her childhood in Jamaica, and she'd go on about going hunting with her dad for birds that they'd "cook up with a little salt 'n pepper." "It was good," she'd say, as Barbara and I were nearly in a coma! But a "good" coma!

The definition of ASMR from lexico.com is as follows: "A feeling of well-being combined with a tingling sensation in the scalp and down the back of the neck, as experienced by some people in response to a specific gentle stimulus, often a particular sound."

MY BESTEST CUBEMATE 4-EVA

Peter Petas and I shared cubicles next to one another, and ultimately called each other "my bestest cubemate 4-eva." Peter also posted a sign on the hallway side of my cubicle that read "Please don't feed the analysts." Since my cube was closest to the entrance of the copy room, people were constantly hanging over the top of my cube asking for staplers, staple removers, paper clips, scissors, and Scotch tape.

My "bestest" cubemate: Peter J. Petas

OUR GROUP COVERED THE ELECTRIC UTILITY INDUSTRY

Our group was responsible for the coverage of the electric utility industry. This is a rather large industry, as every state in the United States has at least one, if not several, utilities that provide electric and/or gas service to their customers. For instance, in New York state, the companies that provided service were Consolidated Edison, Long Island Lighting Co., Orange & Rockland Utilities, Central Hudson Gas & Electric, Rochester Gas & Electric, New York State Electric & Gas, and Niagara Mohawk. While there are also several companies that provide either electric or gas service, they are small, municipally owned companies. We covered the companies that issued corporate debt securities (corporate bonds). Thus, our industry coverage was composed of more than one hundred operating companies, throughout the fifty states. As a result, our group staffing was larger than other industry sectors. When fully staffed, we covered over one hundred electric and gas utility companies, among Paul Parshley, James (Jim) Asselstine, Deborah Grosser (me), Michele Mahoney, Barbara Germain, and Peter Petas. Later on, we added a telecommunications analyst, Tom Aust, to our group.

LEHMAN BROTHERS TRADING DESK

Once we were at Lehman, it was incumbent upon us to learn the new members of the trading desk. Much like DLJ, Lehman had coverage for all of the various industry sectors. There was Herbert (Bart) McDade, a nice-looking blond guy who looked serious. He traded the banking and finance sectors. Gerry Weston and Carmine Urcioli traded industrials. Scott Fahey, Jeffrey Weiss, and Arnie Palatnek traded the utilities sector. It was our job to keep them informed of ratings changes, positive or negative developments in a rate decision, and anything else that might impact their existing trading positions.

Gerry and Lynn Weston, after Wall Street travels

EEI: THE ANNUAL INDUSTRY EVENT

As is custom for other industries, electric utilities had an annual industry conference, sponsored by its industry group, the Edison Electric Institute conference. Each year, the location would alternate between the East Coast and the West Coast. It was held each year during a week in October, from Sunday night through Wednesday afternoon. It was a big deal. All of the sell-side analysts and all of the buy-side analysts would be hosted at a hotel of note (usually, very nice, with four- or five-star ratings). Along with the buy-side and sell-side, all of the industry's companies would be there, too. Plus, there were a number of EEI staff people that participated in all of the activities.

For the companies who were presenting, senior management reps, such as the CEO, the CFO, the treasurer, and others involved with the regulatory and finance areas, would be present. In my first year at DLJ, I did not attend the annual financial conference for EEI. That didn't happen until I was actually doing the research. But that happened pretty quickly, as I was eager to learn, and be part of the "exciting stuff." After I passed muster in performing the daily "Morning Line" ritual and successfully planned a research-investor road show, I was hopeful to get my name attached to a project.

When I arrived at DLJ, Paul Parshley was in the middle of working on his project, related to nuclear power plant construction. In the mid-1980s, there were dozens of electric utility companies in the midst of building new nuclear plants. Nuclear plant construction was expensive. The attraction to building these mammoth projects was precipitated by statements made among industry officials, including regulators at the Nuclear Regulatory Commission. Peter Bradford was quoted as saying that the price per unit of electricity (kWh) produced by nuclear plants would be "too cheap to meter." As a result, the original projections for nuclear capacity in the United States were that there would be one thousand nuclear plants built by the year 2000. A near meltdown at the Three Mile Island Nuclear Generating Station (owned, in part, by General Public Utilities), followed by the Chernobyl accident, in 1986, changed everything for the prospects of nuclear plants in the resource mix for the industry. Ultimately, only 109 nuclear reactors were ever built in the United States. As it turned out, our research group was well-positioned to provide insight on the companies and the overall industry as these projects progressed. As I mentioned, Paul Parshley was working on a book related to nuclear power plant construction, and I was fortunate that Paul asked if I could help him with that task. I was thrilled! This could be my shot! Paul had a very impressive resume: for undergrad, he went to Colgate University, in Ithaca, New York, and subsequently, he entered the Executive MBA program at Wharton Business School, part of University of Pennsylvania, in Philadelphia. Prior to business school, Paul worked in Washington, DC, as a Congressional aide to Morris "Mo" Udall, from Arizona. Mo was the chair of the House Interior Committee on Energy (Paul's tenure with Mo gave him access to some federal regulators, one of whom came to work at DLJ).

I digress. Back to Paul's book on nuclear power plant construction. My task was to contact each of the companies that were involved in the proposed nuclear plant, and go through a checklist of questions related to the project:

1. What is the current projected total cost of the project?

2. How much has been spent so far?

3. Are there any delays foreseen, given the current status of the project?

4. Has there been any opposition to the project? If so, what is it?

5. Have any of the regulatory filings been made to secure the recovery of the company's investment?

6. What is the status of the NRC licensing process?

7. When is it projected that the license will be granted?

Ultimately, the project got completed, the final version went through editing and formatting, and I was so happy to see the completed project—in print! It had a nice gold cover.

I believe it was my efforts helping Paul with his project that garnered me some recognition and demonstrated that I offered some value in the research project, and that was a consideration for me to be included in the next year's EEI conference.

In 1987, the annual EEI financial conference was hosted at The Breakers in Palm Beach. Reservations had to be made for the team: Mariel, Paul, Michele, and me! I'd been to Florida before but not to Palm Beach. When we arrived at The Breakers, I mean, I had arrived! Monday, October 19, 1987, came to be known as Black Monday, as the stock market plunged more than 22 percent. I remember during the conference that everyone walking from meeting to meeting was talking about the latest market report. People were fixated on the television. In years to follow, Paul and I learned, through Fred Fraenkel, that a market strategist in equities research, Elaine Garzarelli, "predicted" the crash, through a model she touted as accurate. It certainly looked that way.

THE WALL STREET JOURNAL.

Calling the Crash: Pessimistic Predictions
By Analyst at Shearson Make Her a Star

YOUR
MONEY
MATTERS

[illegible]

[illegible]

Elaine Garzarelli's claim to fame. Shearson Lehman management loved this kind of press.

1987 EEI Conference hotel, The Breakers in Palm Beach

The EEI financial conference commenced on a Sunday evening and ran through Wednesday afternoon. The Sunday night meeting was a welcome session, and it was usually a packed house. There are typically more than three thousand people from all aspects of the financial securities markets. There was the sell-side, those whose firms would sell the investor-owned electric utilities' stocks and/or bonds, and there was the buy-side, those institutional investors who bought the IOUs stocks and/or bonds. Then, there were the IOU's senior management and investor relations staff. Finally, there were people from the regulatory side, from the State Public Utility

Commissions (they could also be called the Public Service Commissions). There would also be representatives from the federal regulatory agencies: the Nuclear Regulatory Commission (NRC) and the Federal Energy Regulatory Commission (FERC). Representatives from each of these agencies could ultimately be keynote speakers of the various sessions.

Of course, being in this beautiful hotel in the midst of Palm Beach, we took many opportunities to partake in pool or beach activities. One afternoon, Paul and his wife, Cathy, and Gary and I went to spend time by the pool. While there, I noticed that senior management of one of the companies for which we rated their bonds, and for which we co-underwrote several of their first mortgage bond issues, was also at the pool. We struck up a conversation with Don Rayburn, from investor relations, Walter Goodenough, CFO, and a few others who were out enjoying the sun, the pool, and the spectacular environment. At one point, we took a walk inside to get some refreshments, and while there, I looked out by the pool, and I noticed Gary outside with Cathy Parshley, and they were naturally laughing at something. Gary (who always tended to get a bad sunburn on his back) was being aided by Cathy (who always had a beautiful figure, and she was in a black bikini), who was applying lotion to Gary's back. As we watched the interaction, the management from TXU looked at them, then turned to me, and they shrugged, and just said, "Sorry." Gary and Cathy had no idea they were being watched. It was very funny.

One more story about TXU: We were in Dallas for a meeting with the company, staying at the Adolphus Hotel. Later that evening after dinner, we participated in an impromptu game of pool. (Just a note, the Adolphus Hotel was built in 1912, by the founder of the Anheuser-Busch Company, Adolphus Busch). I teamed up with Walter Goodenough, CFO, while Don Rayburn partnered with another guy from TXU. During the game, there was no shortage of drinking, Rémy Martin stingers. And while I did not partake (this time), Walter and the other guys had several Rémy stingers. At the end of the match, I innocently asked Walter if he was okay to be driving home (given the amount of alcohol consumed). Walter, who was always very friendly, simply, but sternly said, "Little lady, never tell a Texan he can't drive!"

In Texas, up until 2001, it was legal to have open containers of alcohol in the passenger compartment of a vehicle. They'd speak of the distance to drive somewhere, as "it was a two-beer or a three-beer ride." (I'm not kidding).

In October 1987, on Monday the 19th, the stock market suffered a huge crash.

In October 1988, EEI hosted its annual conference in Scottsdale, Arizona, at The Camelback Resort. This was an entirely new environment for me. The resort is so named for its proximity to Camelback Mountain, which looks like a sleeping camel, crouched down to the ground.

Camelback Mountain, perfect for cross-training, pre–New York City Marathon

At EEI Camelback, I got to spend time with Melinda Curry (a co-competitor, on the sell-side, at Drexel Burnham Lambert) and Debbie Bromberg (a ratings agency analyst, at Standard & Poor's). It was during this conference that Melinda, Debbie, and I became much more friendly and knew we'd spend more time together upon our return to New York City.

During this conference, one morning, for exercise, Paul Parshley suggested that we hike up Camelback Mountain, and we did! It was this year that I'd be running the New York City Marathon, and this "hike" would be perfect cross-training in advance of my race in a few weeks! I wore a pair of shorts with a blouse (it was actually a matching outfit) and my New Balance running shoes (that I would wear on race day). To maintain hydration, I also brought a couple of water bottles, but where to carry them? My only solution was to carry my shoulder-strapped black leather Coach bag! It wasn't a strenuous climb but it did require a fair amount of exertion. There were multiple places that had railings to hold on to (curious, who put them there?). Along the route, we passed several other people, some families of climbers, who seemed to be strolling casually up the camel's back. Eventually, after a bit more than an hour, we reached the peak of Camelback Mountain. It was quite a view, overlooking Phoenix and the surrounding rocky desert terrain.

MY NEW YORK CITY MARATHON EXPERIENCE

My initial plan had been to run the New York City Marathon in 1987, but I ended up with chronic fatigue syndrome. My symptoms were recurring strep throat infections and fatigue, and I had to postpone it to the next year, 1988. Gary and I had moved to Mahwah, New Jersey, by this time. I viewed the New York City Marathon as the greatest in the world (and still do) and had watched it on TV for a few years before I signed up. I had met Fred Lebow, president of the New York Road Runners club, and he encouraged me to sign up. I'd met him at the Brooklyn Half marathon, in Prospect Park, in the spring of 1987, and he wanted to do the Trevira Twosome together in September, so I couldn't say no.

I started training, a lot, eventually getting up to eighteen miles around the towns where I lived. The day of the race was the first Sunday in November, which that year was November 4. Gary had to drive me, at the crack of dawn, to the Staten Island side of the Verrazano Bridge, at Fort Wadsworth. There were to be about twenty-five thousand runners that day (the crowd grew for several years after that, ballooning to fifty-thousand-plus runners). I stayed involved with the marathon, eventually becoming a race director, and I had to escort other race directors from around the world who wanted to see how New York did it. It was an extraordinary feat, coordinating five boroughs, their police departments, and their parks department people, to run the race course, over 26.2 miles, seamlessly. But Fred Lebow did it: he got everybody to agree, and so the New York City Marathon became what it is today. I loved that they put me in charge of people from all over the world, and I only spoke English. We managed to get through. I just had to speak loudly and hold signs up high. My second year as race director, we had a problem where the human chain that we created to start the race (so runners couldn't get through) broke, and there was a false start.

In 1989, at the end of the marathon, I met someone who would eventually become a friend I still have today. His name is David Dikeman. He was in town to shoot an infomercial for his business, Command Performance. He was a professional dog trainer for commercials and movies. I'd always envisioned that, one day, he could come and train our golden retriever, Samantha. The fact that he lived in Kansas was a bit of a limiting factor. I also thought he was very attractive. I reconnected with David while I was at Gurwin in 2019. We'd sporadically stay in touch via text, and he was the first one to warn of the pandemic. He was already heavily into "prep-mode" and warned it was going to get really bad. He was right. That was in early March 2020. We just reconnected today, August 30, 2020.

David Dikeman, Command Performance, dog trainer

The week before my marathon in 1988, the group I worked with at Lehman called me into the conference room on the Friday before my big race. I went to the conference room, and when the door opened, they'd spread out a yellow crepe paper ribbon like a finish line, and they said I had to break it, like I was finishing the race! I was really touched by their special effort for me, and pizza for "carbo loading" (which is mandatory for marathoners) was perfect!

NEW YORK CITY MARATHON: RACE DAY!

Photo by Ken Shelton Photography, from the Staten Island side, overlooking the Verrazano Bridge. The runners are about to explode into their starts!

When I got to the start, at Fort Wadsworth on Staten Island, everyone there was nervously getting ready for what lay ahead. I ran into my running buddy, Marvin Palmeri, a New York City sanitation worker, who always cracked me up and made running fun, as he made comments to many of the other female race participants, with his signature line, "Dis Game is easy!" And his answer to "Marvin, how's work going?" to which he said, "It's pickin' up." And he had lots of others. We ran many races together, along with his sanitation buddy, Jack, and his girlfriend, Sue Greene. As we drove into the various venues for the races we ran, such as Central Park in a New

York City sanitation van, Marvin would say, "They think we're here to pick up trash, when we just want a spot closest to the start."

We finally got herded into the various "time" groups, which led us to where we would start the race. I anticipated a 3:30 marathon (I was being a bit aggressive), so I started with the eight-minute milers. We were cautioned to start out slowly, as it was a long race, and you don't want to hit "the wall." Marvin and I agreed that we would run the first ten miles together, at which point, he was free to go as fast as he wanted. The start, running across the Verrazano, went well, and we got to watch the fire boats spout out red, white, and blue water streams. We also got to see the many race participants jump up on the short barrier on the lower level of the bridge, to pee—no time like the present to relieve one's self. We finally got across the bridge and were onto 4th Avenue in Bay Ridge. Not far along, I spotted my goddaughter and niece, Lorianne, and my Aunt Joan, with a poster board that read: "Go for It, Aunt Debbie!" (I still have that picture on my nightstand, next to my bed), which made me cry and put a big smile on my face. It was so great and it gave me a huge adrenaline surge! Thank you, Lori and Jax! That made my day!

Aunt Joanie holding a poster made for me by Lori and Jackie in 1988

I must say, the first ten miles were smooth as pie. By this time we had crossed the 59th Street bridge into Manhattan, and from there, the spectators were great! It was such a rush! As we entered Manhattan, the sound of the crowd roaring for us was loud but amazing! They call this point in the race "thunder alley" for the roar of the crowds lining the streets in Midtown. It was at this point where I got my first stomach rumble and cramps. Uh-oh, it felt like diarrhea was coming on. Where's a Porta-Potty when you need one? At mile fifteen, I spotted a row of portable lavatories and knew I had to stop. Once in, quick relief. The only thing I'd done wrong was to drink Exceed, and it was a lemon-lime flavor, and it must have been acidic and causing my cramps. Training for the marathon, I had been told *not* to drink or eat anything I hadn't used during training. And Exceed was the culprit. I had to make a few other pit stops, after which I was fortunate to get back in the groove. Somehow, I passed Gary a couple of times along the route, the last being at Columbus Circle, where there was a bleacher set up. I saw Gary and a friend of ours, Chris Sadler, cheering for me, screaming, "Go, Debbie! You're going to make it under four!"

I was at the entrance back into the park, and I heard the loudspeaker announcing, "This group is the last one to make it in under four hours! Let's cheer them on!" The crowd roared louder, while Bruce Springsteen's song "Born in the USA" was playing, and finally, I saw the trademark clock counting the time, and it was 3:57:17. When I crossed the finish, it was 3:59:24, just under four hours! Wow! What a rush! They stopped me at different points along the finish line funnel to take my finishing number and to put that medal around my neck!

The Wall Street Entertainment Environment

Working for firms like DLJ and Lehman, we got to partake in some of the firms' entertainment practices. Barbara and I have both spoken about working on Wall Street before it became PC, or politically correct, and liking it that way. While the traders and salespeople might have sexualized us a bit, they were like brothers or friends, and we'd feel left out if they were polite all the time. Barbara and I were valued for our brains, not our boobs, and we liked to switch it up now and again. At DLJ, there were a few occasions when strippers were brought onto the trading floor. Typically, trading floors were lined with windowed offices. There was one occasion when a stripper, posing as a person to be interviewed, went into an office for her "interview" with a senior management (whose birthday it was). When the interviewee started her act, all was visible for the trading floor occupants to see. As I thought the firm ought to be "equal opportunity," I decided that a male stripper ought to be brought in for entertainment. One of our administrative assistants was brought up as a strict Catholic and was horrified when I'd put Tom Moore, one of our bond salesmen, up to posing as a male stripper. She ran down the hall at the mere sight of him posing as a possible stripper. Tom was a very nice guy, and he thought it would be funny also, but the "posing" never happened.

Tom Moore: willing to go in on a prank

I remember at Lehman, we once had to go to sexual harassment training, and some of the guys who were waiting to go into the auditorium said to us, "We don't need training in sexual harassment, we know how to do that."

Back to the parties: both DLJ and Lehman had the best Christmas parties ever. For a few years, we had events at the American Museum of Natural History, "under the whale" in the Milstein room. The whale model, which was ninety-four feet long, overlooked our impromptu dance floor. I remember on one occasion, Hazel Talley (new to our group, originally from Jamaica) and Jim Asselstine (one of the "twin towers") literally stood back-to-back and then hooked arms and swayed back and forth, dancing to "Play That Funky Music." I can't remember a funnier visual than that episode.

LEHMAN DID EVERYTHING BIG

When Lehman went public in 1994, CEO Richard (Dick) Fuld gave a speech. It was downstairs, in the Winter Garden, in the World Financial Center. After Dick made his remarks, and everybody cheered, a special event occurred. While everyone was speculating what was happening, we proceeded to move to the front wall of the Winter Garden, where we noticed that a large sliding door had been installed, versus a solid glass wall. As we got closer, we started to hear a helicopter above. There was also a large klieg light shining up above in the direction of the helicopter noise. Who could this be, coming to the WFC? Some were speculating that it was Madonna, but we soon learned that was not it. Instead, the helicopter landed, the door opened, and out of it emerged Grace Jones on a horse! Smiling, she waved to the crowd that had gathered to meet her as she arrived. Mounted on the horse, she rode directly into the Winter Garden and proceeded to make her way toward the marble staircase at the back. She and the horse stopped at the base of the marble steps and dismounted. It was certainly a wow moment! But that was all in keeping with the Lehman way!

Grace Jones appeared at Lehman's big announcement!

OUR NUCLEAR EXPERTISE AND MARKETING TRIPS

While at DLJ, our group had become a formidable entity with expertise in nuclear technology, the construction of new nuclear plants, and, as that moved forward, the emphasis shifted to the operations at nuclear plants. Paul Parshley had had experience in Washington, due to his work experience with Mo Udall at the House Interior Committee on Energy. During his tenure, Paul met Jim Asselstine, a reasonably new commissioner at the Nuclear Regulatory Agency. He'd been appointed by President Reagan and served from June 1982 to June 1987. Paul met Jim Asselstine, and during their discussion, he pitched Jim on the idea of coming to Wall Street to discuss the impact of nuclear operations on a company's credit quality. Their discussion took root, and James Kilburn Asselstine came to work at DLJ in the fall of 1987. We commenced, almost immediately, with work on the next big report from our group: operating nuclear power plants in the United States. There were profiles created for each operating nuclear plant. The data presented included a given power plant's report card, issued by the NRC. These were called SALP (systematic assessment of licensee performance) reports. These report cards for nuclear power plant operations were monitored closely by the buy-side investors in the utilities that owned and operated the plants (both bonds and stocks). If there was a negative, or "bad," grade received for performance at the plant, the respective utility owner's stocks and/or bonds would be impacted negatively. It was the job of research to head off the announcement of said "bad" report, which made research more valuable to the traders and salespeople and their clients (fund managers, who each had their own salespeople, traders, and investment officers). Conversely, if a plant received a "good" SALP report, the opposite would happen: spreads on the utility's bonds would tighten (yields would go down; prices would go up), and stock prices would go up, as well.

James K. Asselstine, former Nuclear Regulatory Commissioner, was appointed by President Reagan

Each year, a big part of the job of research was to go and visit the clients that bought the securities of the utilities we followed. These clients were located throughout the country, but we'd focus our visits on a regional basis. As we had offices in New York, Boston, Chicago, Dallas, Philadelphia, and San Francisco, there was a lot of territory to be covered.

Part of our operating nuclear power plants report was to present and market our conclusions to the buy-side in each region. Thus, we started a series of conferences on the topic. And that entailed enlisting the help of seasoned experts in the area of nuclear power plant technology. When we hosted our nuclear conference in Boston, we empaneled Peter Bradford (former NRC commissioner and head of the Maine Public Service Commission). Also enlisted was Victor Gilinsky, a two-term commissioner for the Nuclear Regulatory Commission. The industry credited Peter Bradford with the remark that launched the US nuclear power plant construction era, that the cost per unit sold by nuclear power plants would be "too cheap to meter." That remark contributed to the launch of an enormous nuclear plant construction boom! Ultimately, the last nuclear plant that came online was in the late eighties. What was supposed to be one thousand reactors by the year 2000 turned into 109 total reactors for "the boom." The bust came with the 1979 near meltdown of Three Mile Island nuclear plant, and the 1986 Chernobyl reactor disaster. The lack of containment at that reactor caused untold deaths from the accident itself, and the aftereffects for more than a decade, rendering all the site land, and much of it around it, unusable forever. Practically speaking, it's unclear if there will ever be the use of nuclear power plant technology in the US power resource mix. Que será, será.

We hosted a conference in New York at the former Vista Hotel, part of the former WTC complex. Its physical address was 3 World Trade Center. It had morphed into different hotel names during its history, ultimately becoming the Marriot World Trade Center, which was damaged beyond repair in the September 11 terrorist attack.

The Vista Hotel, our New York conference venue

We hosted a conference in Boston at the Four Seasons Hotel around Christmastime. There was a smaller group of buy-side attendees, but they were all associated with large, key funds in the Boston area. As it turned out, there were many women on the buy-side in Boston who held key positions at these large funds. As many or most of these funds all bought large amounts of electric utility first mortgage bonds, they all had a vested interest in the underlying companies' financial performance and its prospects. Peter Bradford was also a panelist at the Boston conference. It was there that some of the Boston fund managers were present and cozied up to Peter. Margaret Stapleton, upon seeing Peter, exclaimed, "I love a man with a beard!" Later that evening, post-conference, it was proposed that a group of us go out and have some fun in the Boston area. We went to one place where there was music and dancing, and Peter, upon a request to dance with me, said, "I'm not a big dancer" (he's six foot six inches tall), to which I replied, "You're the biggest dancer I've ever seen!" It was funny, to us.

Our Boston conference venue: The Four Seasons

NINA AND THE FAPWA YEARS

When I started working with Shearson Lehman Brothers, I was excited at the prospect of making much more money, and also the prospect of working together with Ken Ambrecht, Gary's cousin. I saw Ken when I came down to the trading floor, and I also got to meet Nina again. She was friendly toward me, and I took that as a good sign. Not long after being there, Nina invited me over to her apartment for dinner with a "few of the girls." So now I was going to Fifth Avenue and meeting some of her friends. I was being accepted into the blue blood upper class! Wow!

Kenneth Ambrecht, aka the "Senator"

Nina was the first person I ever met that farted with impunity. Forget the fact that she was a woman. At first, I thought I was hearing things when her legs would part, she'd raise a knee, and I could hear the distinct sound of flatulence. She'd always laugh a little at these occurrences, and her shoulders would shake up and down, but there was no mistaking it, that was a fart!

Nina Wainwright and her dear daughter Alex

Later, as I got to know Nina better, she introduced me to her new boyfriend, Lou Lloyd, who was on the equity side. Lou had the distinction of having a barber's chair in his office, one of the many "toys" that high-level managers on Wall Street used to adorn their offices. Nina was also very open with discussions of her and Lou's sex life, like the time Mr. Wong, Lou's houseboy, gave them seven towels, with which Lou and Nina proceeded to saturate with, let's just say, sexual fluids. He didn't flinch, he just put them in the washing machine. Mr. Wong never got the hernia that Lou always feared he would from lifting the heavily saturated towels.

I became very close to Nina, and we had great times together. We began to form a group friendship with other women at Lehman. I decided that we needed to call ourselves something, and I came up with "FAPWA," for Fifth Avenue Professional Women's Association (not exactly catchy, but we knew who we were).

Some of the males at Lehman indicated they wanted to be invited to the FAPWA get-togethers, and sometimes we would oblige, but they had to be cool, and they had to contribute, usually with more wine or something else. And they did.

Nina confided in me quite a bit when she was hoping that Lou would get more serious, and hopefully, marry her. She asked me to "see what info I could get out of him as to which way he was leaning." Naturally, I did what a good friend would do: I asked Lou to a casual dinner and needled him for "how things were, with Nina, etc." My findings were less than satisfactory, and not what Nina wanted to hear, but I did my job.

One day, Nina was quite upset. I took her down to the floor where there was a gym and a row of leather couches, all bunched together, and poor Nina had a meltdown because Lou didn't want to get married, but they did remain very close friends.

Later, things evolved and Nina needed some retail therapy and we'd call each other, saying we "needed to see our good friend Ann," which was our code for shopping at Ann Taylor, right there in the WFC; how great was that? On one occasion, Nina was looking for some holiday party apparel, and "Ann" was good for that. Setting her sights on a short black velvet number, we proceeded into the dressing room, and Nina began to try things on. I was her dressing room attendant, and she sent me out for a bigger size (not that she was big, or anything), and I brought two more back to her. Same dress, different sizes. So she tried them both on, and seemed to like the second one, at which point all hell broke loose! Nina had a hard time getting the dress off and ultimately, tried to get the dress over her head. She bent forward, with the dress partway up and her butt hanging out, and then the farting began! It sounded like a tommy gun, and the more she laughed, the more she farted! Exasperated, and in a panic, she had to rip the dress off, severing the zipper from the dress. So the score was Nina/Deb: 1, Ann Taylor: 0. Oh, and all the while, Nina was imploring me to "get this fucker off me!" It was hysterical to us, but not that way for the onlookers in the dressing room area. It was a story that went down in Nina infamy, and I usually got the stage to tell it, and I did. Those who knew Nina well, all "got it" and laughed along with us. Some were horrified that a woman with her blue blood background could fart (and curse) as much as she could, and that I, as a co-conspirator, could tell the story and make it sound funny. All I can say is that Nina has remained a dear friend and very loyal, coming to visit me at Gurwin, along with a former Lehman Brothers client, Christine Curnan, from Merrill Lynch Asset Management. They made the trip in a snow storm, but they made it, and we had a great time, and I felt a little like "me,"—something I hadn't felt in quite a while. We went out for brunch (a nice treat for me, at the Bonwit Inn where I used to waitress, and I saw a few people there that I actually knew, and who remembered me).

Whether it was at the "numbers," as Nina referred to the 21 Club, Nina and I dined together many times. One of our usual restaurants was Bice, on Madison and 54th Street. It was there that we had two celebrity sightings! The first time, our table was right next to one with actor Armand Assante. He had recently been in the film *Odyssey*, released in 1997, and he was wearing long hair (as in the movie). I'd always thought he was handsome, and loved him in his role in *Private Benjamin* with Goldie Hawn. He was very friendly toward us, and even asked us to have drinks after dinner at the bar. Naturally, we accepted, but we spent only a little more time with him before departing Bice.

On another occasion, we were also dining at Bice. Midway through dinner, I excused myself to use the bathroom, which was downstairs. It was there that I saw Eddie Murphy, who had just appeared in the very funny movie *Coming to America*. It was just released in 1988. Eddie was not as friendly as Armand Assante. Or perhaps he was a germophobe. In any event, he would not shake hands, although he did flash that broad smile!

When I started on Wall Street, walking was a way to meet coworkers. I walked through many airports, while on business travel and on vacation. As we covered the US electric utility industry, I traveled extensively, getting to travel to forty-eight out of the fifty states in the United States of America. Not many Americans can say that. I got to see the many beautiful scenic places in many parts of the United States. I've gotten to see Lake Tahoe; Lake Havasu, in Arizona; and Lake Michigan, in the Great Lakes (while in Chicago), to name a few. Along with Paul Parshley, we flew (in a small passenger plane) over the Grand Canyon. As a result of our research marketing of Conseco Insurance, in Indiana, we twice attended the Indianapolis 500. While not geographically or scenically attractive, I've also visited several nuclear plants, which were being built at that time, as well as other fossil-fuel burning plants, like coal plants with scrubbers, and I also got to see geothermal plants (at the other end of the "clean" power spectrum).

Bert Gutierrez, Conseco CIO; we met at the Indy 500

OUR GROUP MAKES A BIG CHANGE

After three years, at Shearson Lehman Brothers Division of American Express, some changes were being proposed. Martha Dillman, our new research group head, was thinking that our group, with eight people including support staff, was too large; she wondered, "can't part of your group do the equity side?" The previous equity analyst for electric utilities had long been Ed Tirello, famous for his "Tirello tours." He was *Institutional Investor*'s #1 ranked analyst for years, as he took the whole buy-side to meet with the senior management of select electric utilities, usually on a regional basis. He, too, scheduled his events at luxury hotels, and he offered access to company managements that other sell-side firms did not. He was a shoo-in to be placed first in Electric Utilities by an *Institutional Investor* magazine investor poll. It worked like a charm!

Ed had left Shearson Lehman Brothers the year prior and had taken most of his staff with him. He did, however, leave one of his team members, Daria Roullett, and she would be available to work with us, if we moved over from fixed income to equities. Paul thought it would be a good opportunity.

For a short time, he attempted to run both the fixed income and equities groups, but that became too cumbersome to manage, and a bit unwieldy. So, we made the split: Paul and I would move to the fourteenth floor (from eleven), and Jim Asselstine, Barbara Germain, and Peter Petas would remain in the fixed income department. Michele Mahoney was shifted to the investor services department, which she seemed comfortable doing.

Paul and I had to get acclimated to a move to the new world of equities. It was not a slam dunk. While all our company knowledge was still relevant, we had to switch our financial analysis from pretax interest coverage to price/earnings ratios and compound average growth rate. As we covered electric utilities, they were not high growth rate companies, or a high-growth industry as a whole. Electric utilities pay quarterly dividends. Thus, dividend yields had to become another metric that was used to determine the recommendation placed on a given company's stock. For example, Southern Company is viewed as a high-quality investment as compared to its industry peers. The dividend yield of 4.56 is a superior return to the industry average of 3.42.

> The company's trailing twelve-month (TTM) dividend yield calculates the indicated annual dividend divided by the stock price. This value is always expressed as a percentage. This is the return on investment that is specifically attributed to the expected dividends that are paid out over a year. Note: investors should not base their investments on the size of the dividend yield alone. Seek attractive dividend yields, but only on top rated stocks with a solid payment history.

Source: https://www.investopedia.com/terms/d/dividendyield.asp

Stock yields were completely different than the yields on a company's bonds. Corporate bond yields were calculated as a spread off treasuries. Treasury yields were based off of the maturity of the bonds, and based on the triple-A rating of the US Government. The shorter the maturity, the lower the yield. Also, corporate bonds were rated, largely by the ratings agencies: Moody's and Standard & Poor's, and in this case, the lower the bond rating, the higher the spread off treasuries, and the higher the yield. In both the stocks and bond yields, they were used as a measure of the potential return on investment in a particular company's bonds or stocks.

Because electric utilities were stable, mature, cash-flow-generating companies, there was not as much growth in their year-to-year growth rates. The price of a stock was determined in part by the potential growth of its earnings. Every industry had a normalized P/E (price to earnings ratio) for its companies' stocks. The lower the earnings rate, the lower the P/E.

Utilities were regulated companies, regulated by Public Utility or Service Commissions. The commissions would determine the allowable price that companies could charge for the electricity units, kilo-watt hours (kWh). Utilities were deemed to be a public good. No one could go without electricity. It was needed to light our homes, to heat them, and needed to cook our food (gas or electric). Thus, utilities were afforded a monopoly service territory (customers for life) in exchange for a reasonably priced product (kWhs). The companies' costs to build (generation), transmit (transmission), and connect to the customer (distribution) would all factor into a company's rate base. The formula used by regulators to calculate the price per kWh was known as rate-base rate of return regulation.

When we moved to the equities division at Lehman, we joined up with Daria Roulett, who had worked with Ed Tirello, the previous equity analyst at Lehman. Daria had previously prepared a report each month on the regulatory developments within our industry. Her report was called "Regulatory Update," and it was drawn from the various publications that covered these developments on their regular frequency of updates. There were several: "Electric Utility Week," "Electric Utility Daily," and then there was the normal publication by Regulatory Research Associates (or RRA, for short), founded by Wally and Dot French. There was a whole team dedicated to everything regulatory related. It could be decisions made in a given regulatory jurisdiction, by state, or it could be a broad, industry-impacting decision made at the federal level. There was "Inside FERC" (aka, the Federal Energy Regulatory Commission). FERC commissioners were usually appointed by the president, with approval by the Senate. There were five commissioners. No more than three commissioners could be affiliated with one party (Democrat and Republican). Finally, each company was required to produce an interim report of any key developments affecting the company, in Form 8-K. These could be a treasure trove of regulatory or management changes or financial impacts likely to affect the way that a given company's stocks or bonds traded.

Daria Radice Roulett, our regulatory specialist

When Paul and I joined the equities division at Lehman Brothers, we were confronted with a whole new workforce composition, and we were compared to many different industries that were regarded as faster growth companies versus utilities. Compared to tech companies, or Big Pharma, or retail, banks, insurance companies, casinos and gaming companies, utilities were viewed as slow-moving prehistoric creatures; notwithstanding that fact, every company in these competing industries depended on the very product that utilities provided.

There was a whole different methodology of "getting the word out" to the sales force or to investors. There was a First Call note system in the equity department. Like "Morning Line," at DLJ, it was the place to discuss industry or company information that appeared in the *Wall Street Journal* or the *New York Times*, or appeared on TV or Bloomberg, if these developments were likely to effect a ratings change. Stocks were rated on a scale of 1 to 5: 1 = buy, 2 = outperform, 3 = hold, 4 = underperform, 5 = sell; this would necessitate an emergency investment committee meeting. And all of this had to happen before the 7 a.m. call.

The 7 a.m. call was orchestrated by Jane Rosen and Tom Bianco. Jane would announce who the speakers would be, along with the topic or nature of the call: ratings change, industry news story, and the like. Jane would stand next to us at the podium, as we spoke, and she could be annoying. If our story was not moving quickly enough, she would stand next to us, so that we could see, peripherally, that her hand was circling her ear, in a forward motion, as if to signal we should "get to the point!" or "wrap it up!" This could be extremely unnerving when we were already under the gun. We also didn't have a fan in Tom Bianco, as electric utility stocks were dinosaurs compared to tech companies, Big Pharma companies, and Biotech companies; just about every other industry had faster CAGR (compound average growth rates), and he could taunt us with: "Where's the sex, where's the sizzle?" Unfortunately, we didn't have what he was looking for: the sex and sizzle of electric utility stocks was stable, recurring cash flow, and cash dividends. If that's not sexy for you, Tom, sorry.

Lehman Brothers was in a big bid to win the coveted *Institutional Investor* Number One Research Ranking. As a result, everyone and everything within the department was in high gear. The equity department research heads were Fred Fraenkel and Steve Balog. There was also continued input from Jack Rivkin, head of investment research at Lehman. They seemed to be unstoppable! In 1991, they succeeded!

It was in 1991 that Fred Fraenkel, director of equity research at Lehman, presided over a Marketing Research: 101 course. In it, Fred taught us how to effectively market our research product. This could be in the form of First Call notes, produced daily, based on news regarding a given company's ongoing projects, regulatory developments, or financial developments (new issue of stock, or a ruling that dictated a write-off). There were recommendations about the frequency and timing of daily calls to investment funds, analysts, and portfolio managers, while also keeping in touch with the trading desk and salespeople. There were recommendations about the frequency and number of research marketing trips, done on a regional basis near the firm's branch offices. As most of the research people were viewed to be the nerds of the firm, Fred took another perspective and enticed people to join his marketing course with a program-ending dinner, usually at a kosher restaurant in the East Village called Sam's. At Sam's, there were some legendary stories about some of the nerds attending these dinners and getting very, very drunk. Like the time when Teena Lerner (not Tina Turner) drank so much frozen vodka that she lost sensation in her face.

The value of the course could markedly improve one's view and approach toward one's research. The value of the dinner was pure camaraderie.

As Paul and I settled into the rhythm of the equities division, there was a further division among the responsibilities for the companies that each of us would be dedicated to following. Paul opted for the higher-growth companies, known as independent power producers (AES, Calpine, and NRG Energy, as examples), while I stayed with the traditional investor-owned electric utilities. Instead of determining prospective bond ratings for over one hundred operating utilities, I now had to analyze the holding companies that owned the operating utilities. For example, instead of looking at Alabama Power, Georgia Power, Mississippi Power, and Gulf Power, I had to analyze their parent company, the Southern Company, headquartered in Atlanta, Georgia. My favorable rating on the shares of Southern Company's stock was part of the reason that I, along with Gary, was invited to attend the

1996 Summer Olympics. That was a nice perk! Despite the bombing that occurred early in the Olympics, we got to see some amazing track and field events, as well as tennis. We were taken by bus immediately to each venue, and we had great seats!

We set about the annual marketing plans to get the word out on our companies to investors. As a result, we went on "roadshows," meeting with several different groups of fund managers, their analysts, and portfolio managers. We would plan these trips around the branch offices that Lehman had: Boston, Chicago, San Francisco, Dallas, Philadelphia, and Atlanta. The West Coast trips could also land us in Portland, Oregon, and Seattle, Washington. Anywhere there was a major city with state or local funds near those branches, we would go there, too. We'd prepare personalized presentations for each investor we'd meet with. A lot of prep work went into each of our trips. Doing it well, and being prepared, was always the best way to ensure a successful trip (coming back with investor orders to forward to the salespeople and trading desk). All of that factored into how we were compensated. Research had historically been viewed as a cost center, when, in reality, the idea generation that produced recommendations that triggered trading and sales was really more of a revenue generator. Yet, at year-end, the salespeople and traders were polled to determine how a given analyst contributed to their level of trading and sales activity (i.e., revenues). At year-end, there was a process of learning what our year-end "comp" (bonus) was going to be. We'd more or less wait in our offices, as senior management went, office by office; they'd poke their heads in and have "the comp talk." It could be tremendously anxiety-provoking if they walked past your office without stopping in.

There was one year when there was a designated office, down the hall at the end of the row of offices, where windows were blacked out, and one by one, people who got calls to go to that office did not return with a job. That was a bad year.

TRAVEL PERKS

Working as a research analyst could be a tough job. Producing a quality research product, week after week, or month, required much work. While our compensation was high, relative to many other industries, the formula to derive our compensation factored in the revenues generated by the ideas produced in our research product. Yes, it had to be an actionable idea, but most of them produced that. We had to work very long hours sometimes, including having to sleep overnight at the office, as being on the 7 a.m. call made it useless for us to go home to sleep for one hour. I remember one of those nights. Working on a series of First Call notes, during earnings season, and needing to write a First Call note for every company we covered, could be exhausting. Like the night I finished my First Call notes at 2 a.m., and the idea that if I went home and then had to be back by 7 a.m. the next morning, fresh and alert, didn't make sense. I ended up sleeping on a sofa in one of the investment banker's offices. I used my raincoat with a lining as my blanket and a rolled-up sweatshirt as my pillow. But it was the price of being paid well.

Another form of compensation for us was the travel perks. At Lehman, we made our reservations through Corporate Travel, and it was there that we learned that upgrades were possible, for all employees.

Such was the case when we made reservations to travel to Chicago for a marketing trip to visit the Chicago-area pension funds (and there were many). It was decided that we'd stay at a Ritz Carlton. This one was at the Water Tower (one of the tallest buildings in Chicago). Corporate Travel informed us that we could upgrade our regular rooms to a Lakeside Suite. That sounded lovely. We made the reservations and set off for our marketing trip to Chicago. Upon arrival, we took a cab downtown (about a forty-five-minute car ride, or thirty-minute train ride, on the L). Chicago highways could be as bad as in New York, but not always. This day, we had little traffic. We arrived at the Water Tower address, for the Ritz Carlton.

Paul and I went to the check-in desk. When approached by a hotel clerk, I was apprised that, "Sorry, Miss, we don't have any Lakeside Suites available for tonight." Arrgghh. I wasn't happy with that answer. I saw the clerk speaking to another clerk, and overheard him asking: "Is anyone in there tonight?" She shook her head no. When he approached me again, he said, "We think we found you something you'll really like for tonight's stay." What could that be? Paul and I went to the bell stand to request our luggage be brought up. The clerk said: "Twenty-five." Next, we went to the elevators, with bellmen and luggage in tow, and up we went.

Upon reaching twenty-five, the bellman said, "Make a left out of the elevator, to the end of the hall." That's when we saw the double doors! When we got close, I saw the silver plaque: The Presidential Suite! Now that's a really nice upgrade! We entered the room on twenty-five, but soon learned it was a two-story room! Twenty-five *and* twenty-six! It was crazy big! It was 3,500 square feet. In this Presidential Suite, there were two full king-sized suites. It also had a living room, formal dining room, a spiral staircase leading to the second-floor balcony, and it had at least four full bathrooms and two half-baths! In the living room, there was a baby grand piano! And the windows were two stories high! They were overlooking Lake Michigan on a clear day, now turning toward evening. We had really arrived! This could have been a great place for a huge party, but it was just me and Paul. Paul picked his suite, and I took the other. There were dinner reservations with one of the Chicago salespeople, downtown, on the Magnificent Mile, but that was the extent of our big party plans. Still, this was an amazing room! Wow!

Our view from the Presidential Suite at the Ritz Carlton

The Chicago Ritz Carlton, in the Water Tower, Chicago

EUROPEAN BUSINESS TRAVEL

Along with US travel (due to our company coverage), there was a whole new investor base that looked to US utilities as a place for a generous, and stable, return on investment. The investor base was in Europe. Thus, Paul and I went to the UK and the Netherlands. We flew across the pond to London. While there, we met with some UK-based pension funds. We had prepared some presentation materials for each meeting, with personalized covers for the name of the fund and the fund manager. I can remember that one area of interest for Scottish Widows was Duke Power. While driving around and through London, we did get to view Buckingham Palace.

In a bit of off-time, we were able to go to Edinburgh, in Scotland. Edinburgh Castle was the same castle where William Wallace (Mel Gibson's character in the movie *Braveheart*) was drawn and quartered. There was a plaque, detailing the story of William Wallace's execution (see below). There was also a plaque that said, "This is the site where witches were burned." It sounds like it was an equal-opportunity "fun house." Not.

The Castle at Edinburgh, Scotland

Plaque that cites the execution of William Wallace; he was drawn and quartered in the year 1305 AD

By Steve F-E-Cameron. https://commons.wikimedia.org/w/index.php?curid=1633258

We also got to travel to the city of Amsterdam, in the Netherlands. While there we stayed at The Grand Hotel, which was the site of the early Parliament and city hall in Amsterdam.

The Grand Hotel, Amsterdam, the Netherlands

My Big Fat Greek Business Trip?

Finally, my big trip came as the result of my coverage of a company called Thermo Ecotek, a spin-off from a company that Lehman had been the principal investment bank, Thermo Electron. Founded by two Greek-born brothers, George and John Hatsopoulous, Thermo Electron did several IPOs (initial public offerings) over several years. Thermo Electron was a very lucrative investment banking client. Thus, when a new spin-off and potential IPO was coming down the road, Lehman made sure to treat the Hatsopoulous brothers, and their spin-off companies, well.

My tough duty was to accompany one of the founders and the company's CFO to visit prospective investors—in Athens, Greece! This happened in the summer of 1996. I would give it my all. On this trip, John Hatsopoulous made the travel arrangements. We flew first class from JFK in New York to Athens, Greece. Upon arrival at JFK, I met up with John, and he was pleasant, as always. This was my first time flying first class internationally. I was excited. The much larger seating area and the meal service was amazing; we dined on filet mignon, and of course, Champagne, followed by wine, throughout the flight, and there were good movies to view. When we arrived, in the bright light of day, I was awakened by John Hatsopoulous, who informed me that I slept "through all the commotion"! Apparently, a passenger in the rear of the aircraft had had a heart attack. There were announcements: "Is there a doctor on board?" There was even a possibility that we would land in a neighboring country, but alas, the passenger had died. Even worse, the man's wife was seated next to him and had to stay in her seat (next to her deceased husband) until we landed! Upon arrival, sadly, the man's family had come to meet him and his wife at the airport, only to learn that their family member had died en route to Athens. That was the beginning of our trip!

Upon arrival, we were transported to downtown Athens and made a stop at the place we'd stay for the trip's duration, at John Hatsopoulos's apartment. By the time we arrived and got to Athens, it was already time for lunch. John had a regular chauffeur, who would be escorting us around Athens while we were there. We had several investor meetings scheduled, and our first would be mid-afternoon.

Our first meeting was with a group of investors who were all longtime friends of "Yanni," as they called John Hatsopoulous. I made a brief presentation about Thermo Ecotek. It was an independent power company, slightly different than some other Thermo companies. Its financials were good, and plus, they'd have the ongoing support of the parent company, Thermo Electron. We had a number of other investor meetings over the next couple of days. In the evenings, we went to dinner. John made reservations for a place in Cape Sounion, which I later learned was the location of the Temple of Poseidon. Dinner was delicious (I had a whole fish called branzino, deboned and cooked to perfection). In Greece, the after-dinner drink is fairly common, as is the drink ouzo (a fairly high-octane alcohol; it's an acquired taste). Afterward, we went to another place for bouzouki dancing. Bouzouki might be compared to the Electric Slide or another line dance, but it is much more elegant, coming from Greece. I also noted that while in Greece, it was not unusual to see a Greek man with a much younger girl on his arm. Perfect: John was about sixty-eight at the time of our trip, while I was thirty-six. It was so exciting to be in another country, on another continent, going to enjoy some bouzouki dancing. Spending time with the Hatsopoulos brothers, I also got to experience plate breaking. While in New York, we went to a place in "Little Greece" and purchased a large box of unglazed plates, which we would throw at a brick wall. It was actually tremendously stress-relieving! In New York City, there are the Break Bar and The Wrecking Club, where one can schedule group parties for plate breaking!

The IPO spin-off came off successfully, and Lehman could check off another offering, along with its fees, for the books. Deb could check off another desired travel destination with thoughts of returning there again.

Cape Sounion, near Athens, Greece

The Temple of Poseidon

S-CLASS SERVICES: MY RELIABLE TRANSPORTATION FOR OVER THIRTY YEARS PRE- AND POST-ACCIDENT

Throughout my time at DLJ, Lehman Brothers, and Salomon Brothers, as well as my foray into hedge funds through Veritas Partners, one thing, and one person, has been a constant: my reliable driver. I call him "Driver Dan," at S-Class Services. Always the driver of an S-Class Mercedes sedan (currently a 550), Dan has been a fixture for the literally hundreds of rides I required over thirty years. He was a sight for sore eyes at Newark or JFK airports, ready and waiting for my ride home. Dan is quite a professional driver, one I would trust in virtually every situation. Dan is Romanian, a married man, with two twin daughters, now grown, married, and with children of their own.

Even after my accident, Dan made himself available to me for rides to various doctors while I was undergoing surgeries. We made many trips back and forth from Garden City to Paramus, New Jersey. My mom, Grace, while she was still here, was very comfortable with Dan's driving. Thank you, and God bless you, Dan! You are the best "Autobahn" driver I was ever fortunate to know! I have and would recommend you, and S-Class Service, any day of the week.

MY STARTLING (TO ME) DEPARTURE FROM LEHMAN BROTHERS

At year-end 1996, I was awaiting the presence of Lehman's senior management to divulge what my year-end bonus would be. I had what I believed to be a successful year. I published my first book, an industry report on the restructuring of the US electric utilities industry, which was well-received; the firm generated more profits from trading in the equity securities of the "utes." I'd traveled in the United States and Europe to market electric utility securities and for a new IPO offering for Thermo Ecotek. Instead, Carolyn

Moses (our UK research management counterpart) informed me that "due to no fault of my own," I was being terminated, as the whole of investment banking coverage for utilities had been disbanded! I was stunned! I was told I could seek out an employment attorney and was given a few names. I consulted with one, and after several rounds of revisions, we finalized a "Separation Agreement," which would pay me about $80,000 over a period of a few months. I was still very devastated by this news. I contacted Paul Parshley (still my boss).

Fortunately, I had a good reputation as an analyst covering the utilities sector, and it wasn't long before I'd heard from a few places about coming to work for them. The next gig for me turned out to be Salomon Brothers.

SALOMON BROTHERS: HOW I GOT THERE

Salomon put on a big push for me to come to work for them. After leaving Lehman in December 1996, I got a call from Carlotta Chan, and she asked if I'd be interested in talking to them. I was recommended by Carlotta Chan, whose position I would be taking, and Hal Clark, the head of power-related investment banking called me while I was on vacation in Sanibel Island, Florida, and he was very influential in his efforts to sway me the "Solly way." I called John Melesius and told him that Hal had called and we made plans to get together when I got home, but I gave an indication that I was leaning toward "Solly." At the time of Hal's call, I was lying on the beach, basking in the warm, not-too-hot sun, and while talking to Hal and looking up at the sky, I realized I'd made my decision.

I had done a little research on Salomon, as I'd read and heard about the treasury scandal and wanted to make sure the firm had regained its footing. Both Carlotta, and then John, assured me that it had. So I said yes to their offer, including a signing bonus of $10,000, just to come there! I was amazed and grateful. I was back in fixed income, but my income would not be "fixed."

When I started at Salomon, I felt like I had to prove myself all over again. I had to get my fixed income "sea legs" back. Having switched to equities for nearly five years, I had to get back to my rating agency relationships and re-establish things, like where trading levels were and so on. It was a bit like starting over, but I was excited for what lay ahead. I was introduced to my new traders, who would trade the bulk of the utilities sector. Their names were Brian Riano (the head of the desk) and Jon Eckerson, aka Brian and Eck. They were big guys, in height, and I was a little taken aback, not just by their size but more so by their demeanor. They were friendly enough toward me, but they let me know that if I came down to the trading floor, I should have something to tell them, and even more important, what to do with the news I just told them. They said "buy" or "sell"; "hold" was not an option. Yikes, sounded like I would have my hands full with these guys. ("Nice to meet you, too.") Time would tell! Who knew it wouldn't be until September 11, 2001?

WHERE WERE YOU ON 9/11?

Lady Liberty waves to the Twin Towers, for the last time before they died, 9/11/01

MY "BIG CALL" ON TXU BONDS

The utility sector was undergoing a wholesale fundamental change, resulting from FERC Order 636, which required utilities to split up their companies, according to the line of business they were in: generating assets (power plants) were in the production (P) business, transmission wires (T) transport electric current over long distances, and distribution (D) were the wires connected to houses or other physical buildings to which utilities provided power. All of the assets built and used to transmit electricity to customers accounted for a given utility's "rate base" and were regulated by State Regulatory Commissions, called Public Utility Commissions, or Public Service Commissions or boards of public utilities or some other nomenclature designed to indicate their basic function: to set the rates or price that utilities could charge customers, based on the type of service, based on the accumulated cost of property, plant, and equipment, to provide that service.

Utilities got what most thought was a sweet deal: they were afforded a monopoly service territory, where customers were bound to a utility that provided service to them for life, as electricity was considered a public good. No one could be turned away as a customer. Power was essential for survival. The rates were set as a price per unit delivered. In this case, cents per kilowatt-hour (kWh). The rates had to be fair, and the service had to be reliable. That was the trade-off. You, the utilities, get customers for life, but your product (electricity) had to be reasonably priced (in its units, kilowatt-hours) and reliable. And that got measured by customer satisfaction. Electricity is simple yet complex to provide. Yet, we flip a switch and expect our lights to come on, or we turn a faucet and expect our water to be warm, or we expect our homes to be warm, or cool, depending on the season. It is something so essential and ingenious, yet we take it for granted (see, this is my ongoing theme).

For companies to split along business lines, they had to split structurally (draw a new corporate diagram, legally), and they also had to restructure all the outstanding debt (for many, it was in the billions of dollars), most of which was covered under their first mortgage bond indenture. As utilities were still in the middle of building new nuclear plants, these companies had billions of dollars of outstanding debt, with the bulk being in the form of first mortgage bonds (FMBs), and the remainder of their debt being unsecured debentures.

Upon further examination, we discovered that most of the bonds were out of the five-year non-call protection and were in the still above-par pricing, but under certain provisions, under the FMB indenture, bonds could be called at par. The provision was called the Maintenance and Replacement Fund (or M&R fund). This provision was a fund created for the annual maintenance of the very property that secured the FMBs, and that was a good thing. From the bondholder's perspective, having bonds called prematurely, at par, was a bad thing. In my "big call" at Salomon, I made the case that companies who had issued lots of FMB debt, to build all those nuclear plants, were likely to remain "bondholder friendly," as they were likely to issue more first mortgage bond debt, or debentures, and they didn't want egregious pricing when they issued new debt. TXU was a big issuer of debt during the 1980s and early 1990s, and were likely to issue more in the future, and I believed they were likely to remain "bondholder friendly." In this era of restructuring among electric utilities, there was likely to remain a group of companies who could see the potential impact of doing cheaper but unfriendly things to bondholders, and they knew they'd be back in the market again. Historically, TXU always had a good relationship with both the "buy" side and "sell" side, and they didn't want to ruin that in the future.

On September 10, 2001, TXU made a late-in-the-day announcement, via press release, that they would "tender" for all of their FMBs, and that they would be hosting an analyst breakfast the next morning, September 11, at the St. Regis hotel, on Fifth Avenue at 55th Street. As a result, I knew my "big call" had turned out to be right. And not only that, my traders (Brian and Eck) had positioned the desk well, by buying all the FMBs they could find! So, not only was the call right, but "Solly" stood to make a ton of money on their position. I pictured the high-fives and the victory laps I would be taking on September 11, after the TXU breakfast. But after what really happened, the high-fives were the last thing on the traders' minds. Oh well, my victory laps would have to wait. Understandably so.

The morning of September 11, I got ready for work, and then got in my car (that BMW 5-Series, I mentioned earlier) and made the trip to the big city. I remember that morning with great clarity—the sky was so vividly blue, the air was so crisp—it was going to be a spectacular fall-type day! I parked in my usual garage on Greenwich Street, and then emerged to get a cab to go to the St. Regis. I got to the hotel and went to the meeting room, located an empty seat, and I got a press release and a book with slides about the tender offer for each bond and what it would cost the company. Just a few minutes into the meeting, TXU made an announcement that a plane had crashed into the North Tower of the World Trade Center, and they would keep us updated as they received more news. I immediately thought it was a small, passenger plane, but I/we had no idea of the enormity of what was to unfold!

We were all on our cell phones (now common at the time), and I saw Kimberly Blue, who also worked at Salomon and was in debt capital markets coverage for TXU. We nodded to each other, our eyes expressing fear and bewilderment, and I was looking for a fax machine to send the slides to the trading desk (victory lap, here I come!). I remember the first-ever cell phone I had, back in the early nineties: it was a large walkie-talkie style phone, and we were so proud to place them in the center of a table where we'd be dining for lunch or dinner, and it would be like a cell phone bouquet. ("See, we have cell phones, over here, we're important and need to be in constant contact with the world," so there!) But I was looking for a better phone signal, as the call kept getting cut off when I tried calling the desk. Kimberly mentioned to me that all the bridges and tunnels to and from Manhattan were shut down, and that the Pentagon had been bombed! Was the world coming to an end? The breakfast participants all started to scatter, and the breakfast meeting (which I didn't eat) came to an abrupt end. People started to try and figure out how they were going to get home or to their offices.

WATCHING THE DISASTER UNFOLD

I remember going out on a hotel balcony, overlooking the Fifth Avenue side, and when we looked south toward the World Trade Center, we saw the second plane hit the south Tower! 8:46: Plane crashes into North Tower. 9:03: Plane crashes into South tower. 9:59: Tower 2 (the South Tower) collapses in nine seconds. 10:28: Tower 1 (the North Tower) collapses in eleven seconds! Oh my God! I probably knew people in there! The towers were hit fifteen minutes apart and collapsed thirty minutes apart. It was as if one twin saw the other being fatally shot and couldn't bear the thought of being without its twin and collapsed in spectacular grief! I imagined there being debris all over downtown, so much so, that downtown would be closed for about ten years! The Battery tunnel would probably get closed for ages! How would Manhattan survive?

Finally, I started to get a signal on my Blackberry, and Bob Waldman had sent me a message to call into his office, along with everyone in corporate bond research department, to get a headcount. I believe I was able to make a call to his office, on my Nokia cell phone, and we each got to hear the others announce where they were, and if they were okay. All were okay, so that was a relief, but I still hadn't gotten to the desk. Finally, I got Ronnie Matteo, a relatively new trader on the desk (and an assistant to Brian and Eck), and I was able to get the fax number to the trading desk. First, I had to find the business office in the St. Regis. I was also trying to figure out if we should stay put until we learned more. By this time, I was also with Brian Schmidt (our wicked-smart research assistant at Salomon) and somehow, someone had arranged for a room for us, till the next day. I also had somehow gotten a call from Gary, who called me from home, and told me about the disaster unfolding at the World Trade Center. He had been in Manhattan also, and told me about a group of AT&T people who were right around the World Trade Center when those incredible clouds of debris went down the surrounding streets. Gary and others were covered with dust and dirt from when the towers came down. Not to be deterred, I thought about ways to get back to Greenwich Street, so I could get my car and then head home, if all was clear. Greenwich Street was not far but right down West Street from the World Trade Center. If we could get downtown, we'd be golden. If we could somehow get downtown, and I thought, if we offer some cabbie a few hundred dollars, then he could get us back to Greenwich Street.

MY ADVENTURE WITH JULIANNE CAPPOS

Unfortunately, all the reports continued to get worse, and I bumped into Julie Cappos (she'd previously also been at Lehman Brothers but she was now at Morgan Stanley), who was looking to get back to her apartment in Battery Park City. Foolishly, I thought that some driver, in some car, could get us where we needed to be. So, not finding a cab, we settled for the next best thing (or so we thought), a bicycle-driven rickshaw who was surely looking for a good fare, and Julie and I were it! I remember when we got loaded into the seats of the rickshaw, Julie and I realized that the streets were entirely deserted. But that became even clearer when we were driving down 6th Avenue (normally an uptown-bound avenue), in the midst of Times Square. We were howling with laughter, thinking of the sight we must be: two oblivious chicks, sightseeing around Times Square, while catastrophe awaited us downtown. Julie had been able to reach someone in her building, and they said that there was debris all over the place, and she wouldn't be allowed in the building. So, on to plan B: call some friends with whom she could stay. They lived on the west side. She called them next, and from what I could tell, she would be headed that way later. In the meantime, we would make a quick stop at Morgan Stanley, on 44th Street at 1585 Broadway. We stopped quickly at 1585 Broadway, and she got her laptop and filled her briefcase with a bunch of stuff that she thought she'd need. We got back in the rickshaw and resumed our trek downtown.

Julie and I were only able to get as far south as Houston Street, at which point we were stopped by police. We were told we could go no further, as everything around the World Trade was closed, from Canal Street down. Crestfallen, Julie implored the police that she had to get some things to stay with friends for a while, but it was a no-go. I told them I had to get home to New Jersey, and the police told me I could walk west until West Street, and then I could walk north until 42nd Street, where I might be able to find a ferry to get across to the Jersey side. So my BMW would be held hostage for a while (I didn't have much choice). I finally got to the west side, and then north to 42nd Street, and then we heard a group of people screaming and gasping, as they looked south and saw what turned out to be 7 World Trade Center, my old building, collapsing. There was a rumbling sound as the building came down. It was 5:20 p.m. There went my old building at Salomon Brothers. I pictured the beautiful view we used to have from the 42nd floor at 7 WTC. It was a beautiful cross-section of the west side and Midtown Manhattan, now gone forever.

Julianne Elizabeth Cappos, my 9/11 Rickshaw Rider

Finally, after much walking I was (sorry I wore high heels that day), I made it to 42nd and 12th Avenues (also known as the West Side Highway), and looked out to see that there were, indeed, some ferry-sized boats out in the water from where the Circle Line boats normally depart. As long as it would get me closer to home, I wasn't about to be particular about my mode of transport. I boarded the boat (which was a Circle Line), and we departed for the Jersey side, at Weehawken. The boat was well-populated, but not crowded, and we departed Manhattan. There was an eerie silence on the boat, as everyone seemed to be shell-shocked and exhausted. When we got out to the middle of the Hudson, everyone was looking south at the smoldering ruins. The World Trade Center, and any of its inhabitants, now presumed dead, were buried under a pile of wreckage, the likes of which one couldn't even imagine. There was another rumble, of 7 WTC coming down, the last gasp, and a cloud of smoke, above what was once a beautiful complex: the symbol of World Trade and a symbol of America's great freedom.

As I continued to stare downtown, my cell phone started to ring, and I thought it might be Gary, so I picked it up. Instead of Gary's voice, after I said hello, I heard, "Oh my God, I can't believe you picked up, I was sure you were dead." I recognized the voice. It was Doug, an old boyfriend, with whom I'd had a brief, but very intense, relationship. It was comforting to hear his deep voice.

I said, "No, I am alive, but it's been a scary day. I was Midtown, at a meeting, when Armageddon happened at the World Trade, but thankfully, I'm finally on my way home. How are you? Were you anywhere near Manhattan?" The called dropped off, and I never learned the answer to that question.

Finally, we reached Weehawken, and I looked out for my friends, who were coming to meet me at the Chart House Restaurant (one of many in that area). I finally spotted them, and they saw me at the same time! It was like a scene from a movie, where I was coming from a war and they were there to welcome me home! It was Joyce Timko Becker; her husband, Donald; and their kids, Caroline and Brandon. We ran toward each other and we hugged really tight, and we kissed, and we were crying as we attempted (unsuccessfully) to deal with the confluence of emotions: shock and grief, relief, but remembering panic, as we witnessed the trauma that unfolded before our very eyes. This would be a day I'd never forget, nor would the rest of the free world.

SALOMON BROTHERS (HISTORY)

As Wikipedia notes, "Salomon Brothers was a Wall Street investment bank, known as a bulge bracket company. Founded in 1910 by three brothers (Arthur, Herbert, and Percy) along with a clerk named Ben Levy, it remained a partnership until the early 1980s, when it was acquired by the commodity trading firm Phibro Corporation and became Salomon Inc.

"Eventually, Salomon (NYSE:SB) was acquired by Travelers Group in 1998; and, following the latter's merger with Citicorp that same year, Salomon became part of Citigroup. Although the Salomon name carried on as Salomon Smith Barney, which was the investment banking operations of Citigroup, the name was ultimately abandoned in October 2003 after a series of financial scandals that tarnished the bank's reputation."

The firm's top bond traders called themselves "Big Swinging Dicks," and were the inspiration for the book *The Bonfire of the Vanities*, by Tom Wolfe. Salomon Brothers' success and decline in the 1980s is documented in Michael Lewis's 1989 book, *Liar's Poker*. Lewis went through Salomon's training program and then became a bond salesman at Salomon Brothers in London. The last years of Salomon Brothers, culminating in its involvement in the Long-Term Capital Management crisis, is chronicled in the 2007 book *A Demon of Our Own Design*.

All I know is that at bonus time, my big call on TXU bonds resulted in a $250,000 bonus for me, which was nice. At the same time, I got visual confirmation that both Brian Riano and Jon Eckerson received bonus checks of $4 million each, as they had assumed the risk in buying all of those TXU FMBs and unsecured debentures. However, their purchase of all of those bonds was based upon my recommendation that TXU would do the right thing. I'd hoped that there would have been more to recognize my contribution to taking on all that additional risk, which paid off handsomely.

https://en.wikipedia.org/wiki/Salomon_Brothers

RETRIEVING MY BMW-540

After 9/11, we were instructed to work from home for at least the first week. At some point, I'd need to get back to my parking garage on Greenwich Street. I didn't venture back in until Friday, September 22. The ride in to New York City wasn't bad. I traveled in the evening, and traffic was a breeze. I arrived at my parking garage on Greenwich Street in an attempt to retrieve my car. Fortunately, given the circumstances, the garage only charged me for two nights instead of a week and two nights. I retrieved my car, and up the ramp to the street I went. I made a left onto Greenwich Street, and I stayed straight up until Canal Street and made another left, and then a right, onto West Street. Behind my car, a fire truck had its headlights on full force, and the light cut right through the interior of my car. I was completely visible to the outside world! As I traveled north on West Street, I had several lights to get through before reaching the right turn for the Lincoln Tunnel. At every intersection, I noticed groups of people on the center median, and they seemed to be calling to me. The fire truck with its headlights illuminating the entire interior of my car, I saw people leaning toward my car, and yelling, "Thank You!" "You're a hero," as they threw bottles of water and Clif bars into my car window! They must have thought that I was working "down at the pile" at Ground Zero, and I was trying to help find any survivors! Meanwhile, here I was, just trying to retrieve my BMW 5-Series and high-tail it back out of town!

In the days following 9/11, an iconic picture of firefighters "working on the pile" was taken at Ground Zero.
Source: https://groundzeromuseumworkshop.org/photo-gallery.html

AFTER SEPTEMBER 11: CHANGES IN MY INDUSTRY COVERAGE, AND AN END TO MY TIME AT SALOMON BROTHERS[3]

The September 11, 2001, terrorist attack was a huge blow to the world, especially New York City. The world somehow didn't feel safe anymore. Coming into Manhattan every day once we returned to the office had a very tentative feeling about it. It was as if New York had lost some of its confidence and bravado. The New York tough attitude seemed a bit squeamish

3. For a complete discussion, please see "The Wall Street Years."

about what had just happened. How to get the good feeling to return? For starters, people started being kind to one another. On their commutes to downtown Manhattan, drivers started letting other drivers cut in line (something completely unheard of in the past).

People genuinely seemed happy to run into neighbors or even coworkers, checking in with them about how they fared through the attack. People were kind to one another.

In 2001, our industry conference, hosted by Edison Electric Institute (EEI), was in New Orleans. The conference hotel was the Hilton Riverwalk. In October 2001, here we were, about to get on a commercial airliner jet for the first time since the flight ban was lifted. One notable event at that year's conference was a presentation at the National World War II Museum. The speaker that evening was General Norman Schwarzkopf, a famous Gulf War general. He gave a very moving speech that night, bringing many to tears. He spoke about the various Gulf Wars during which he presided over US Military forces (Desert Shield and Desert Storm). Here was a tough guy, a patriot, and he stood for all great things American. At the end of his speech, we were invited to have our pictures taken with him, and I availed myself of the opportunity. The general had very large and powerful hands, which I held as we crossed over a "bridge" in our picture. That picture remains somewhere in my many boxes of pictures.

General Schwarzkopf was not the first general I'd ever met. In 1996, while I was an equity analyst at Lehman, I was invited to a Southern Company event with the utility's industrial customers. The conference was hosted in Point Clear, Alabama (Alabama Power was the operating utility in the area). I remember it was blistering hot in Point Clear that day. And at the water's edge, you could see what looked like oil patches at the shore (almost looking like tar, it was so hot). My presentation was to discuss the need for utilities to be competitive in their pricing, as new power options would be coming down the pike. The morning of the conference, I met my co-panelist presenter. It was General Colin Powell. He had recently published a best-selling book, *My American Journey*. Upon meeting him, I asked if he would mind if I addressed him by his first name, to which he replied, "You can call me General." Thanks for answering that question. Nice meeting you, too, Colin!

Back at the office, some news started swirling about the power marketing companies and their accounting and business practices. Enron came to the forefront of those news stories. What were their businesses really worth? Instead of hard assets like utility companies, Enron had used an accounting practice, known as "special purpose entities," which was specifically used to hide billions of dollars in debt. The company was ultimately unveiled as a house of cards, and on December 2, 2001, Enron filed for Chapter 11. At the same time, Arthur Andersen, its accounting firm, had its license to audit public companies voided by the SEC. Many of its companies' officers and directors were sent to prison.

Our group's research assistant, Brian Schmidt, had a background in forensic accounting, and he aggressively pursued the truth about Enron's accounting practices. Brian was head and shoulders smarter than I was in forensic accounting. John Melesius sought out Brian to attend conference calls and meetings related to Enron, Dynegy, Calpine, NRG, and other power marketing companies. Truth be told, I became very paranoid that Brian would take over my role as a senior analyst. But it didn't excuse my reaction, which was to increase the amount and frequency that I was drinking. Ultimately, John requested that I come and speak with him. In our conversation, he asked, "What is going on with you? Let's talk about this before it goes too far." He told me of someone else with whom he had worked who also had a problem with alcohol but eventually sought help before it was too late. He suggested that I speak with EAP, the employee assistance program. They could recommend a therapist for me. We called and I was referred to Beth Meehan, who had an office in the East Village, on 14th Street. I met with Beth a few times, and I discussed my drinking history and my recent fears about whether it could impact my job. After one of my visits, John was adamant that I'd been drinking, as I came in late that day. While I wasn't drinking at that moment, John and others were on to me and my drinking habit. I remember that Carlotta Chan, whose position I took upon coming to Salomon, had admonished me, "You better be honest with John because he's a great guy, and it could save your job."

A couple of weeks had gone by and I thought things had settled down. I was dead wrong. One afternoon, my phone rang, and on the liquid crystal display I read the dreaded words: Diane Arber, from HR, was calling. Tempted to ignore the call, instead I picked up: "Could you please come down to the third floor, in the 390 Greenwich Building?" This was it! I was screwed! I went downstairs and next door to 390 Greenwich to Diane Arber's office. She told me to go into an office on the right side from her office. As I peered through the door window, I saw Bob Waldman (director of Corporate Bond Research at Salomon Brothers) and John Melesius (my direct boss). This was it—I was going to get fired!

Bob had been a lawyer in the Marines. At one morning meeting, he made a sarcastic comment about someone's behavior (not mine): "I've sent soldiers to Leavenworth for less." Bob was a tough guy but a great guy, too. If you were on his "team," you were "in." Today, I was about to be cut from the team. When we spoke, Bob mentioned that, at year-end, I was put up for a promotion to managing director (equal to being a partner at the firm). He told me: "You're killing me to have to do this, but you are being terminated." I heard the words coming from his mouth, but I was in a haze—not from alcohol but because of the reality of what was happening to me. "You gave me no choice." "You were one of my guys." "How could you screw this up?"

Yes, those were the words that were tearing me up inside. John came into the office and also expressed his disappointment: "Grosser, we were such a good team, but you ruined it." He asked if I had any thoughts of hurting myself (I did not). It was surreal but too real for me at that moment. I spoke to HR one more time and they also asked if I would be okay.

I said, "Yes, I'll be okay." It was July 2002, and I'd been fired from a job I loved. I had worked harder at that job than at any other job on Wall Street that I'd had, over the course of my bulge bracket firm career. I'd made a huge Texas Utilities (TXU) call, and the firm made tens of millions on that "bet" based upon my recommendation! At bonus time, I got a $250,000 bonus (on top of my regular bonus), but the head traders on the desk each received $4 million bonuses. What would I do now? First, I called Gary and told him what had happened. He told me, "Go get your car, and come home. I'll make you a nice dinner." And so I did. As I drove home, I had a big cry most of the way. I had to blow my nose numerous times along the way. Since it was early afternoon, traffic was a breeze. I just wanted to get home and contemplate what to do next.

Gary did make me a nice dinner that night. He barbecued some chicken, along with veggies and a salad; it just felt good to be at home, a little relaxed, and safe. Gary felt terrible for me, and the phone started ringing; people calling with consoling thoughts about what had happened. In the end, the worst was over, and I'd be okay again. It was mid-summer, and I took the opportunity to cool off, calm down, and get my head together. Several months later, I was contacted (by Ron) about a job working with a consulting company as a business development person. The firm was located in Glen Rock, New Jersey, right next to Ridgewood, New Jersey. The firm was called Stanton Walker & Company. It had two partners, Richard Stanton and Richard (Dick) Walker. Their focus was on mergers and acquisitions. They became consultants for pink sheet companies (companies whose stocks traded at less than one dollar per share) that were seeking to grow their businesses. They had a unique compensation formula: they'd get paid by the pink sheet company in restricted stock. When the company merged with or acquired another company, the shares would become unrestricted, and could be sold, usually for significantly higher prices. There was also a trader that worked with them in their office. His name was John Forsythe. Also working in the office was Ron, who had started his company, Strategic

Working Capital. His business model was to fund "working capital" needs to small businesses, which were also usually pink sheet companies. He had raised several million dollars to fund his strategy, largely from business associates and friends from his time at Goldman Sachs.

Around the same time, I'd received calls from someone named Bryan Emerson. He and his wife, Laura, had set up a boutique broker-dealer, Starlight Capital, in Houston, where there were a number of energy company prospects, and did that sound interesting to me to get involved in. Apparently, he'd gotten my name through Mariel Clemensen, my first boss at DLJ, so I thought, why not see what comes of this? Ultimately, I signed on with Starlight Capital in mid-2003. Right off the bat, Bryan had an opportunity for me. It was to work with an energy company that built stand-alone power generators, which the owner manufactured himself. The man's name was Hank Leggett, and he was willing to pay the $10,000 per month retainer and success fees if we were successful at finding a partner or acquisition target. His company was called USCO, a manufacturer of diesel generating units. The company was based in Longview, Texas, about 400 miles from Houston. Eventually, I got on a plane to Houston, and Bryan and I drove out to Longview. The 400-mile trip would take over seven hours. The meeting with Hank was fruitful. I would work with Hank and set about looking for business prospects for USCO. Shortly into our consulting agreement, Bryan received Hank's first check for $10,000. I thought I was "back"! Bryan had suggested that I think about working with some others in Starlight, and that I look at our database of fifty thousand investors for possible investors for Hank's project. In coming on board with Starlight, we needed to make sure my securities licenses were in order. I'd had my Series 7 and 63, but my 7 was about to expire. We had to petition the SEC with a letter about my wealth of experience in the financial markets, in research, and state that I would be utilizing my skills going forward. This negated my need to take my Series 7 again, a six-hour test that would have been a huge headache. I did, however, have to take my Series 24, a Securities Principal exam, that would allow me to supervise others (if that became necessary). In the end, I carried a Series 7, Series 63 (blue sky rule), a Series 24, and Series 79 (research analyst). Unlike working with the bulge bracket companies with whom I'd been affiliated, Starlight had no infrastructure, or any support. We had to do everything for ourselves. Plus, we had to pay Starlight $150 every month for them to maintain our licenses and be compliant with FINRA.

Shortly after I joined up with Starlight, I attended one of their conferences. Aimed at private equity and small institutional investors, Starlight's conferences were designed to match up investors with companies in need of their cash. Bryan and Mike Segal had been hosting these conferences for several years. They were hosted at the Yale Club, right near Grand Central Terminal. It was an afternoon series of meetings and presentations made by small companies in need of capital to fund their projects. The meetings were followed by a cocktail hour/reception with hors d'oeuvres and other food. It was perfect for networking. At the first conference, Bryan introduced me to Murray Froikin and Gubin. Murray and had been partners for several years.

Being back in an investment banking environment and at a conference venue made me feel that, somehow, I'd been able to reinvent myself once more. (Keep that skill set, Deb, you'll need it again.)

Murray and I got more involved in several projects: some profitable, some near misses, and some a crying shame. But working with Murray, I found another loyal friend. He was a good man, a very smart man, and he could produce a full-blown financial model for a project in record time! He was a very skilled forensic accountant. Together, we worked on a geothermal project that almost sold to a New York–based private equity firm called Riverstone Energy (part of the Carlyle Group). In one conference call, the firm was ready to bid on a geothermal energy project in California, only to learn they had been outbid by US Renewables Energy by a very small amount, but it was too late.

Then, we spent a year trying to find a private equity firm to buy Vanoil, a coiled tubing company in Edmonton, Alberta, Canada. In this instance, a bid was submitted by Cadent Energy, in Connecticut, but the bid was rejected by the owners of Vanoil.

Other deals came our way. For more than a year, we worked with Gateway Energy in Houston. We assisted them with some structural changes to their common stock, moving it from the pink sheets to the American Stock Exchange. We also sought acquisition targets in an effort to grow their business. While Gateway did not pay us a cash retainer, we were awarded shares of their stock, which was later sold at a reasonable level, and which made for a healthy profit for our work.

There were several other projects that Murray and I worked on over the next several years, even up to just before my accident in 2011. We worked for more than two years on a geothermal project in Bali, Indonesia. Murray actually traveled to Indonesia for further due diligence and possible negotiations with vendors for the project.

Murray has had a long-term relationship with Judy Werble Weiss. They've been together for roughly twenty-one years. Judy has lived with Murray at her rent-stabilized apartment, on the upper East side. They had two Shih Tzus, named Gracie and Georgie (like the '50s show). Now, they have Georgie (now seventeen years old, or 102 years in human years) and Abby (eight years old, or forty-eight in human years).

Judy is a longtime "fan-atic" of Jon Bon Jovi. She procured tickets to our first concert at MetLife Stadium in East Rutherford, and to a second one (courtesy of *The Ellen DeGeneres Show*), also at MetLife Stadium. For the first concert, in 2010, my role was to make dinner reservations. We went to the Bonefish Grill, in Secaucus, New Jersey. We made 6 p.m. reservations. The concert was at 8 p.m. My sister-cousin, Gigi Burrows, came to my house in Mahwah, and we drove to Secaucus together. Of course, much like teens on their way to their first concert, we had Bon Jovi CDs blasting for the whole ride from Mahwah to the NJ Transit station in Secaucus. "Whoa-whoa,

Livin' on a Prayer." First to pick up Judy and Sue Ollander at the train station in Secaucus. Then, on to Bonefish Grill. During the course of our dinner and the ease with which Gigi blended into our group, we ultimately decided that we'd become "the Jovi girls" (a name that's stuck, over time). Sue was immediately enamored with Gigi and her penchant to tell of stories from back in her day, much like Mercedes Ruehl in *Married to the Mob*.

Judy Werble Weiss, our Jovi ticket connection

Sue Ollander, sultry

The Jovi girls and their guys at MetLife Stadium, 2013

ANOTHER ITERATION OF REINVENTION: THE WORLD OF HEDGE FUNDS AT VERITAS PARTNERS

While I was working at Starlight Investments (as Starlight Capital was now called), I had yet another opportunity to reinvent myself. It is here that I became involved with Ron, on a business level. For a couple of years after his stint with Strategic Working Capital, he began working with an emerging investment fund manager called Iron Mountain Capital Partners. They were located in Ridgewood, New Jersey. The managing partner was Nicholas Lattanzio. Apparently, Nick had secured funds to allow him to pay Ron and others at the firm a reasonable weekly salary. There appeared to be some new funding prospects that Nick asked Ron to pursue. He was required to travel to the West Coast to pursue it for Iron Mountain.

In March 2008, there were some abrupt negative developments, as it related to Nick, personally. His wife, Whitney, died suddenly, and Nick was left to care for his two young children. There was much speculation about what was really happening, and in short order, Iron Mountain was closing its doors. Ron had been somewhat friendly with a young attorney at Iron Mountain, Benjamin C. Browning. Ben, Ron, and I conferred about what to do next. There was the possibility of raising funds to manage, otherwise known as AUM (assets under management). After much discussion, and a little bit of my organizational skills, Veritas Partners was born. All it really took was some browsing on the web to come up with the availability of the name: the existence of other companies with that name, and not finding many, or any, we took Veritas (which means "truth") Partners and submitted to the state's IRS revenue division.

We then made business cards. We agreed upon the design:

This began a whole new chapter in reinventing myself.

Ron was conversant on all aspects of hedge fund strategies, and in which markets they performed well or what conditions would have a negative impact.

My strength was on the marketing side, searching for likely sources of funding. All my years at bulge bracket firms, and my knowledge of funding sources of capital through that arena, came in handy: start at the state pension level, or even higher—start at the state. Every state has multiple pension fund organizations that compensate its public employees. But we needed to start with state government structure: the governor of the state and the mayors of the cities.

We needed to network with the necessary groups. This opened up a whole new arena in which to participate. I looked online and found groups and organizations that sponsored hedge fund conferences. I found Opal Financial, located in Midtown, on 36th Street. I knew from experience that by volunteering for a speaking engagement at one of their conferences we might get "comped" versus having to pay a hefty conference attendance fee. These could run into the thousands of dollars. As he was a knowledgeable source on hedge fund strategies, I volunteered Ron to speak at several Opal Financial conferences. They were usually at great locations with amazing conference hotels in each location. In getting to know the folks at Opal, I met its founder, Abe Wellington, and at least two of its young associates. There was Jaime Lane and Lauren Sharabi. Both were incredibly knowledgeable and helpful. In Newport, Ron spoke at the Family Office and Private Wealth Management forum. We stayed at the Inn at Castle Harbor. We had lunch with LaRoy Brantley, from Cambridge Associates, a hedge fund advisory firm.

For another one of the Opal conferences, the Investment Trends Summit, the sponsor hotel was the Four Seasons Resort, the Biltmore, in Santa Barbara. It looked beautiful. As a matter of fact, the Biltmore was the basis for scenes (filmed in New York City) from the movie *It's Complicated*, with Meryl Streep and Alec Baldwin. Also, I knew that Mariel Clemensen had once had a house in Santa Barbara. I asked her where we ought to stay, as an alternate to the conference hotel. She suggested the San Ysidro Ranch,but said it was very pricey. Undaunted, I looked it up, and made a call to inquire about the hotel and to make a reservation for two nights. It was a definite splurge, but I was willing to go for it and I am glad I did.

Santa Barbara (San Ysidro Ranch)

Santa Barbara (the restaurant at San Ysidro Ranch)

Another big conference sponsor was Skybridge Capital, founded by Anthony Scaramucci in 2005 (Anthony worked in the Trump administration for a brief period eleven days). Skybridge hosted an annual conference out in Las Vegas: it was called Skybridge Alternatives, or SALT, for short. It was a huge, must-attend event for emerging hedge funds, or funds of funds. The SALT conference was typically hosted at the Bellagio hotel. There were a number of great venues where conference events were hosted. At each conference, Anthony Scaramucci ("the Mooch") was the master of ceremonies. His energy level was unmatched. From start to finish, he participated or commented on every panel discussion. In between, he participated in live broadcasts on CNBC, along with Maria Bartiromo and others. Also, at each conference, the president from the previous administration would be a keynote speaker. In 2011, I got to meet and speak with George W. Bush. He had just published his memoir, *Decision Points*, which chronicled the many hard decisions he had to make post-September 11, and how easy it was for people to second-guess (and be critical of) his choices. It was true what people say: he really was a guy you'd want to have a beer with. The SALT conference attracted a huge audience. Roughly two thousand people would fill the vast Bellagio Ballroom. When we went to SALT for the first time, I had no doubt this was the place to be! At every break between sessions, Ron and I got out there to meet and greet potential investors in Veritas. It was at SALT that we found a potential strategic opportunity. Having been voted the fund of funds for the year, we met Daniel Freedman from London & Capital (L&C). While schmoozing a bit with Daniel, Ron and I started to discuss our need for funding and the potential to have some discussions with L&C about working together. We exchanged contact details and not two weeks later, I was contacted by Daniel Freedman, who suggested that we come to meet with L&C, in London, that fall. It was decided that we visit them on Labor Day weekend in 2009. That was Monday, September 7, 2009.

Ultimately, Daniel had in his mind that Ron and I would become the New York office of L&C, marketing their fund of funds product. They would arrange and pay for our new office space. We agreed that there would be a nominal salary; the rest of our compensation would be determined by the amount of additional AUM that we attracted. There would also be a small portion of equity in L&C as compensation for us. In the end, Ron felt that the equity percentage was inadequate for the risk that we would be taking on ourselves. Daniel and Ron agreed to disagree, and we parted ways, reasonably amicably.

Back to square one. I began to go back to some of the other investment managers with whom I'd been in contact over the last year. I contacted Krista Ward from Calhoun Asset Management. Calhoun was based in the Chicago area. In my discussions with Krista, she indicated that they had about $20 million in AUM. It was a start, and it could attract further assets to manage.

SEEKING LEGAL COUNSEL

Along with our conference participation, and as we were seeking opportunities to raise new capital to manage, our paths crossed with a very impressive and well-known attorney in the alternative asset arena: Ron Geffner. Ron was a partner at Sadis & Goldberg. Ron was a former SEC Enforcement attorney representing clients in some high-profile cases, generally in the alternative asset or hedge fund space. One notable transaction: Sadis & Goldberg represented Skybridge Capital in its acquisition of Citigroup's alternative asset business. (Source: https://en.wikipedia.org/wiki/Ron_S._Geffner).

Ron Geffner has an impressive background. He began his career with the SEC, where he investigated and prosecuted violations of the federal securities laws with an emphasis on enforcement in connection with violations of the Investment Advisers Act of 1940 and the Investment Company Act of 1940. He also assisted federal and state criminal agencies, such as the Federal Bureau of Investigation, US Attorney's Office, and the Attorney General's Office, in their investigations of criminal violations of federal and state securities laws. When we met with Ron, he seemed to take a liking to us and the way we presented ourselves. He seemed to be impressed by Ron, his appearance, and his knowledge of all things hedge fund strategy and their likely performance in different market environments. As we were not yet funded, we sought his advice and he made recommendations but we were not yet ready to engage his services. Since the first time I met him, Ron Geffner reminded me of Richard Gere in *Pretty Woman*.

Ron Geffner, Sadis & Goldberg

NAVIGATING A NEW BUSINESS WHILE MAKING A BIG MOVE AT HOME

It was 2009, and I was in the process of selling 17 Seminary Drive. I was using Margaret Gregorek as my realtor, who did an excellent job of dealing with the sale amid a difficult real estate market. It was in the midst of the 2008 global recession, as Lehman Brothers had collapsed and the markets were roiled with fear. We successfully sold 17 Seminary at what turned out to be a sizeable premium relative to our initial purchase price in 1994. Still, it was a bit difficult to manage both selling my home and moving forward with a completely different business venture. I was excited that the prospects could bring sizeable growth and success to Veritas Partners. I sold 17 Seminary in 2009, and closing took place in early December. I literally closed on 17 Seminary and moved in right away into 22 Airmount

Road, in Ramsey, New Jersey. There were beautiful, brand-new three-story townhouses built there; Margaret Gregorek and I went to check out the new place. We went to all the units there, and I chose the unit next to the end unit: #6. The unit I chose was not the largest, but it was still over three thousand square feet. Entering the front door, there was a small stairway on the right, which led to the downstairs; there was plenty of room for the new office space Ron and I would need. On the left, there was a stairway that led up to the first-floor landing (where I was found, face-down in a pool of blood, on August 31, 2011).

On the first floor, there was room for the living room, and behind it, the dining room. There was a powder room, and the kitchen, right behind that. Off the back of the kitchen was a small deck, perfect to sit out in the sun and take in the view. Finally, we went upstairs, on the very steep staircase that I would eventually fall down, almost to my death. My friend Robin even told me that, upon seeing the townhouse, that I'd stated about the staircase: "These stairs could be the death of me!" (How prescient.) Upstairs was a spacious master bedroom, with a master bath on the right and another large bedroom on the left. That would become my office. I enjoyed 22 Airmount Avenue very much. I took to entertaining quickly, once I got settled in. Settling in meant unpacking everything myself, and that was a big job. I had at least twelve large wardrobe boxes, packed to the gills, with all my clothes, shoes, boots, sneakers, bags, accessories, and personal care products. It took a couple of days to fully empty those boxes. I just started with one box at a time, emptying the contents into every closet, cabinet, or drawer that I could find.

Before I moved into 22 Airmount Road, we made a stop with the moving truck to where Ron would be moving in. As I was moving out of a large home with too much furniture for my new townhouse, I gifted Ron with several pieces of furniture that I could no longer use in my new place. Thus, a beige leather circular sofa, a queen-sized bed, two wicker dressers, a butcher-block cart for the kitchen, a coffee table, and some bedding, towels, and other domestics got dropped off at Ron's new place.

Off we went to 22 Airmount Avenue. Of course, my sweet baby girl, golden retriever Kayla, came to move into our new home. She was now three years old. The first thing to get set up in the new townhouse was the bedroom. The movers helped with setting up the headboard and footboard on my king-sized bed. As there was no longer Huffman Koos, I'd graduated to using Raymour & Flanigan, in Paramus. In one fell swoop, I ordered a new dining room table (pub-height, with six chairs), a hutch, a side hutch, a new sofa for the living room, and a new mattress for the king-sized bed. When Ron came over to check out my new place, he said, "You've outdone yourself." Over the next few weeks, I began to procure more items: some paintings, a large rectangular mirror for over the side table, some lamps, and a few other items to adorn the new place. Christmas was coming in just a few weeks. I went to Michael's, a craft store in Ramsey Square. There, I purchased some Christmas decor and a small tree that I would call my townhouse Christmas tree. (It was a far cry from the eight-foot balsam fir at 17 Seminary Drive.) It was perfectly adequate and fine. This was my new place!

My extraordinary Realtor, Margaret Gregorek, and her husband, Mark

22 Airmount Avenue, Ramsey, New Jersey

Once settled in, I came to like living at 22 Airmount Avenue in Ramsey. It was certainly convenient to downtown Ramsey and the Main Street thoroughfare that one can find there. I quickly found a new running route through downtown Ramsey, on Main Street, past all of the shops that I would frequent. I would take that to Central Avenue and make a right on N. Island Avenue, and I could continue onto Darlington Avenue. Or, I could stay straight, on Main Street, which would turn into Wyckoff Avenue. Most often, I would run the course myself, but other times, I'd make handy use of Kayla, as my running "guide dog." As a young golden retriever, she needed and loved to run with me. At times, it felt like it was just me and Kayla, out to explore the world. There were other times, on Main Street, where Kayla and I would make a pitstop at the local downtown Carvel, owned by Joel Occhiuto (previous owner/co-owner with Johnny Occhiuto, Joel's son), of Totally Tan, where Gary and I both frequented often. At the Carvel, I treated both me and Kayla—she would get her favorite, her own waffle cone with vanilla ice cream. I loved to take this walk with Kayla on late summer evenings, as kids and families still stayed out a bit late on Sunday evenings, before the kids were headed back to school.

While still unpacking at 22 Airmount, right after Christmas, I went to Chicago to meet with Krista Ward and the others at Calhoun. Our decision, early on, was to retain the name Calhoun Asset Management, while later we might transition back to Veritas Partners (based upon the assets brought in to manage). Krista picked me up at Chicago O'Hare, on Monday, December 28. I would stay there for a few days, returning on New Year's Eve, that Thursday. Krista drove us in to the place where she leased office space for Calhoun. Turns out the name Calhoun came from the name of one of the many lakes at which she and her family had vacationed as a child in Minnesota, the land of ten thousand lakes. During my stay, I met Krista's administrative assistant, Corrie, as well as a research analyst, Mushir Shaikh. Rather than recommending a hotel, Krista invited me to stay at her home, in Park Ridge, Illinois, an upscale suburb of Chicago. I met her three lovely children, and we played board games and had dinner.

While we were together under the banner of Calhoun Asset Management, we traveled to Philadelphia, Baltimore, and Chicago (for a conference at which Ron spoke), and to Omaha, Nebraska (where a number of Calhoun investors resided). As there had been some preexisting investments made prior to our forming a combination, these "Madoff" investments became problematic for Calhoun investors. Ultimately, between an SEC review and a personal disagreement between Krista and Ron, we parted ways in early 2010.

2009, Veritas Partners merger partner, Calhoun Asset Management

I entertained with some new friends and some of my core group. The first time I entertained, however, was with a group from AA. I ordered some of the usual staples: a platter of pinwheel sandwiches (turkey, roast beef, chicken salad) from Bagel Boys. I ordered a tray of chicken Française and baked ziti, at the Ramsey Deli, and for the rest, I asked everyone to bring a dessert of their choice. That usually resulted in a great variety to sate our sweet tooths! As it was a group from AA and I was staying sober at the time, there were no alcoholic drinks: seltzer/sparkling water with cranberry juice, ginger ale, Diet Cokes, and a big pot of coffee (just like at meetings). It was a great gathering and house-warming with my AA home group friends. It was a nice way to start to entertain at my new place.

My next gathering consisted of some of my triathlon friends, and friends from New York Sports Club. I even invited some of my Cornerstone friends. I ordered and prepared the food for this gathering. While I was not drinking at this time, I knew that people in attendance might want some red wine, white wine, or some beer to accompany their dinner. This is where things got dangerous. In the guise of buying "for them," I went to the Saddle River liquor store, on Route 17, and ordered a variety of red and white wines and a twelve-pack of St. Pauli Girl beer. I was fully stocked for my next gathering.

It was really a successful gathering! Everyone enjoyed an evening with good food, good conversation, and, for those who had a drink, good drink. I did not drink for that gathering, but danger was lurking. Everyone mingled with each other and got along fine. People were generally very happy with my first "friend" gathering at 22 Airmount Road Thank you, Alyson, Peter, Rob and Jill Isabelle, Jim and Karen Riley, Cathy and Gary Konner, Deborah and Marc Schwartz, Amy McLennon Marklin and Michael, and Lizabeth Cirillo and Nick. I believe even Stacey Lopis showed that night.

You made my first independently hosted gathering a great success.

My Triathlon friends:
Jim Riley, Peter Skutnik, and Rob Isabelle

2011: A Collision Point

In January 2011, I contacted Kirsten Kincade and proposed the idea of working on an event for the Matthew Larson Foundation, ironmatt.org.

She liked the idea and suggested we meet to talk about it. On January 13, 2011, I had a surgery scheduled, an upper and lower lid blepharoplasty, in New York. Kirsten volunteered to drive me in for the surgery. Interestingly, it was Ron's fiftieth birthday. My surgeon was Dr. Theodore Diktaban, who was referred by two other doctors who were in my group therapy, with Dr. Arnold Washton. That therapy was intended to treat my dependency on alcohol. Given the benefit of hindsight, I realized how many lies I'd been telling as reasons why I was missing sessions, often.

I went for my eyelid surgery, which eventually turned out very well, but I spent three weeks looking like I'd just gone sixteen rounds with Rocky Balboa. The extent of bruising was awful. From the top of my forehead, down my cheeks, and to the base of my chin, my face was black, blue, purple, green, and red. For my recovery process, it was recommended that I apply cold ice packs and to use Arnicare Gel (which I swear by). In a week or so, I was able to go to Shop Rite with sunglasses on. As I approached the checkout cashier, I warned her, and dipped my sunglasses to display the ugly picture beneath my glasses. But it was temporary, and the results were lasting. Despite my need to be a bit covert, I continued to meet regularly with the IronMatt Casino Night group: Kirsten Kincade, me, David Baker, Jayne Abramson, Stacey Lopis, Nancy Silverman Flaum, and many others. Right around my birthday is when I needed to go to detox at Valley Hospital. It didn't take very long and I was discharged the same day.

Right after that, Ron and I attended the 2011 SALT conference in Las Vegas, to be hosted at the Bellagio. This year, I'd heard about a brand-new, all-suite hotel, at City Center. It was called Vdara. As it was new, they were offering extremely low rates per stay to attract new customers. I called there and made reservations for May 10, a Tuesday. I'd reserved a two-bedroom "Loft," which turned out to be a duplex, on the top floor of the hotel! When inside and looking out of the window, our view was incredible! It was like being suspended in a helicopter, overlooking the entire Vegas Strip! We had an amazing view of the conference hotel: the Bellagio, right next door, Paris Hotel, across the way, and all of the MGM properties!

Vdara, an all-suite hotel, in City Center, Las Vegas

Anthony Scaramucci (the Mooch), SALT Conference MC, founder of Skybridge Alternatives

Source: https://www.usatoday.com/story/news/politics/2019/08/11/donald-trump-and-former-aide-anthony-scaramucci-engage-twitter-war/1980716001/

The conference commenced the next day, and as in years past, it was amazing. The Mooch, as in Anthony Scaramucci, did his usual amazing job as MC. It turns out that there were evening events, right back at City Center, and thus our hotel was very conveniently located.

We arrived back in New Jersey on Thursday, and the casino night event was the next night, Friday, May 13. While in Vegas, I remained in contact with the last-minute sponsors and donors for the evening. Tom Potenza at Tech-Link became the sponsor of a special "gaming room," cordoned off from the rest of the blackjack and roulette tables. The big evening we had all worked so hard on had commenced.

Ron and I continued in our quest to make something of Veritas Partners, LLC. In our downstairs office, Gary's desk from his office at 17 Seminary became Ron's desk, at Veritas Partners. Between attendance at conferences, and studying all of the industry publications and work done for us by Risk-AI, we were keeping busy. Risk-AI was an alternative investments research company with two partners, Aleksey Matiychenkyo and Alexandr Mazo.

Aleksey Matiychenkyo

Ron and I continued in our relationship, although one day, sitting at the kitchen table, he announced that he didn't want to be in a relationship. Not wanting to hear that, I employed denial as my protection. It set inside me feelings of great sadness and self-pity for all we'd done together. Thinking only of the good times, these feelings set in motion a dangerous need to squelch the pain and self-pity. While it did nothing to alleviate these feelings, I went to that which I'd always reached for in the past: alcohol. This was along with my "screw AA" mentality, and so I began doing the worst thing—after my last two-year sobriety anniversary, I picked up a drink again, under the worst circumstances for an alcoholic; I was living alone, and I knew where to call to have alcohol delivered to my front door: Saddle River Liquors. I ordered several bottles of Pinot Noir, a couple of bottles of Veuve Clicquot (Champagne), and that was it for my first delivery.

Upon delivery, having paid for it over the phone, I scurried to hide the alcohol in my garage (hide it from whom, as I was living alone?). There it would stay, until I got the urge to "just feel relaxed." That would become the pattern over the next several months, until August 31, 2011, when the amount of alcohol in my system became so great that a middle of the night bathroom stop turned into a near-death accident, the likes of which would change the course of my life history. I'd learned in AA that drinking over a resentment or out of self-pity was like "taking poison and hoping that the other person dies." How true was that? Alcohol became my poison.

Importantly, my life did not end, as many thought was likely. Thanks to God and my excellent neurosurgeon, Dr. Roy Vingan, I was given an eleventh-hour reprieve and a second chance at life. The rest of my story is yet unwritten. The possibilities of how I can live my life in a positive manner are endless! To be continued.

My story could have been a simple one. If I'd just stopped drinking way before I was ever in danger of a near-deadly fall, none of this would have happened, and my life would have continued on with its own uncertain conclusion. That wouldn't be much of a story. Instead, I had a nasty near-death accident and, with the help of God and my excellent neurosurgeon, I survived, and yes, I (along with my family) had to endure my six-week coma, the nineteen surgeries, the need for years of intense therapy—physical and occupational—and all the treatments that corresponded with them. I've come to see my accident as a gift, for had it never happened, I wouldn't have had the opportunity to gain a whole new perspective in life, to always be grateful no matter what the situation, and to finally have sustained clarity, to see things for the way they really are. Along with all of that insight, I see that alcohol can never be part of my life again, and this time I am happy for that. I'd never been able to let go before, but now I am finally free, and my life can once again be based on a happy objective.

I promised there would not be a happy ending because it's not my ending, yet. Until that day comes, I can be a productive, vital person in society and in the lives of those closest to me for my remaining time on the earth. There are many amazing things in my new life that I intend to accomplish. There is nothing standing in my way, and if there is, just as before, God will show me the way out, up, and over. I am an overcomer. Instead of a traditional Happy Ending, mine is a "happy new beginning." Thank you, Jesus. Amen.

Appendix

Remarks to Honor my Mother, Grace Feltman, before Faith Evangelical Free Church

Good morning. My name is Debbie Grosser, the firstborn daughter of Grace and John Feltman. I am here today with my siblings: Donna Maida, John Feltman, Robert Feltman, and Michael Feltman. Also here are my two sisters-in-law, Kelly Feltman and Eileen Feltman, and one brother-in-law, Ronnie Maida. There are also many other loving family members and friends who share our sorrow but rejoice in my mother's entrance into Heaven.

For anyone who knows my mom, you know she'd be the last person on earth to be made a fuss over!

Well, Mom, we're doing just that this morning!

My mom was the most humble woman I'd ever known. She epitomized what Jesus Christ preached in His Sermon on the Mount: the Beatitudes. The meek shall inherit the Earth.

My dad spoke about his and my mom's relationship spanning over 60 years. And they were blissful years! Not something you see often at all, these days. A relationship built on a deep forever love for each other and a love for Jesus Christ.

Another reason I'm standing up here is because after I had my near-death accident on August 31, 2011, my parents asked Faith's congregation to pray for me. And pray you did! I can honestly say that I am living testimony that the Power of Prayer works! I think it's nice to report that back to the entire congregation of Faith Church!

Being given a second chance at life, to me, is miraculous! Being born again spiritually is the most amazing thing I could ever imagine. Thank you, and thank you, Jesus!

But let's get back to the matter at hand: honoring my mother, Grace Anne Feltman!

Her humility preceded everything she did in her life. She was kind to everyone who came in contact with her. Being parented by Grace and John Feltman was an idyllic life: we took vacations in the Catskills. Staying at the Rip Van Winkle Motel, my mom became their housekeeping department, making the beds and cleaning up after us. It didn't matter that the motel had its own housekeeping department; she became it!

We had a wonderful childhood, just like the movie with Donna Reed and Jimmy Stewart, *It's a Wonderful Life*.

The holidays are coming now, and that's going to be hard for all of us. My mom always worked tirelessly to get that perfect turkey on the table for my dad, and us! Rising sometimes at 4:00 or 5:00 a.m., she'd get that turkey defrosting in the kitchen sink, so it could get in the oven. My Mom and Dad were a team in regard to the holidays. She'd do most of the cooking, while my dad was the master carver and stuffing disher-outer. We were always nearby to get our fair share!

After a big holiday, like Thanksgiving or Christmas, there was always a mountain of dishes! We had no dishwasher; instead, Grace would put on those rubber gloves and just start washing, until the last glass, dish, spoon, fork, or knife was done! Phew! What a workload she bore, in order to please her family. How could we not appreciate every single thing that she did?

Well, Mom, I know you're hearing all of this, and watching it all, from Heaven.

We love you with all of our hearts, Mommy! We will never ever forget you, and we'll carry you in our hearts forever.

Your loving daughter, Debbie!

Memorial for John P. Feltman, Jr. and Remarks by Debbie Grosser

Good morning, and thank you all for being here. Here we are, again. Yes, just 161 days, or 5 months and 10 days ago, I was here, delivering a eulogy for my mom, Grace Feltman, and it is because of that, that we are here, again, today. After my mom passed, my dad was devastated and distraught, yet he was calm because of his intense faith in Jesus Christ. He knew that my mom was out of pain, and now, with Jesus. That brought him, and all of our family, much comfort, just as it's doing today: the knowledge that my mom, Grace, and my dad, John (or Jack), are together again, in the presence of our Lord, Jesus Christ. That must've been a glorious reunion for both of them!

I also want to note that my remarks today are from me, about my relationship with my dad, what he meant to me, and what I will miss most about him. Following my remarks, I will be followed by my siblings: Donna, John, Robert, and Michael, who was with my dad during his final moments.

John and Grace Feltman. Theirs was an enduring love story, one that could not, nor would not end, even when the physical presence of each was no longer there. And it is the physical presence of John Peter Feltman that we will surely miss, from two weeks ago, and for many years to come. I don't think that sense of loss will ever leave us; it will just lessen in its intensity over time. My brother Michael had the very emotional task of picking up my dad's ashes at the crematorium. He described my dad as his best friend. He also mentioned that, in the last couple of years in caring for my mom, and then my dad, that he had come to know him more than he ever had before. Yes, Michael, the youngest of us five children of Grace and John Feltman came to be with my parents at precisely the time they needed him most!

I just wanted to note, that my dad had always instructed us that he didn't want any fanfare when he died. He said, "Just bury me in a pine box." His final instructions were that he wanted his ashes combined with my mom's. Well, Dad, I think we'll be following through with your instructions!

My dad, John Peter Feltman, Jr., was an amazing man. Before he was a loving husband to Grace, and our dad, he was a son, of John Peter Feltman, Sr., who was an amazing man himself. We kids all called our grandfather Gramps or Poppy, and my grandmother, Nanny, called him Zahnny (pronounced "Zawny"). John, or Jackie, was also a beloved brother to his sister Joanie. He was also a grandson to "Mutter" (Marie Dietz Feltman) and cousin to many on both sides of his parents' families.

John, or Jackie, as many called him, also had many friends throughout his school years and his time in the Air Force. He made friends easily, but once married, John was a completely devoted family man, forgoing any "buddies" to hang out with. He loved his Gracie, and he loved each of his kids. He always provided for his family in every possible aspect. When we made the move from Bay Ridge, Brooklyn, to North Babylon, we'd moved into a baby-boomer, kid-packed neighborhood, called the Poet Section, as the streets were all named for poets: Powell, Irving, Brookes, Beecher, Taylor, Harriet, Longfellow, and Poet Avenue.

When we moved into our house, at 100 Powell Court, in 1964, we got our first swing set in our backyard. Around it, my dad built a sandbox. Being the dad he was, no ordinary sand would do. No, he took two guys that worked at the plant he owned, called High Strength Composites, down the block from his plant, in Copaigue. Together, they filled more than a hundred large bags of nice, white beach sand to put in the new sandbox. He wanted us kids to have the best he could find, and that day, the best could be found down the block from his plant in Copaigue.

He didn't stop there. Once the swing set was firmly planted and the nice white sand was deposited all around it, we needed a clubhouse on the lot, didn't we? My dad set about building a Swiss Chalet house, designed with a steep A-framed roof, built with plywood, and painted white with plastic glitter, so it would look like snow in the Swiss Alps. Just as every kid in the neighborhood had, right?

He installed a six-foot wooden stockade fence around the backyard perimeter. Kids were able to stand on the back of it in order to view the many activities that the Feltman's had going on. In the hot Long Island summers, my dad thought of different, fun things to do. There were the times when he bought the 55-gallon drum (the size of a barrel of oil), which he would fill with water, and drop in several silver dollars (sometimes half dollars). He'd invite the neighborhood kids over to dunk for dollars! We were very popular at these times.

My dad was our biggest cheerleader, in every year of school, in every sport or activity we tried. Dad was there for us. We'd get feedback from every parent-teacher night. Our father and mother both helped to build our sense of self, or our self-esteem. My dad was amazing with his ability to do that for all of his children.

When I participated in the Ironman in Lake Placid, NY, my family was there to cheer me on. My dad, being 'Dad', wanted to be there when I finished the second leg of my Ironman, my 112-mile bike ride. My dad told the race officials navigating the course that he was on the board of the Ford Motor Company (Ford was the title sponsor), so that they would allow him to be there when I came in at the end of that ride. He would be there to wish me well as I set off on the third leg of my Ironman, the 26.2-mile marathon. Only John P. Feltman was capable of pulling that one off, but he did!

He was also the first one to hug me when I crossed that finish line after 15 hours on that course.

Without exception, my dad was also our wonderful counselor, when things in our lives didn't work out the way we hoped. When our marriages had troubles, when our careers took an abrupt turn, he was always there to listen, to counsel, and to offer suggestions and encouragement. He always guided us to talk to Jesus, in whatever life change was happening for us.

In August 2011, I had a near-death accident, falling down a flight of steep stairs, during which I broke my skull and suffered a traumatic brain injury. The prospects for me to survive did not look good. So much so that the organ donation teams were called in to parcel out my organs to potential recipients. The good news: I still need them, and I have survived! But not without my loving family, whom I'm so fortunate to have stuck by me the whole time!

I mentioned this when I spoke at my mom's service, that the call for prayer, for me, went out to Faith Church; and yes, those prayers, and the power that comes from it, clearly worked.

I thank you, again, Faith Church! Your prayers worked! And Jesus is all powerful! Amen!

My dad was a very smart man, with a high I.Q. He met Albert Einstein, in Germany, while in the Air Force. He'd also met Werner von Braun, the rocket scientist. They had lunch together.

Being informed that my dad had died, Donna, John, Robert, and Michael all showed up at my room at Gurwin on Sunday, March 31, 2019. I knew it couldn't be good news.

I wrote to them after they left Gurwin: Thank you guys for coming to tell me in person about Daddy's passage. It's like he snuck away when no one was looking to be back with the woman he was so lost without. Much as he tried to put on the "brave dad" persona, I could tell he couldn't wait to be back with her. And now, he is. I could cry just imagining their first moments, together, in Heaven, he, the smiling, handsome Jackie that made her heart quicken when she saw him, and he, embracing her tenderly yet strongly, because he's never going to let her go ever again. Look, there was no drawn-out, lengthy illness (which he was never good at handling without Mommy). There was no abrupt sudden trauma that would be more shocking for us to bear. No, this was simply Daddy leaving to be back with his Gracie, forever!

Thank you for coming to tell me. Our worlds will never be the same with both Mommy and Daddy gone from the Earth. I'm just glad that we have the faith that we do: knowing our parents are reunited, and now with Jesus, to begin eternity together! I feel very blessed and grateful that we could share this all together! I love you! Let's be strong and keep Mommy and Daddy proud and treat this with the respect and honor they deserve.

Love, Sister Debbie

POSTING ABOUT DAD'S PASSAGE ON FACEBOOK

After the initial shock about the news of my father's death, I did what most many Americans do: I posted the information on Facebook.

WE RECEIVED 445 COMMENTS, AND I'VE ATTEMPTED TO RESPOND TO EVERY ONE

Many of you may have seen the post.

It is with the heaviest of hearts to tell you that my father, John Peter Feltman, Jr., died last night, around 5:00 p.m. He died peacefully, at home, of an apparent heart attack. This, only five months after losing our mom, Grace, in October. From what I observed, I think my Dad's heart attack was really a broken heart following the loss of my mom. He was so lost without her. At least tonight, I can say through our faith, that we know that he is with my mom. It's the only reason why I'm not sobbing hopelessly, because there is hope, and his passage just demonstrates that by choosing Jesus as our Lord and Savior, we can be certain of eternal life! With Him! We are here today at this memorial service, to celebrate the life of John Peter Feltman, Jr. This picture was at their 50th anniversary, ten years ago. We will be celebrating that this happy couple is together again, tonight!

March 30, 2019

Our loving father, John Peter Feltman, Jr., died at 4:59 p.m. on March 30, 2019, at his home in North Babylon. He was 88, just four months away from his 89th birthday, in August 2019. He died peacefully at home, just five months and ten days after the passage of his late wife, Grace Anne Feltman, who passed on October 17, 2018.

He was a loving husband to Grace, for more than sixty years, and he and Grace were the most loving parents, survived by five children: Deborah Grosser, Donna Maida, John P. Feltman III, Robert W. Feltman, and Michael J. Feltman. He was also a loving Grandfather to John Gregory Feltman, Matthew Thomas Feltman, Natalie Grace Maida, Nicholas Michael Feltman, and James Philip Feltman. John is also survived by daughters-in-law, Kelly Feltman and Eileen Feltman; former daughter-in-law, Melanie Feltman; and son-in-law, Ronald Maida. He is also survived by many nieces and nephews and godchildren.

John was born and raised in Bay Ridge, Broolyn. He was a highly-decorated staff sergeant in the US Air Force from 1952–56 while stationed in Germany. During his Air Force tenure, he also played golf on the Air Force team in several European countries. Those were some of the best memories of his life, and he told us stories of that period, many times. After an honorable discharge, he returned home and met Grace in 1957. They married nine months later, on June 7, 1958.

Wasting no time, they started their family with the birth of first daughter Deborah Anne in May 1959, followed by Donna Marie in 1961, John Peter in 1964, Robert William in 1966, and Michael Joseph in 1971. They provided us a wonderful, idyllic family life. Since my mom didn't like to fly, our vacations were always within a few hours' drive, except for our Hilton Head trip in the mid/late 1980s, which was more like ten hours. We'd travel in our Ford Country Squire Station Wagon. That car came in handy, because not only did we take vacations while driving that car, but it was also the place where my brother Michael was born. It was about the time, prior to my brother's birth, that the prospect of five children meant it was going to be more expensive in the Feltman household.

John's professional career had been largely focused on computers and then chemical engineering. He made a complete career shift in 1970, becoming a registered representative for then-Merrill Lynch, Pierce, Fenner, and Smith, and joined their trainee program. He was number one un his class. John became one of the first Registered Options Principal (Series 4) on the CBOEX.

After retirement, John became a published author, writing both *Toga* and the *Kingdom of Croone*, a highly acclaimed children's book, and, more recently: *Nuclear Jihad, My Predictions*, by Tate Publishing.

What will I miss most about my Dad?

I would say the most significant thing I'll miss is his voice. On the phone, when he'd hear it was me, he'd always have that upbeat tempo to his voice: "Hello, Debbie! How are you?!" He was a good listener, always quick to offer wise counsel and an empathetic response.

I will miss his voice of reason. He always knew the solution to a problem, along with the method to deliver that solution, and he'd offer words of comfort and consolation, if necessary. He always offered his counsel, in concert with what he believed my mom would want. It was never, if my dad said no, ask your mom. They were a team, through and through. She did, however, know how to manage my dad's emotions regarding different situations.

I will miss his voice of encouragement. As I've had numerous events throughout my life—especially since my accident, and now, as I consider my future life—I always would run my ideas past him. I've followed in his footsteps, both professionally, and now, as I start over, I've followed suit, in that I'm writing a book about my life, especially since my accident. I will miss his wise counsel, on how to go about completing my project and seeing it come to fruition. For that, I will now rely on my siblings, and I'm fortunate to have them, by my side, these last seven and a half years.

I will miss his voice of competition and his continual cheerleading for his children.

I will miss his unconditional love. My dad meant the world to me, and second from Jesus, he was the most unconditionally loving dad I could have ever had. There were plenty of mistakes I've made during my life, and times I've gone seriously down the wrong path. My dad was upfront about the displeasure and hurt that I caused my family. Yet, he was my dad, forgiving, loving, and supportive through all these things. He told me, "We're your parents, and I'm your dad, and we'll love you, no matter what you did. Just get on the right path, stay there, and you can be with Jesus, and all of us, for eternity. Jesus forgave you. Stop looking at the past. Just continue walking your path, with Jesus." That's what he meant to me. That's what I'll miss, until, as I continue on the right path, I will get to see him, and my mom, again, in eternity.

I'll miss you, Daddy!

VALEDICTORIAN SPEECH: JUNE 27, 2019

I literally made it just in time, having had surgery this morning. Thus, I come to you from Gurney to Gurwin!

Welcome to Stuart Almer, Joanne Parisi, Shua Sauer, who are members of Gurwin's administrative board.

I'd also like to welcome some of my family members who chose to attend, despite their busy jobs and family requirements. Thank you to my brother Robert, who's just starting a new job.

Gurwin was started in 1986 (that's when they broke ground, and the Center opened in 1988), by Joseph Gurwin and his wife, Rosalind. Lithuanian-born, Mr. Gurwin came to the US at the age of sixteen with $100 in his pocket and a plan to send back for his parents once he was on his feet financially. Unfortunately, his parents perished in the Holocaust. Mr. Gurwin, along with his wife, Rosalind, ultimately set forth to build a center for caring for the elderly. His initial mission statement for Gurwin was, "Caring for those who cared for us." It basically said that he couldn't take care of his own parents, but he could care for the parents of others. Mr. Gurwin went onto a career in textiles, with contracts from the military. He prospered from those large contracts, and he did make a lot of money, but ultimately, he invested with notorious Bernard Madoff and lost a significant sum of money, around $36 million. But Mr. Gurwin never stopped his efforts to help others. He is quoted as saying, "I'd rather sell apples in the street, rather than not be able to give others money who needed it." That statement says everything about the kind of man he was: generous to a fault and always caring for others.

Education has always been extremely important to me and my family.

In all my years, which now measure at sixty-one, as of May 6, 2020, education and being smart was highly valued in my family.

My wonderful father, who passed away in March 2019, just five months after my mom, used to call me and my sister Donna the brain and the star.

My sister Donna Lee, who performs here at Gurwin, is the star, and by default, I was the brain.

I graduated high school in North Babylon, with high honors and a year's worth of college credits because I took AP classes in biology, chemistry, and physics. My initial plan was to go pre-med, but after looking at the curriculum, I knew it was going to be too long and too involved, and I had my sights set on getting married and having a family. In my second year, I switched majors to economics and business. That ultimately led to my thirty-year career on Wall Street. I worked at DLJ, Lehman Brothers, and Salomon Brothers. I used my smarts throughout my career. I became a highly regarded analyst covering electric utilities. It was a very lucrative career. Because of my career in covering electric utilities, I was fortunate to have traveled to fourty-eight out of the fifty states. Alaska and Wyoming are the only two I missed. I also was fortunate to travel to a number of countries in Europe, including Greece, for my coverage of a company called Thermo Ecotek.

That life nearly ended on August 31, 2011, when I fell down a steep flight of stairs, broke my skull, and suffered a traumatic brain injury. I've been recovering ever since. I've had nineteen surgeries and tons of rehab over these last eight years.

Many people who work here and see me walking around tell me how far I've come and what a miracle I am. They've become the mirror into which I need to look to measure my progress.

I'm going to give credit to the man whose footsteps I'm going to follow in as valedictorian, Irving Fuchs. From day one when I arrived at Gurwin, three and a half years ago, Irving told me, "You've got to get involved. You've got to participate in the card games (three-card poker, and blackjack), the Bingo, the word games, the trivia." And so I did. Who knew it would take me coming to Gurwin to become a degenerate gambler. Fortunately, we didn't play for money, and our best haul was to win, after thirty-eight games of winning the Bingo or the cards, a scratch-off lottery ticket. Rarely did we have any big winners—maybe a dollar or two, except for Frank Bodensky who won $20 one time.

The Adult Ed program here at Gurwin is something I've really enjoyed. I love the Therapeutic Recreation Department! They do a great job putting together a variety of programs, including the Adult Education program.

Of the Adult Ed programs, most were topics I've always wanted to take, because they'd be useful in my dream to be on the program *Jeopardy* as a contestant! I loved the history of Long Island class taught by Avery, the history of New York taught by Kaitlyn Carvalli, Presidents 40–45 taught by Patti Dowsett (recent Employee of the Month at Gurwin), and last but not least, Art: From Michaelangelo to Modern taught by Johanna Cutolo. They were all very informative and were accompanied by good videos about the subject as well as handouts prepared by the instructors.

I thoroughly enjoyed the programs, their content, and the accompanying videos. I think I became valedictorian because I asked lots of questions and showed real interest in the topics. There are no quizzes or finals, so there is no numerical grade for the Adult Ed Program, but I'm very pleased that the Therapeutic Recreation Department puts it on and that they elected me valedictorian.

I am starting a new chapter in my life and will begin to follow through on my longer-term plan to give back to those who have given me so much, and so freely. In July, I will begin taking an online class in human anatomy and physiology. It is instructor-led and accredited, and that will round out all of my prerequisites to begin a nursing program, to get my RN. Who knows, I might be coming back here to Gurwin, only this time, it will be for a job.

Thank you all for this honor! Much love to all the Gurwin staff and dignitaries. Thank you and love you, all of my family!

Love, Debbie Grosser